Spirit Possession
Modernity & Power
in Africa

Spirit Possession Modernity & Power in Africa

Edited by

HEIKE BEHREND
&
UTE LUIG

The University of Wisconsin Press
Madison

James Currey Ltd
73 Botley Road
Oxford
OX2 0BS

The University of Wisconsin Press
2537 Daniels Street
Madison, WI 53718-6772, USA

Fountain Publishers
PO Box 488
Kampala

David Philip Publishers (Pty) Ltd
PO Box 23408
Claremont 7735
Cape Town, South Africa

First published 1999

1 2 3 4 5 03 02 01 00 99

British Library Cataloguing in Publication Data

Spirit possession, modernity and power in Africa
1. Spirit possession – Africa 2. Religion and sociology
Africa
I.Behrend, Heike II.Luig, Ute
299.6'7

ISBN 0852552580 (paper) (James Currey)
0852552599 (cloth) (James Currey)

9970-02-196-6 (paper) (Fountain Publishers)

Library of Congress Cataloging-in-Publication Data is available from the
Library of Congress

ISBN 0–299–16630–9 Cloth (The University of Wisconsin Press)
ISBN 0–299–16634–1 Paper (The University of Wisconsin Press)

Typeset in 9.5/11 pt Palatino by Saxon Graphics Ltd, Derby
Printed in Great Britain by Villiers Publications, London N3

Contents

List of Figures

Contributors

Heike Behrend is professor of anthropology, Institute for African Studies, University of Cologne, Germany.

Jean-Paul Colleyn is anthropologist, filmmaker and *maître de conferences* at the Ecole des Hautes Etudes en Sciences Sociales in Paris, France.

Linda L. Giles is an assistant professor in the anthropology program of the Department of Sociology and Anthropology at Illinois State University, USA.

Ute Luig is professor of social anthropology, Institute for Ethnology, Free University of Berlin, Germany.

Susan M. Kenyon is associate professor of anthropology and director of the anthropology program at Butler University, Indianapolis, Indiana, USA.

Matthias Krings completed his MA in anthropology at the University of Mainz, Germany, and is engaged in doctoral research at the Institute for Historical Ethnology at the University of Frankfurt, Germany.

Adeline Masquelier is assistant professor at Tulane University, New Orleans, Louisiana, USA.

Alexandra O. de Sousa is a medical doctor and anthropologist, completing her doctorate at the Ecole des Hautes Etudes en Sciences Sociales in Paris, France.

Lesley A. Sharp is assistant professor of anthropology at Barnard College, New York, USA.

Tobias Wendl is a member of the Külturwissenshaflikes Forshings Kolleg 'Medien und Kültürelle Kommunikation', University of Cologne.

Introduction

Heike Behrend
& Ute Luig

In the last decades, a vast amount of literature on spirit possession has substantially increased our knowledge and understanding of its manifold discourses and practices. In this introduction, we do not intend to give an overview of the history of writings on this topic. This has been achieved already in a more than satisfactory way by Janice Boddy (1994). Instead, we would like to concentrate on a few subjects that informed the contributions to this volume:

1   Spirit possession and modernity
2   Complexities and proliferation of spirit possession
3   Spirit possession and gender
4   Spirit possession as performative ethnography and 'history from below'

Spirits and modernity

One intriguing experience of modernity is that spirit possession cults are proliferating the world over, not only in African, Asian and Caribbean countries (see Kapferer 1991, Ong 1987, Littlewood 1992), but also in the midst of New York (McCarthy Brown 1991), Toronto (Boddy 1995) and various towns in Europe.

The disenchantment of the modern world and the disappearance of spirits, as foretold by Westerners, has not taken place, either at home or in other parts of the world. In Africa as well as in Europe, many spirits and their mediums are part of local as well as global or transglobal cultures. Thus, we find Christian spirits named Hitler and Mussolini or King Bruce after Bruce Lee, the Kung-Fu actor, in a pantheon of new Christian holy spirits in Northern Uganda, who are waging war against the government (Behrend 1993). And, in Central Africa, we find spirits of aeroplanes, engines, guitars and angels (see Colson 1969, Luig 1993), while thunder, snakes and rain as well as playboys and prostitutes are inhabiting the spirit world in West Africa (see Rouch 1978: 1010). Yet, in Cologne and other towns in Germany, spirits from Ashanti, Yoruba and Brazilian Candomblé are taking possession of local women and men (Ring 1994) and in Paris, spirits from abroad as well as spirits of the dead – for instance, the spirit of Alain Kardec whose grave forms the centre of a cult in *Père Lachaise* – are incorporated and give their messages to the living (personal communication from Barbara Keifenheim). Bearing in mind the increasing interconnectedness of local cultures, we might interpret modern spirits as the (quint)essence of cosmopolitanism, in a world that is not a replication of uniformity but an organization of diversity (Hannerz 1990: 237).

Despite the exotic fascination it still exerts on Westerners, spirit possession, like magic or witchcraft, represents no archaic past. While some cults have existed since the sixteenth century (Janzen 1992, Heintze 1970), or are the product of the colonial encounter, spirit possession is not a premodern or 'traditional' phenomenon. Africa too is producing its own modernity (Bayart 1993: 12). This is demonstrated by the various contributions to this volume which show that spirit possession cults are not in opposition to but rather supportive of modernity, be it in an affirmative or critical way.

Thus, in Lesley Sharp's example, royal *Tromba* mediums are given due consideration in the economic policy of the postcolonial state in Madagascar; they contribute significantly in development projects. Heike Behrend's contribution explores the relationship between spirit possession and modern warfare in Northern Uganda, confirming the importance of spirit mediums in organizing militant resistance towards the state which Ranger (1985) and Lan (1985) described for Zimbabwe as well. However, other spirit mediums developed a rather sceptical attitude towards modernity and its consequences. Adeline Masquelier, for example, describes the *Dodo* spirits' negative reaction and critique of the capitalist market economy and modern consumerism which leads to their distancing from the dominant *Bori* cult whose mediums rather supported money and the market. In her chapter, Ute Luig finds the same ambivalences towards modernity in the Gwembe Valley in Zambia. The hesitant or even reluctant reactions of rain prophets (*Basangu*) against imported European goods and services are counterbalanced by other spirit mediums who directly favour the consumption of these goods. These ambivalent and contradictory processes of modernization the world over find an arena in spirit possession cults and are acted out among healers and believers in endless variations according to local contexts.

Complexities and proliferation of spirit possession

In the history of the anthropology of religion, there have been various attempts to explain and understand spirits and spirit possession. Evans-Pritchard interpreted spirits as 'refractions of social realities' (1956: 106ff); John Beattie called them 'abstract qualities' (1977: 4); for I.M. Lewis spirits were 'hypotheses which, for those who believe in them, afford a philosophy of final causes and a theory of social tensions and power relations' (1971: 205); Andreas Zempleni tried to interpret the ancestor spirits which took possession of a Wolof priestess in reference to the psychoanalytical 'family story' (1977), and Michael Lambek referred to spirits as 'products of imagination, partial constructions that are fictional but not simply fictitious' (1996: 238).

These various attempts to relate spirit possession to an idiom of sickness or to take it as an index for social conflict or as a means to generate power etc., give evidence that it is impossible to explain spirit possession in reference to one or the other institution of our division-of-labour society – for spirit possession is, at the same time, more and less than healing, art, entertainment, social critique, profession, fashion, and ethnography (Kramer 1987). Spirits are produced in a complex process of reciprocal interpretations in which the spirit and its medium, the interpreter and the public, take part. Of the many spirits who make their appearance, only a few succeed in standing their ground and showing their power, while others are forgotten. Thus, in the various contributions to this volume the full range of different domains in which spirits can become active is displayed.

In addition, spirits and spirit possession cults are not seen in isolation. Instead, they are situated in a synchronic as well as diachronic perspective in a wider field of power relations with various competing discourses and practices. Thus, some contributions in this volume focus on the interdependence of various cults and religions in space and time that developed their discourses and practices in opposition to each other or borrowed from each other.

In many regions, Islam has a long history of cultural interchange with other cults, leading to the Islamization of African cults and Africanization of Islam. Despite these mutual exchanges the hegemonic Islamic discourse expressed its rivalry and competition often in prejudices of backwardness and superstition. It appears that Islamic communities 'tolerate' spirit possession cults as long as they are not powerful competitors, but when these turn out to be politically influential, tensions can turn into conflicts and open power struggle. A case in point is the *Nya* cult in Mali, which is not a cult of affliction but draws on the formal elements of a secret society for organizing spirit mediumship. As Jean Paul Colleyn describes (in chapter 5) its main adherents are men who were in a position to control the power structure of the community until Islam got deeper entrenched in this region. Responding to the latter's success, to the hostile attitude of Muslim leaders and to the politics of the Malian state, many *Nya* elders converted to Islam in order not to lose their political influence on the younger generation. The consequences of this seem (at least at this time) ultimately detrimental for *Nya*.

Relations between Christian churches and spirit possession cults exhibit the same features of intense competition, but also a long tradition of reciprocal relations and borrowings. Many African independent churches have integrated aspects of spirit possession and witchfinding cults into their services – former missionary churches were more reluctant in this regard (Luig 1997). Vice versa, spirit possession cults have been Christianized in various ways, using the Bible for divination, integrating the cross and other Christian symbols into their cults' practices. However, the conversion of African spirits into Christian ones is often accompanied by their devaluation, turning, for instance in Zambia, former respectable *Basangu* spirits symbolizing fertility, health and wealth into malevolent spirits or the devil himself (Colson unpublished fieldnotes). In chapter 2 Heike Behrend describes the appropriation and indigenization of Christian discourses and practices by spirit mediums in Northern Uganda. She shows how in a highly complex process the *Christian Holy Spirit* was adopted, but then split into a variety of holy spirits which were used for healing and killing in the three *Holy Spirit Movements* waging war against the government at the end of the 1980s up to today. In addition, she gives the example of the *Holy Spirit Movements* of Severino Lukoya and Joseph Kony, which in strong opposition to other more secular movements intensified the process of Christianization to such an extent that spirits took over some aspects of Catholic saints, martyrs and biblical figures.

For comparative reasons it seems useful to differentiate between local and regional/translocal cults as well as more or less hierarchical and acephalous cults (Kramer and Marx 1993). Although regional cults are rooted in local traditions, their organization and membership is often translocal or inter-regional (Werbner 1977), which accounts for regional variations and transformation in the cult's ritual. But since they tend to be organized along hierarchical principles, change is more controlled, at least at the orbit of the centre, while it peters out at the periphery. Acephalous cults – often synonymous with cults of affliction, begin as local cults, but due to labour migration, dislocation as well as 'cultural flows' between town and country may extend their influence beyond local communities. The successful among them become also translocal spreading their centres over large regions, like *Bori*, *Zar* and *Masabe*. They build up highly complex networks and develop their discourses and practices along lines of inclusion and exclusion, fusion and fission.

A constant drawing and redrawing of boundaries is thus characteristic of these cults. In some cases, Ute Luig observed, healers and prophets try to assume roles and privileges in competing cults in order to increase their power. To include foreign spirits into local or translocal pantheons, a 'strategy of affinity' (see Schoffeleers 1978) may be used as Krings demonstrates in chapter 4 on the integration of European spirits into the *Bori* pantheon. In addition, often through functional differentiation, spirits are interrelated and categorized in opposition to each other. Thus, for example the rivalry and opposition between different spirits in the Gwembe Valley is expressed through additional differentiation of colour among the same category of spirits (see Luig chapter 9).

In his chapter, Krings illustrates how the European *Turawa* spirits in a complex play of oppositions change their various identities and affiliations in time and space until in the 1990s they finally became African spirits which adopted the European way of life.

Adeline Masquelier (chapter 3) discusses the invention of new spirits in opposition to the dominant *Bori*. She relates the popularity and power of the new *Dodo* spirits to their moral rejection of undue commoditization of *Bori* mediums who seem to be interested above all more in money than in the well-being of their clients. *Dodo* spirit mediums present themselves as guardians of an anti-capitalistic moral tradition. They thus create a moral space for negotiating modernity. Their rejection of consumerism – known from other cults as well (Lan 1989, Luig 1995) – is however only partial since just special commodities like cars, buses, plastic sandals etc. are disdained. Masquelier points out the intricacies of this form of resistance as *Dodo* spirit mediums themselves were caught in relations of the market economy which when they became too commercial caused their spirits to abandon them.

Likewise in Northern Uganda, where a brutal civil war has been waged for more than a decade, Christian spirits were attempting to create a new moral space that put an end, above all, to witchcraft and sorcery (see chapter 2). It is therefore not so much modernity as such but the negotiation of a new moral order that is debated in these various cults. In opposition to capitalist values like individualism, selfishness – often expressed in witchcraft accusations – and commoditization, a new and at the same time old morality is discussed in an idiom of truth and betrayal that constantly reworks understandings of tradition and modernity.

Spirit possession and gender

The relation of spirit possession and gender formed an important subject in the theoretical discussion of spirit possession cults. That the great majority of the possessed were and are women (although in the last years the numbers of men have increased) caused anthropologists to ask for explanations. In addition, feminists recently discovered that spirit possession was used by women not only to challenge and appropriate male power, but also to confirm and subvert gender categories. Spirit possession dealt with the resistance and empowerment of women and other marginalized groups, but also with the dislocation of gender categories thus denaturalizing male hegemonies through spirit possession. It allowed alternative models of agency which displaced the hegemonic association of masculinity and femininity (Cornwall 1994: 116).

In many regions in Africa, spirits are gendered. In forming hierarchies, they often replicate the inequalities between women and men. However, spirits of various pantheons often establish their masculinity or femininity as fluid rather than fixed, offering gender as a continuum of qualities found in both females and males. Thus, male spirits in the Brazilian Candomblé, for instance, are associated as much with emotion and softness as with forceful dominance, while female spirits include images of the fierce and the powerful, as well as the sensuous and gentle (Cornwall 1994: 126).

In the contribution of Jean-Paul Colleyn on the *Nya* Cult in Mali only men are possessed by an androgynous divinity named *Nya* who according to the context is referred to as 'she' or 'he' thus oscillating between the two sexes. Members are married to *Nya* and call him or her 'my husband' while becoming his or her wife. Thus, as in many other regions in Africa, the gender of the possessed is also dislocated. Initiation, continuous contact and incorporation of the spirits through marriage may alter or shift the medium's gender. In Northern Uganda, for instance, the relationship between spirits and their mediums was seen as a marital and sexual relationship, the spirit being the medium's spouse. As such, male spirits were said to feminize male spirit mediums while emasculating female spirit mediums. In contrast, among the Lugbara permanent or temporary asexuality was an essential characteristic of spirit mediums enabling them to mediate between the human and the spirit spheres (Middleton 1969: 224); while in Lamu on the Swahili coast the gender of women and men married to *Jinn* spirits was not changed at all. Men would marry female jin and women would marry male jin (El-Zein 1974: 71ff). Perhaps because these unions were thought to be fertile and to produce spirit children they did not shift the heterosexual matrix.

In many regions, male and female spirit mediums own spirits of their own and of the opposite sex. In one session, various spirits of different sexes may enter the medium and provide alternate versions of gender, thus displacing the dominant gender hierarchies. In the selective recombination of gendered traits, the person possessed by spirits is given the chance to play, to present a range of choices and alternatives within which people can locate themselves (Cornwall 1994: 127). Thus, spirit possession can be a stage for enacting tragedies, comedies, travesties and parodies of gender that are constantly recreated and dislodged.

This highly flexible aspect of spirit possession is worked out in Susan Kenyon's chapter on *Zar* spirits in Central Sudan. In her careful case study of a butcher's wife possessed by various male and female *Zar* spirits she offers insight into the contradictions and complexities of ideas about women's multiple-gendered identities, about autonomy and power in relation to possession by spirits.

In addition, in her discussion of possession in Madagascar, Lesley Sharp gives the example of female royal *Tromba* spirit mediums that undermines the dominant assumptions in anthropology that participation in what are often assumed to be marginal cult activities is generally regarded as proof of the structural weakness of women. Instead, she shows that among the Bemazava, women embody local power in the political arena that enables them, for instance, to make substantial decisions on local development projects.

In Alexandra de Sousa's chapter on spirit possession on the Bijagós Islands the bodies of women serve as vessels to accomplish the initiation of young men into full ancestors. The spirits of these young men who because of their premature death could not accomplish their initiation into full personhood take possession of women. The possessed women undergo an initiation and thus establish and fulfill not only their own personhood but also the one of the spirit they embody. Thus, female initiation is in fact a post-mortem male initiation. While in everyday life women's bodies become the location of a future child, during initiation they harbour the spirit of a defunct who died too early. Pregnant women are not allowed to undergo initiation because it is impossible to carry at the same time a foetus and a defunct.

Here possession surely is not sex war. On the contrary, it is concerned with the social reproduction of the community, women's bodies not only producing babies but also ancestors. During the time of initiation women change into warriors, the age group of the young men they have incorporated. While being pregnant with a defunct they display the virile qualities of warriors thus relating to the longstanding warrior tradition of the Bijagós Islands. By doing so they dislocate the dominant gender norms while at the same time confirming the productive power of women's bodies.

As in other African regions, the self, the body and the person are not unitary concepts but open to a constant reformulation through mutable entanglements with others. In this context, spirit possession could be seen as one of many practices that inscribe *dividuality* (Strathern 1988; Battaglia 1995: 3).

Spirit possession as performative ethnography and history 'from below'

Several of the authors of this volume in various ways refer to the problem of mimesis, ethnography, history and spirit possession that Fritz Kramer explored (1987). Kramer interpreted the performances of alien spirits as mimetic ethnographies making use of the Other to differentiate the self. However, although mimetic actors do not lack agency, Kramer, refering to Godfrey Lienhardt's theory of *passiones* (1961) strongly stressed the point that in a local perspective the spirits are the ones who are acting and not the persons they possess. According to Lienhardt and

Kramer (1984), *passiones* are the opposite of actions, the inversion of action that is, being acted upon by others. Certain experiences, events or things which impress a person may appear to him or her as images of *passiones*, as a power from the outside, that will or may be accepted as a spirit by the possessed person. That images of *passiones* are in no way limited to Africa is born out by another example of Fritz Kramer's. He pointed out that in our Western languages, remnants of a cosmology are found in which extraordinary or outstanding experiences can be interpreted as images of *passiones* as well, such as, for example, in the context of love when we speak of being possessed by the beloved person. It seems that, when due to 'God's death', man as a subject became empowered and the centre of the world, the world itself was reduced to a collection of objects which lost their force or power and could be manipulated and dominated by man. Kramer suggests that modernity located agency within the self, replacing cosmology with psychology, passion or better *passiones* with action (compare Lambek 1996). Thus, when interpreting spirits and their performances as condensed ethnography or history, we have to keep in mind the inversion of agency. In local perspective, it is certain aspects of history or ethnography becoming *passiones* or spirits that are experienced as so strong and compelling that they carry away and take possession of their host or medium.

Yet the dialectics of possession rituals allow the possessed also to become subjects in their own right again. It is this change of positions and roles which provides the interstices of not only repeating but critically or ironically commenting on dominant historical versions as well as ethnographies.

In chapter 10 Linda Giles explores the various categories of spirits in Swahili society. While the spirit pantheon gives insight into the various ethnographic, historical and cultural components of Swahili society, it marks at the same time the permeability of its boundaries. *Kiarabu* and *Kipemba* spirits reproduce the difference – characteristic for Swahili society – between Islamic and African elements, which correspond to the opposition between coastal (urban) and interior (rural) spaces. Relations of dominance and hegemony, as between the *Kiarabu* and *Kipemba*, are inscribed into the symbolic realm of the spirits as well as their former historic relationships. Giles is thus able to document a rich mimetical ethnography which is historically informed and relates forgotten events to present everyday life. In the last years there has been a shift of interest from 'real and true history about which historians are obliged to write' (White 1997: 325) to local representations and 'unofficial' versions of history that sometimes run counter to the dominant discourses. Following this line of argument, various contributors to this volume have tried to interpret spirits and their performances as histories 'from below' (Fabian 1990).

Tobias Wendl discusses in chapter 8, about the *Tchamba* spirit cult among the Mina in Togo, how the dominant version of history that excluded the slaves was reformulated in the context of the cult through the drastic presence of spirits of former slaves. He views the *Tchamba* spirits as referring to a repressed part of Mina history, a part which has been expelled to the wilderness. It seems, however, that the repressed and excluded take revenge by returning periodically – by means of a possession cult – into society's ritual consciousness. Yet it is not only the powerless and marginalized but former kings or heroes as well who are given the chance to tell their story in performances of spirit possession. In various central and peripheral cults, spirits embody historical personalities thus transcending death by giving back a body and a voice to (the spirit of) the dead. In spirit possession ritual biographies of historical persons are reformulated and reinterpreted. In Buganda, the mediums being possessed by the spirits of dead kings have to speak in a voice resembling that of a dead king and to manifest the king's mannerisms and facial expressions (Ray 1991: 147; Behrend 1997). Lesley Sharp gives the striking example of the *Tromba* spirits who represent well-known, historical personalities. Their origins are remembered and preserved in royal genealogies. The institution of *Tromba* possession is firmly rooted in Sakalava history, and today, participation in *Tromba* possession is not an experience of the marginalized; instead, *Tromba* spirit possession is one of the central institutions that define Sakalava identity. *Tromba* possession ceremonies, in addition, provide a recording of battles in the late eighteenth and early nineteenth centuries between Merina and Sakalava. In these ceremonies spirits of Sakalava royalty who chose suicide by drowning because of submission to Merina rule can be seen embodied by their mediums.

Other case studies draw attention to the fact that the biography of a historical person is less documented or recorded but rather reinvented 'for the better' through spirit possession. In chapter 2 on the Holy Spirit Movements in Northern Uganda Heike Behrend gives the ironic example of the spirit of a former soldier called *Ojukwu* (nicknamed after the Biafran leader) who during his lifetime vehemently refused to join the Holy Spirit Movement of Alice Lakwena. After his death, however, he fulfilled the demand and became a spiritual fighter in the Holy Spirit Movement of Alice's father. Thus, in the idiom of spirit possession, history is retold and turned – as in wishful thinking – into a success story that fits local aspirations.

In chapter 9 Ute Luig takes a diachronic perspective in order to analyse the construction of locality and local history in two different possession cults. Individual *Masabe* spirits present important social and historical events in Tonga history – for example colonial politics, the time of resettlement and labour migration as well as the challenge of modernity. In contrast, *Basangu* spirits who as spirits of the wild embody the fertility and health of the community, display concern for the moral order and reproduction of society. Both cults are intimately linked with the production of locality and its contexts but proceed in different ways. While *Basangu* rituals are rather formalized, *Masabe* performances are more theatrical in nature commenting upon local history either as affirmation or through ridicule and mockery. In this way, they construct and reconstruct local identities and situate them in the wider context of the outside world.

The full complexities of spirits and their complicated relationship to history are explored in Matthias Kring's contribution on the *Turawa* spirits, a group of European spirits of the *Bori*-cult in Northern Nigeria. He not only constructs the history of these spirits out of the large body of ethnographic literature relating to the *Hauka* cult in Niger in the 1920s, but also describes the history of their gradual transformation and integration into the pantheon of *Bori* spirits. Through marriage-alliances these European spirits in the last few years became 'africanized', transforming themselves into spirits of African descent who adopted European manners and customs. In this example, we have not only an account of spirits who as complex and contradictory personalities condense and represent 'the lessons of history' (Boddy 1994: 417) but also give insights into the logic of the imaginary that transforms them and integrates them into a larger pantheon.

References

Battaglia, Deborah (ed.) (1995) *Rhetorics of Selfmaking*, Berkeley, Los Angeles, London: University of California Press.

Bayart, J.-F. (1993) *Religion et modernité: politique en Afrique Noire*, Paris: Karthala.

Beattie, John (1977) 'Spirit mediumship as theatre', *Royal Anthropological Institute News*, June.

Behrend, Heike (1993) *Alice und die Geister. Krieg im Norden Ugandas*. München: Trickster Verlag.

—— (1997) 'Geistbesessenheit und Geschlecht. Königsfrauen in Buganda'. *Sie und Er: Frauenmacht und Männerherrschaft im Kulturvergleich*, G. Völger and J. Engelhard, (eds) Köln: Rautenstrauch–Joest–Museum.

—— (1994) 'Spirit possession revisited: beyond instrumentality', *Annual Review of Anthropology* 23: 407–34.

Boddy, Janice (1995) 'Managing tradition: superstition and the making of national identity among Sudanese women refugees'. *The Pursuit of Certainty: Religious and Cultural Formulations*, (ed.) Wendy James, London & New York: Routledge, 15–44.

Colson, Elizabeth, unpublished fieldnotes.

—— (1969) 'Spirit possession among the Tonga of Zambia', *Spirit Mediumship and Society in Africa*, J. Beattie and J. Middleton, (eds) 69–103. London: Routledge & Kegan Paul.

Cornwall, Andrea (1994) 'Gendered identities and gender ambiguity among Travestis in Salvador, Brazil', *Dislocating Masculinity*, 111–32, A. Cornwall and N. Lindisfarne, (eds) London: Routledge.

El-Zein, A. H. M. (1974) *The Sacred Meadows: A Structural Analysis of Religious Symbolism in an East African Town*, Evanston: Northwestern University Press.

Evans-Pritchard, E. E. (1956) *Nuer Religion*, New York & Oxford: Oxford University Press.

Fabian, Johannes (1990) *History from Below*, Amsterdam & Philadelphia: John Benjamins Publishing Company.

Hannerz, Ulf (1990) 'Cosmopolitans and locals in world culture', *Theory, Culture and Society* 7, 2–3: 237–51.

Heintze, Beatrix (1970) *Besessenheitsphänomene im Mittleren Bantu-Gebiet*, Wiesbaden: Franz Steiner Verlag.

Janzen, John M. (1992) *Ngoma: Discourses of Healing in Central and Southern Africa*, Berkeley: University of California Press.

Kapferer, Bruce (1991) *A Celebration of Demons*, Oxford: Berg Publishers.

Kramer, Fritz W. (1984) 'Notizen zur Ethnologie der passiones', *Ethnologie als Sozialwissenschaft*, Ernst W. Müller, René König et. al (eds) 297–312. Opladen: Westdeutscher Verlag, Sonderheft der Kölner Zeitschrift für Soziologie und Sozialpsychologie, vol. 26.

—— (1987) *Der rote Fes. Über Besessenheit und Kunst in Afrika*, Frankfurt: Athenäum.

Kramer, Fritz W. und Gertraud Marx (1993) *Zeitmarken. Die Feste von Dimodonko*, München: Trickster Verlag.

Lambek, Michael (1981) *Human Spirits. A Cultural Account of Trance in Mayotte*, Cambridge & New York: Cambridge University Press.

—— (1996) 'Afterword: spirits and their histories', *Spirits in Culture, History and Mind*, J. M. Mageo & Alan Howard (eds), New York & London: Routledge.

Lan, David (1985) *Guns and Rain: Guerrillas and Spirit Mediums in Zimbabwe*. London: James Currey.

—— (1989) 'Resistance to the present by the past', *Money and the Morality of Exchange*, 91–208. Jonathan P. Parry and Maurice Bloch (eds), Cambridge & New York: Cambridge University Press.

Lewis, Ioan M. (1971) *Ecstatic Religion: An Anthropological Study of Spirit Possession and Shamanism*, Baltimore: Penguin Books.

Lienhardt, Godfrey (1961) *Divinity and Experience: The Religion of the Dinka*, Oxford: Oxford University Press.

Littlewood, Roland (1992) *Pathology and Identity. The Work of Mother Earth in Trinidad*, Cambridge: Cambridge University Press.

Luig, Ulrich (1997) *Conversion as a Social Process. A History of Missionary Christianity among the Valley Tonga, Zambia*, Hamburg: Lit Verlag.

Luig, Ute (1993) 'Gesellschaftliche Entwicklung und ihre individuelle Verarbeitung in den affliktiven Besessenheitskulten der Tonga', *Tribus* 42: 109–20.

—— (1995) 'Gender relations and commercialization in African possession cults', *Gender and Identities in Africa*, 33–50, G. Ludwar-Ene and M. Reh (eds), Münster: Lit-Verlag.

McCarthy Brown, Karen (1991) *Mama Lola. A Vodou Priestess in Brooklyn*, Berkeley & Los Angeles: University of California Press.

Middleton, John, (1969) 'Spirit possession among the Lugbara', *Spirit Mediumship and Society in Africa*, 220–32, John Beattie and John Middleton (eds), London: Routledge & Kegan Paul.

Ong, Aihwa (1987) *Spirits of Resistance and Capitalist Discipline: Factory Women in Malaysia*, Albany: State University of New York Press.

Ranger, Terence (1985) *Peasant Consciousness and Guerilla War in Zimbabwe*, London: James Currey.

Ray, B. (1991) *Myth, Ritual, and Kingship in Buganda*, Oxford: Oxford University Press.

Ring, Irene (1994) Typische Beziehungen in einigen fremdkulturell gespeisten Therapien und Konsultationen unserer Tage, MA Thesis, Philosophical Faculty, University of Cologne, Cologne.

Rouch, Jean (1978) 'Jean Rouch talks about his films to John Marshall and John W. Adams', *American Anthropologist* 80: 1005–22.

Schoffelleers, J. Matthew (1979) *Guardians of the Land*, Gwelo: Mambo Press.

Strathern, Marilyn (1988) *The Gender of the Gift*, Berkeley & Los Angeles: University of California Press.

Werbner, Richard P. (ed.) (1977) *Regional Cults*, A.S.A. Monograph 16. London: Academic Press.

White, L. (1997) 'The traffic in heads: bodies, borders and the articulation of regional histories', *Journal of Southern African Studies*, 23,2: 325–38.

Zempleni, Andreas (1977) 'From symptom to sacrifice', *Case Studies in Spirit Possession*, Vincent Crapanzano and Victor Garrison (eds), New York: Wiley & Sons.

I

Spirit Possession
& Modernity

1

The Power of Possession in Northwest Madagascar

*Contesting Colonial
& National Hegemonies*

Lesley A. Sharp

In 1975, employees of a state-run fishery in northwest Madagascar were pleased to report the success of their annual harvest: they had pulled in a sizeable catch of *makamba*, a giant prawn that can be as large as an adult's fist. After reporting their net yield to the main office in the nation's capital of Antananarivo, the managers turned their attention to local royalty, hosting a two-day – and very expensive – ceremony to honour the spirits of royal dead ancestors. All were pleased with the outcome – fishery managers as well as living and dead royalty agreed that they should proceed in the same manner during the next year's season. A similar pattern of events occurred three years later in the same region in response to an epidemic of an unusual possession illness that had struck students in local schools. Just two months before national examinations were to be held, three spirit mediums were called in to purify school grounds and to heal the most severe cases affecting approximately ten students. The two schools were significantly different, one being a public, state-run institution, the other a private Catholic school. Following the hosting of appropriate ceremonies, outbreaks of school possession declined considerably, much to the relief of all concerned.

These two related events are deeply rooted in the symbolics that characterize simultaneously the culture of a local northwest community, and Madagascar's national culture, particularly since the mid-1970s.[1] Embedded in these and other related events is the dynamic nature of religious experience, and, more specifically, spirit possession as a dominant institution in political and economic arenas. Indigenous forms of possession, involving *tromba* spirits and female mediums, challenge anthropological assumptions about the relevance of religious experience and gender to the dynamics of power. In the Sambirano Valley of northwest Madagascar, spirit mediums are crucial actors in the daily operations of localized national economic development. As representatives of royal authority, they are recognized as embodying local power, while their actions are inadvertently sanctioned by national policy. As a result, they are able to contest two hegemonic forces: the former colonial and current national regimes. As primary actors working in a (local, royal) state within a (nation) state, the actions of *tromba* mediums lead us to reconsider the meaning of such terms as *power* and *economic development* in non-western settings.

3

Re-examining the power of possession

The dominant paradigm in anthropological studies of spirit possession is that it is a marginal experience of the weak and powerless, an assumption made explicit in the seminal works of I. M. Lewis (1966, 1971, 1986). Possession has often been described in the literature as a 'safety valve' mechanism that enables those occupying subordinate social status to assert themselves temporarily without being held responsible for their actions, the logic being that the possessing spirit, and not the individual, is responsible for any words uttered or deeds committed. In turn, women's preponderance in possession activities cross-culturally is described as evidence of their subordinate status in contrast to men, who occupy formal positions of power, an argument bolstered by earlier writings in feminist anthropology (see Ortner 1974; Reiter 1975; Rosaldo 1974; Rosaldo and Lamphere 1974). In the few instances where men are recorded as being active in possession activities, they are regarded as marginal for other reasons: for example, they may be disenfranchized within their own society because they are members of the urban poor (Crapanzano 1973, 1983).[2]

Biological determinism may overlay this argument of the political or social-structural weaknesses of possessed women, and we find this in both anthropological theory and indigenous accounts. Women may be viewed as more appropriate vessels or recipients for possessing spirits because they are conceived of as physically or intellectually weaker than men and thus are more easily possessed or controlled by invasive spirits. This is certainly a dominant argument in Madagascar, where Malagasy women are often described as 'weak' or 'soft' (*malemy*), while men are 'hard' or 'strong' (*mahery*). A tangent of this argument in the cross-cultural literature is the postulate that perhaps this 'weakness' for possession and trance experiences is rooted in women's physiology and requires medical 'solutions'. Thus, Kehoe and Giletti (1981) have suggested that a calcium deficiency may account for the preponderance of women as spirit mediums (compare Raybeck *et al.* 1989). Ong has also described the manner in which Japanese and non-Muslim factory managers have medicalized possession, relying on psychiatrists to medicate and thus silence young, possessed female workers in Malaysia (Ong 1988; see also Zola 1978).

Almost universally, however, it is assumed that possession provides an appropriate means for voicing minority, disfavoured, and thus potentially dangerous opinions while simultaneously avoiding the risk of facing the repercussions, since the spirit, and not the medium, is held responsible for any actions or deeds that occur during possession. As anthropology has become more keenly focused on issues of power and political agency (see, for example, Apter 1992; Comaroff 1985; Comaroff and Comaroff 1993; Nash 1979), similarly possession studies emphasize modes of political consciousness that are embedded in religious experience. More specifically, we find rich and compelling accounts that reinterpret possession states as critiques of capitalist labour relations in Free Trade Zones in Malaysia (Ong 1987, 1988) or, as documented particularly well in Muslim societies, as an awareness of sexual exploitation (Morsy 1978) and as feminist responses to patriarchal oppression (Boddy 1989). Nevertheless, the dominant paradigm is that possession shrouds critique in symbolic gesture and language and thus offers no permanent alternatives to the existing order.

Only a few writers have questioned these pervasive assumptions, insisting that possession may be a central, rather than marginal, cultural phenomenon. Significant examples of such exceptions are Giles' (1987) work from the Swahili coast of Kenya and several pieces generated by a conference on *zar* possession in the Sudan (see the articles in Lewis *et al.* 1991). Madagascar offers yet another refreshing counter-example, forcing us to reconsider our assumptions concerning possession as a form of oblique political protest. In the Sambirano Valley, female spirit mediums are recognized as embodying local power, enabling the indigenous Bemazava-Sakalava[3] to challenge both colonial and contemporary national hegemonic systems. As the discussion below will reveal, *tromba* spirit mediums wield substantial power in the Sambirano, where they dictate the direction of national economic development projects. In order to understand this phenomenon as a process, however, it is necessary to address, first, the manner in which possession is indigenously defined in Madagascar and, second, the historical developments that have led to the preponderance of mediums in these politically-charged arenas.

Forms of Sakalava *tromba* possession in the Sambirano Valley

Spirit possession is a widespread phenonemon in Madagascar. The term *tromba* is employed throughout the island as a generic label for all forms of possession.[4] Purists, however, only apply this term to a specific form that characterizes the culture of the Sakalava, who are organized into a series of kingdoms that, over time, have expanded northward, primarily in response to disputes over succession. The northernmost of these kingdoms is that of the Bemazava lineage, which encompasses the area known today as the Sambirano Valley. The Bemazava established their dominion in this region in the early nineteenth century, led here by their founding ruler, Andriantompoeniarivo (r. 1820–21), and his sorceror (*moasy*) and advisor, Andriamsara. Under Andriantompoeniarivo and his successors, the Bemazava were organized hierarchically as royalty, commoners and slaves. Commoners were further divided into exogamous clans. Markers of non-royal status were most significantly defined in reference to obligations of service to members of the royal lineage (for more detailed discussions of the Sakalava social and political orders see Baré 1980; Feeley-Harnik 1982, 1991; Sharp 1997). Andriantompoeniarivo established his residence near the seacoast, with his subjects' settlements scattered throughout the Sambirano Valley. Subsequently, the Bemazava built their royal tombs on the small, offshore island of Nosy Faly ('Taboo Island'), where both Andriantompoeniarivo and Andriamsara, as well as other successive Bemazava royalty, are entombed today.

Throughout Madagascar, ancestors are central to indigenous concepts of collective and local identity. This honouring of ancestors takes precedence over, or may eclipse, all other beliefs: regardless of one's religious affiliation, level of education, or (European) cosmopolitan experiences, Malagasy throughout the island make painstaking efforts to honour their dead. Among the most celebrated of (non-royal) ceremonies is the elaborate *famadihana* or reburial of the Merina of the high plateaux (Bloch 1971; Graeber 1995). Sakalava differ from other Malagasy speakers in that they are not particularly concerned with their individual or personal ancestors.

Rather, they focus their attention and efforts upon the *tromba*, or spirits of their royal dead.

Tromba spirits are well-known historical personalities whose origins are documented and preserved through royal genealogies. The institution of *tromba* possession is firmly rooted in Sakalava history and has been recorded as early as the sixteenth century by Portuguese travellers and explorers. As a result, the historian R. Kent recognizes *tromba* as one of several significant markers of Sakalava culture (Kent 1968; see also Ramamonjisoa 1984). Today, participation in *tromba* possession is not an experience of the disenfranchised. Rather, it epitomizes what it means to be Bemazava in the Sambirano: it is perhaps the central institution of local culture that defines collective identity (see Sharp 1993).

Tromba possession in the Sambirano assumes a variety of forms. The first consists of what I will refer to as royal possession, involving the greatest and oldest spirits (*tromba maventibe*) who appear only in a select group of mediums or *saha*. *Saha* are generally Sakalava women who, upon showing signs of being possessed by the most powerful of these spirits, travel in a trance state to the island of Nosy Faly where the royal Bemazava tombs are located. Here they must undergo complicated and arduous examinations designed to determine whether they are truly possessed by these spirits. If so, they live out the rest of their lives on Nosy Faly, rarely leaving the royal village. Here they serve as the advisors for living royalty. In so doing, their recommendations, decisions, and actions likewise affect more generally all who live within the boundaries of the kingdom. A far more widespread or popular (as opposed to purely royal) form of *tromba* possession involves a multitude of spirits who appear primarily in women living in town. Mediums for these spirits generally work as healers, serving the needs of local commoners. The first wave involving the popularization of *tromba* possession occurred around the 1940s, when *tromba* spirits began to possess a few women living in Ambanja, the Valley's colonial post and booming urban centre. By the 1950s the incidence of possession began to increase dramatically, marking a shift away from the more staid, older spirits of Nosy Faly towards new, less fearful (and less powerful) ones. This was followed by yet a third wave of change, beginning in the 1960s, involving a wide variety of young playboy spirits who today appear frequently in young women in their teens and early twenties.[5]

There also exist a variety of forms of possession sickness that are caused by bad or evil (*raty*, *ratsy*) spirits. From 1975 to 1980, possession by volatile and dangerous *njarinintsy* spirits reached epidemic proportions. Their primary victims were adolescent schoolgirls, where as many as ten or more students would become possessed at one time. *Njarinintsy* possession is highly contagious and, at the height of these incidents, possession attacks spread from Ambanja's junior and senior high schools into the elementary school across the street (Sharp 1990). Spirits that cause possession sickness are sometimes referred to as *tromba hely* or 'little *tromba*'. Genealogically speaking, however, they are unrelated and in several ways operate as a negation of *tromba*. *Tromba* possession is a permanent fixture in a medium's life and involves powerful and honoured ancestral spirits. In contrast, these evil spirits must be driven out of their victims before they can cause serious and potentially permanent harm, driving their victims mad or even killing them. Bemazava (particularly royalty) emphasize that *njarinintsy* do not belong in this region, labelling them as alien spirits that were brought by Tsimihety migrants from the south.

The responses from concerned adults to these crises set in motion a sequence of events that led to the reassertion of royal spiritual power in the Sambirano. When local healers (including *moasy*, or herbalists, and mediums for popular *tromba* spirits) were unable to solve the problem by treating cases individually, school officials eventually brought other more powerful spiritual specialists on to school grounds. These healers declared that the French during the colonial era (1896–1960) had desecrated sacred territory by moving or destroying tombs of commoners in order to construct school structures. Displaced and forgotten ancestors had been angered and were now attacking these young girls. The responsibility for cleansing this soiled (*maloto*) ground fell with the royal *tromba* spirits of Nosy Faly. Subsequent actions led to the reaffirmation of royal *tromba* possession, which until then was under threat of displacement by more popular forms of *tromba* and other destructive spirits of foreign origin. Paired with the fishery's earlier actions, together these two events established a patterned response that provided the model for major development projects in the future. As a result, today royal *tromba* spirits and their *saha* mediums are actively engaged in monitoring economic development in the Sambirano. The evolution of this process is rooted in the recent colonial and postcolonial history of this region.

The colonial impact on the Sambirano

Madagascar is a nation of peasants, where approximately eighty per cent of its estimated twelve million inhabitants acquires some proportion of its subsistence needs from farming. Agriculture is the backbone of the national economy, similarly comprising over eighty per cent of all exports. Major crops include rice, coffee, cocoa, vanilla, cloves and sugar; other exports consist of manioc, lima beans, pepper and other spices, as well as lobster, shrimp and other seafood and beef (Covell 1987, esp. 85; The World Bank 1980). Nearly all of these commodities can be found in the northwest, making it among the most prosperous and profitable regions of an otherwise extremely economically-depressed nation.

The original transformations within the agricultural sector are rooted in colonial policies. Under the direction of General J. S. Galliéni (1900, 1908; see also Rabinow 1989), the French first conquered Antananarivo, the capital of the Merina[6] kingdom in the central highlands. The French then led military campaigns throughout the island to 'pacify' other groups of indigenous Malagasy. Lt. Dury was responsible for the campaign in the north. When he arrived in the Sambirano in 1897, he remarked on the richness of the region's alluvial soil, the fatness of the cattle, and the ease with which one could travel up river:

> Dans ces plaines l'herbe est abondante en toutes saisons, ce sont des pâturages magnifiques, qui nourrissent les troupeaux les plus beaux et les plus nombreaux qui existent de la Mahajomba [Mahajanga] au Sambirano. Les boeufs y sont superbes et donnent de 100–150 kilos de viande; on les vend sur place 20 Francs du maximum ... Cette region du Sambirano est donc aussi très riche. Le débouché vers la mer, qui donne dans la large baie de Passandava, est commode et la construction d'une route simplement.
>
> (Dury 1897: 443, 445)[7]

Dury's assessment was correct: it was fairly simple. By the end of that year a military post was established in what is now the town of Ambanja, which lies approximately fifteen kilometres inland and is the urban centre of the Sambirano. Within twenty years of Dury's arrival, much of the valley had been converted into foreign-owned plantations of manioc (for tapioca) and sugar, two crops that later gave way to coffee (since the 1920s) and cocoa (beginning in the 1940s and 1950s). The French relocated the Sakalava and their cattle to settlements (reserves indigènes) that were pressed up against steep hillsides to make way for these plantation lands.[8]

The French wished to undermine – and destroy – any sense of Bemazava auton-omy and tradition, and they sought to accomplish this in several ways. An impor-tant thrust of colonial power involved the desecration of local territory. This was a central aspect of the relocation of Bemazava villages and the expansion of the plan-tation economy. As is characteristic of all Malagasy speakers, Bemazava identity is linked to the land. The Sambirano is sacred space, defined as their *tanindrazña* or 'ancestral land'. Second, the French also targeted tombs and other sacred sites. Today structures built by the French – including colonial office buildings and school houses – rest upon tracts of land that were once occupied by tombs of Bemazava commoner clans. Third, they sought to undermine local royal authority: during the mid-century years of colonial occupation, the ruler Tsiaraso II (r. 1945–66)[9] was forced to relocate his palace from the sacred coastal village of Ankify to the new colonial administrative town in Ambanja. It is here that Tsiaraso Rachidy IV (r. 1993–), the grandson of Tsiaraso II, now presides (Sharp 1997; cf. Feeley-Harnik 1991 for a similar discussion on the Analalava region).

In response to these colonial policies, the Bemazava of the Sambirano did not abandon their rulers or traditions (*fomba*). Rather, as Feeley-Harnik (1982) has noted for the Analalava region, they shifted their attention from living to dead royalty, honouring with greater intensity the *tromba* spirits and their mediums who embody the royal dead. Europeans had long recognized possession activities in Madagascar as politically-charged and thus potentially revolutionary events, especially when they involved large numbers of participants.[10] Following the failed insurrection of 1947, which began on the east coast and then spread throughout the island, *tromba* possession was outlawed in the Sambirano, and mediums were required to obtain permits from the colonial administration to hold possession ceremonies. This policy continued after Independence in 1960 until the Socialist Revolution in the 1970s; only then were the bans lifted. During the colonial period *tromba* possession did not vanish, however: it simply went underground, no longer held outdoors in village squares but rather in the private homes of mediums, behind closed doors. In fact, it is at this time that popular forms of *tromba* possession first began to appear in town, whereas the more powerful *tromba* spirits and mediums of Nosy Faly continued to receive occasional visitors from members of the local royal lineage. Nevertheless, since the French did not perceive women as a political threat, the continued activi-ties of the great *saha* mediums of Nosy Faly insured the preservation of their ances-tral knowledge and power.

Ironically, because the Bemazava maintained rights to small parcels of land, they were also able to resist plantation labour. As a result, the French brought in migrants from other parts of the island, and the first were Antandroy prisoners from the south. Today migrants continue to come to the Sambirano Valley because, as they explain, the land is rich and, *misy vola*, 'there is money'. They come here 'to seek their fortunes' (*hitady harena*), either sending remittances home or saving their earn-ings to pay the transportation costs so other kin may join them. Whereas at first they come in search of jobs, many eventually hope to settle permanently, acquiring a small plot of land that will enable them to be independent of the plantations. This, however, is extremely difficult for all but Sakalava. The reasons for this lie in local and national rules of land tenure.

An urban community and its tensions

Ambanja is a community that is rife with tensions which are in turn significant for understanding the dynamics of nationally versus locally-rooted power. Local power hinges first and foremost on the control of and access to land. In turn, local power dynamics involve two general social categories: the indigenous Bemazava-Sakalava, and non-Sakalava migrants. Sentiments attached to these competing statuses of 'insiders' and 'outsiders' are expressed locally through the terms *tera-tany*, meaning 'children' or 'possessors of the soil'; and *vahiny*, or 'guests,' a polite form of identification that obscures the ambivalence that surrounds host-visitor relations. Throughout Madagascar, *vahiny* are individuals one welcomes into one's home, offering them food, shelter, and other basic needs. One hopes, however, that they will not stay too long (see Linton 1927). From the point of view of the Bemazava, the *vahiny* of the Sambirano are guests who have overstayed their welcome. During my fieldwork in 1987, Bemazava, fearing the ever-increasing number of outsiders coming to their territory, often reacted with consternation to the recent paving of the national highway that runs from the capital and up through the Sambirano. No longer a muddy and treacherous path in the rainy season, it had now become an all-weather road, facilitating the ever increasing in-migration of *vahiny* into their territory.[11] Bemazava *tera-tany* of the Sambirano often define themselves in reference to *vahiny*, stating that they, in contrast, are 'people who do not move' (*olo tsy mandeha*).[12]

The tensions that exist between these two general social categories are rooted in policies that characterized the colonial period from 1896 to 1960. The most highly charged arena of contention involves land use. In turn, this is compounded or exacerbated by more recent national policies following independence. The most significant and deeply-rooted problems exist between Bemazava and another group of Malagasy speakers, the Merina, who occupy the island's central highlands. Bemazava resent the Merina for several reasons. First, the Merina attempted to conquer Sakalava territory along the west coast in the late eighteenth and early nineteenth centuries (for a discussion of Merina expansion see Mutibwa 1974; and Thompson and Adloff 1965: 4–6). *Tromba* possession ceremonies provide a recording of these battles, where one may encounter the spirits of Sakalava royalty who chose suicide by drowning over submission to Merina rule. Second, the Bemazava of the Sambirano view the Merina as being favoured by the French, groomed as indigenous civil servants who dominated the colonial administration. Third, since Merina territory coincides with the national capital of Antananarivo, Merina are perceived by Bemazava as maintaining access to the best education, jobs and health care.

In Ambanja the tensions between these two groups are explicitly clear in several arenas. First, religious affiliation is a marker of ethnic origin: while Merina in the Sambirano tend to be Protestant, the Sakalava, if they 'pray' (*mivavaka*), are Muslim or Catholic (see Gow 1979; Mutibwa 1974; Sharp 1994). Difference is also under-scored in activities involving the *fomba-gasy* or 'Malagasy religion' or 'customs'. In response to events that occurred during the Merina wars of the nineteenth century, royal ceremonies and many *tromba* possession ceremonies are now *fady* or taboo for Merina participants.[13] Education is yet another important marker of difference. Beginning in 1975, in response to a national policy called malagasization, the cur-ricula of all state-run schools up through high school (*lycée*) were to be conducted in standard Malagasy, which is based primarily on the Merina dialect. Bemazava have been highly resentful of this policy because they see their children being schooled in the language of their oppressors. Furthermore, they stress that Merina children have had an advantage over Sakalava and other coastal peoples, since they speak essentially the same language in their homes, while other children must mas-ter two dialects. In turn, Merina school teachers have dominated the local schools in Ambanja, since they far outnumber Bemazava (and, more generally, Sakalava) who have been able to complete their work in pedagogical studies (for more details see Sharp 1990).[14] Health care is yet another source of tension and resistance: because the majority of doctors trained in clinical western medicine are Merina, Bemazava are reluctant to visit the local state-run hospital.

Following independence in 1960, many of the colonial policies were continued, whereby French advisers were maintained in their posts to assist Malagasy in their transition to self-rule. This first decade was followed by an important – and volatile – transitional period of the mid-1970s, now referred to as the Socialist Revolution. This was characterized by the expulsion of expatriates from government posts, the alienation of much foreign-owned private property, and the conversion of the national economy to state capitalism. Among the most significant effects in the Sam-birano was that the local ethnic-based tensions over land use worsened. Plantations that were once owned by foreigners now became state-run farms or enterprises managed by Merina elite.[15]

Thus, the Sambirano continues to be simultaneously a rich and prosperous plan-tation zone as well as the sacred ancestral land (*tanindrazña*) of the Bemazava. As the region's *tera-tany*, Bemazava struggle to preserve their claims on local territory. The *tromba* spirits, as the royal ancestors (*dady*), are today recognized as both the guardians of this sacred space. Ironically, it is in this last arena where we see that significant tensions exist and interesting innovations and solutions have evolved.

Local challenges to larger hegemonies

In the mid-1970s, the national policy of malagasization arose, facilitating the resur-gence of spiritual power in the Sambirano. The original intent of malagasization was to assert a new, unified sense of a national Malagasy culture and identity in opposition to former French colonial practices. Since customs (*fomba*) may vary from one region to another, ultimately this national philosophy has taken an important turn, assuming a more flexible form, where local custom is often honoured by local and distant authorities alike over other subordinate (or, at times, competing national) ones. Thus, today the Bemazava *tera-tany* are recognized as the proper spiritual authorities of the Sambirano. Here collective ethnic identity, religion, and common territory are all primary defining principles of Bemazava culture. The royal *tromba saha* mediums have become the guardians of this local sacred space and often the directors of subsequent attempts to develop their territory by Merina, whom they regard as persistent invaders from the outside.

As a result, malagasization has led to some interesting forms of cooperation and partnership between otherwise competing factions. When school children were struck by possession sickness in the 1970s, local ritual authorities argued that these epidemics were caused by displaced – and forgotten – local ancestors. These angry, evil *njarinintsy* spirits sought to harm the living and thus the most vulnerable members of the community: its children. Through malagasization these spirits had found a voice. Responses reflect the multifaceted dimensions of the local community. Parents, school officials, and the children themselves participated collectively in ceremonies that honoured these spirits. Participants included not only Sakalava but also Merina, and the two schools that became most heavily involved were a state-run school and, surprisingly, the Catholic mission. The early actions taken by the fishery set the stage for subsequent development projects involving new factories and, as illustrated below, the building of a new school.

The fishery in Nosy Be

Seafood is among the more important exports of the northwest, with *makamba* or giant prawns being a particularly prized commodity. Early in the 1970s a fishery was built on the offshore island of Nosy Be in order to harvest and process local sea products. In 1973 it started to fish in this area for *makamba*. The allocation of fishing rights was a touchy issue, however, since the richest waters surrounded the sacred island of Nosy Faly. Fishery management consisted primarily of Merina elite and a few French expatriates. They knew that if they approached Nosy Faly without permission they would enrage the Bemazava. They were faced with a serious dilemma, however. Merina employees, as Malagasy, were most familiar with local customs, yet taboos associated with the Merina wars of the nineteenth century made it impossible for them to approach Bemazava royalty. For this reason they decided to hire an emissary, and so they chose a man who was a member of a related royal lineage and who was knowledgeable in both financial and royal affairs.

Gaining initial and continued access to the waters of Nosy Faly involved complicated negotiations and private conferences with both living and dead royalty. The emissary first approached the ruler TsiarasoVictor III (*r.* 1966–93) and his advisors, who eventually granted him permission to visit Nosy Faly. There, in the village of the royal tombs, the emissary had to confer with the tomb guardians (male: *ngahy*; female: *marovavy*) who, in turn, helped him gain access to the *saha* mediums and thus the *tromba* spirits themselves. The standing agreement that was reached between the fishery and the royal *tromba* spirits required that at the opening of each season the emissary must visit Nosy Faly and acquire permission to fish in the local waters. If the fishing season is a successful one, the fishery must then host a *joro* and other ceremonies to honour and thank the royal Bemazava ancestors. The first ceremonies were held in 1975 and have been held every year since. Each time the fishery hosts these ceremonies, both living and dead royalty preside.

The new high school

Similar events occurred in the early 1980s when the townspeople of Ambanja decided that they needed a new high school. Already having one in town was an advantage, because it meant that many local children no longer needed to relocate to the provincial capital of Diégo-Suarez, 240 kilometres to the north to continue their studies. The existing school, however, had exceeded its capacity and was poorly constructed. Decisions surrounding the new school involved similar participation by *tera-tany* and *vahiny*, where two issues were especially important.

First, given that outbreaks of possession sickness had occurred on school grounds several years before, many school officials and parents were concerned over the decision of where to place the school. Eventually land was donated by a local plantation. This involved a precious sacrifice, since the plantation gave up a large plot of cocoa fields for this purpose. In this way 'state-owned' *tanindrazña* land was given back to the local community. The second issue involved naming the school, and here two factions emerged. *Vahiny* wanted to name the school after a *national* hero from the 1947 insurrection. The Bemazava, however, wanted to honour a *local* figure, Tsiaraso I (r. 1887–1919), whose reign coincided with the period of French conquest of their territory at the turn of the century (see Sharp 1997). After the Sakalava won the vote, the question that remained was whether to use the name this ruler bore when he was alive (which is *fady* or taboo), or the praise name (*fitahina*) he was given following his death, which is *Andriamandilatrarivo* ('The ruler who is honoured by many'). To complicate matters, placing his praise name on the side of the building was regarded as an even greater breach of tradition: it is a sacred name since it is the one that his *tromba* spirit now bears. The ruler at the time, Tsiaraso Victor III, went to Nosy Faly to consult with this *tromba* spirit,[16] and it gave permission to use the name Tsiaraso I.

Today the school is an imposing structure on the edge of town. It is also a source of great civic pride: June 1987 marked the first year that Independence Day celebrations were held on its grounds. A lengthy parade was held where nearly everyone in town – including school children, workers from all of the enterprises, different elements of the national party and local clubs – filed past a grandstand of local government and enterprise dignitaries who watched from the shade of the school's veranda. The school opened its doors to students in the autumn of 1987.

It is important to stress how differently the French would have viewed such events. They would have considered it ludicrous to consult spirit mediums (after 1947, such actions were made illegal). Likewise, in the early years of post-Independence Madagascar, these actions would have been perceived of as backward and as running contrary to national progress. As essentially the inheritors of French power in 1960, why is it that by the 1970s Merina state employees ceased to ignore or overpower Bemazava needs and demands? The answer lies in a newly constructed national identity that characterized the island's socialist era: to do so would have been read as a deliberate attempt to exacerbate Bemazava hostility towards Merina as outsiders. In doing so, Merina would have been identified with the oppressive former actions of their predecessors of the French colonial regime. As a result, following the years of the Socialist Revolution in Madagascar, the early actions taken, first, in 1975 by fishery management and, again, in 1978 by school officials plagued by cases of mass possession, provided a natural model for all future development projects.

Analysis: the resurgence of spiritual power and identity

Analyses of the symbolics of religious experience and ritual form may reveal indigenous conceptions of rapid social change and oppression. In such contexts, ritualized responses cannot be viewed simply as archaic forms of traditionalism that arise in times of desperation and hopelessness (cf. Apter 1992; Comaroff 1985; Comaroff and Comaroff 1991; Nash 1979; Taussig 1977, 1987). Rather, they reflect a keen awareness of existing power structures and hegemonic forces. Usually, however, these sentiments appear as expressions of 'symbolic discontent' (Pred and Watts 1992) which operate as more oblique – and thus politically safer – forms of protest. As these examples from Madagascar reveal, however, this need not always be the case, leading us to re-examine our assumptions about religious experience and political agency cross-culturally.

Identity, land use and local autonomy are intrinsically linked in many cultures. Thus, the frequent desecration of sacred territory often leads to the permanent destruction of local culture. For example, in Foster's study of a US Appalachian community (1988), the re-routing of a river cut the lifeline of a community, not so much because its members needed the river for economic reasons, but because they defined themselves as 'people of the river'. Without the river they ceased to exist. A more devastating account offers Shkilnyk (1985), who records how a Canadian Ojibwa community was completely undermined by being relocated to land that was deamed unnatural, dangerous, and spiritually impure. The effects were horrifying: children are now raised without parents, there is rampant alcoholism and drug abuse, and gangs of teenagers rape other children and deliberately burn down the houses of their own grandmothers. The poisoning of their waters with mercury was simply the 'last nail in the coffin' (1985: 192).

These are, fortunately, a far cry from the Madagascar case, where we actually see the opposite occuring. As Lan's (1985) work reveals, spiritual authority can at times reassert local authority and undermine larger hegemonic forces. During the struggle for independence in Zimbabwe in the 1960s and 1970s, Shona spirit mediums served as vessels for royal ancestral spirits, who are the guardians of local, sacred ground. Spilled blood can pollute the land and harm its inhabitants, and thus Shona mediums imposed restrictions on and served as advisers and ritual specialists for ZANU (Zimbabwe African National Union) guerillas, teaching them about the terrain and monitoring their access to the land and its people. Following Mugabe's victory, Shona mediums were recognized as heroines of the revolution. I am not arguing that *tromba* possession is revolutionary; nevertheless these events parallel those in the Sambirano, where ritual authority works to assert local land rights and autonomy.

Malagasization greatly enhanced the prestige and power of the *tromba* spirits and *saha* of Nosy Faly as the guardians of sacred space by both *tera-tany* and *vahiny*, or Sakalava and Merina. Unwanted Merina migrants, perceived by Sakalava as representatives of the national government, wish to distinguish their actions from those taken by former French colonial officials. Thus, malagasization put in motion an interesting dynamic – one that involves satisfying national economic needs while simultaneously respecting local authority and autonomy. It is only through indigenous religious institutions that this can be accomplished successfully. Since the mid-1970s, the role of the royal *tromba* spirits has become increasingly important in the Sambirano. Prior to constructing any new building, the state must have the Bemazava's approval, where construction is sanctioned and controlled by local authorities, both living and dead. Deferring to the *tromba* spirits of Nosy Faly became an aspect of local protocol – in 1987, for example, a new coffee factory bore evidence of a *joro* ceremony, with cow skulls mounted on the surrounding fence.

These events underscore the need as well to re-analyse the dynamics of local power in reference to gender hierarchies. The activities of these specialized spirit mediums undermine dominant assumptions in anthropology, where participation in what are often assumed to be marginal cult activities is generally regarded as proof of the structural weakness of women. As this example from northwest Madagascar reveals, the success of local development projects initiated by state agencies hinges on a subtle understanding of Bemazava experiences of conquest from outsiders. Merina, as the dominant ethnic group of Madagascar and the current directors of large-scale enterprises in the Sambirano, must tread softly on local land. Should they choose to disregard Bemazava authority, they will only confirm local constructs of their identity as yet another group of conquerors who continue the destructive policies initiated by the French. Thus Merina must respect and honour local royalty, both living and dead, who represent Bemazava collective identity and therefore are the voice for local needs and concerns. Most importantly, since the *tromba* spirits speak through a select group of *saha*, it is women who embody this local power.

As has been shown, malagasization's purpose was to assert Malagasy customs over those of foreign origin. In this Bemazava kingdom, however, it has led to the assertion of local custom over all others. Thus, this is not a story of the marginal and powerless seeking a temporary voice. Nor do *tromba* spirits and their mediums represent an oblique attempt to control but, rather, a vital force during times of deliberate social and economic transformation. It is they who are the true guardians of sacred space who may manage and control the means of production in the context of state capitalism. Since Merina managers of state businesses rarely occupy their positions for more than a few years, the extent of their influence is limited. These outsiders must maintain a delicate balance with the *saha* and their *tromba* spirits if they are to proceed smoothly in their pursuit of profit in Bemazava territory.

Acknowledgements

An earlier version of this paper was delivered at the Annual Meeting of the Canadian Association of African Studies in Toronto on 14 May 1993 for the session entitled 'Recent Anthropological Research in Madagascar: History and Ritual Knowledge in the North and Highlands', organized by Michael Lambek. The bulk of the data reported here were collected throughout 1987 during twelve months of anthropological fieldwork in Madagascar. Financial support for this endeavour was generously provided by the US Department of Education Fulbright-Hays Doctoral Dissertation Research Abroad Program; the Wenner-Gren Foundation for Anthropological Research; the Sigma Xi Foundation; and the Lowie Fund of the University of California, Berkeley. Additional, supportive data were collected in the Summer of 1993 with generous funding from a Butler University Academic Grant; the American Philosophical Society, and the Joint Committee on African Studies of the Social Science Research Council and the American Council of Learned Societies with funds provided by the National Endowment for the Humanities and the Ford Foundation. I would like to thank the many inhabitants of the Sambirano Valley who have made my research activities both possible and enjoyable. Space limitations prevent me from mentioning them all by name, but special thanks must go to H.T., my research assistant, and to the many mediums (and their spirits) for their patience and forthrightness. This article is dedicated with love to Maman'i'Soa (Berthine), who was a most kind and generous spiritual guide. Finally, I wish to thank Sue Kenyon, Heike Behrend, Ute Luig, and Janice Boddy for their insightful comments on earlier drafts of this manuscript.

Notes

1   I wish to stress that the data reported here are based primarily on research conducted throughout 1987 during the era currently known of as Madagascar's Second Republic, or Socialist era (under President Didier Ratsiraka), which spanned the 1970s and 1980s. The 1990s have been characterized by major political changes that, in turn, are affecting social and economic institutions at local and national levels. In March 1993, President Zafy Albert was sworn into office; during a brief six-week visit to Madagascar in the summer of this same year I found that perhaps the most significant change within the field site involved the privatization of state-owned farms that were such a mainstay of the previous administration's socialist (or state capitalist) policies. This trend continued to be true during subsequent field research in 1994 and 1995. Zafy was subsequently impeached and removed from office in late 1996, and Ratsiraka re-elected as the nation's President in early 1997. It is still too early to know the effects of such political changes on possession, and thus 1987 will serve as the 'ethnographic present' for this article. It is my understanding that malagisization's effects on the spiritual realm persist into the present day (1998): that is that the subsequent administrations under Zafy and, again, Ratsiraka, continue to bolster rather than undermine local spiritual authority. For general information on recent developments in the sacred realm of royal affairs see Sharp (1997).

2   Marriage may be yet another structural difficulty of mediums' lives that is expressed through possession institutions. In some cultures a spirit may be defined as a medium's spouse. In such cases the spirit spouse is often regarded as superior to or more powerful than the man to whom the medium is married in daily life. This is generally interpreted in the literature as a relationship that offers her new, albeit temporary and indirect, forms of leverage over others who are more powerful. For example, a Korean shaman's dead spouse may be incorporated into her spirit repertoire (Kendall 1988). In Haitian *vodou* a medium may choose to marry a spirit, reserving particular days of the week when she cannot date or have sexual intercourse with living partners (Brown 1991: 248, 306ff). Relations between *zar* mediums and their spirits in the Sudan and Morocco likewise may involve marriages and sexual relations (Lewis *et al.* 1991: 3; Crapanzano 1983), or possession rituals may mirror marriage ceremonies, as in parts of the Sudan (Boddy 1989, Kenyon, this volume). Finally, romantic encounters can occur between spirits (that is, possessed mediums) and onlookers (see Wafer 1991: 2–3). In each of these cases a spirit marriage is once again generally interpreted in the literature as an escape from or replacement for the drudgery or failures that characterize daily life. As I have argued for Madagascar, however, spirit marriages operate as permanent forms of empowerment; a full discussion of this phenomenon is beyond the purview of this article (see, however, Sharp 1993: 182ff).

3   Madagascar is the fourth largest island in the world, measuring approximately 1,500 km in length, and lying about 550 km off the east African coast, opposite Mozambique. The Sakalava are the fifth largest group of this island's Malagasy speakers and comprise approximately 5.8 per cent (Covell 1987: xiii, 12) of a current total population of about twelve million. Throughout this

article I will use the term *Bemazava* when referring to the northernmost branch of *Sakalava* who inhabit the Sambirano Valley, and Sakalava when speaking more generally of the larger ethnic category of people who populate the island's west coast.

4 Sakalava apply the term *tromba* in a number of ways, using it to refer to the spirits of dead royalty, the mediums possessed by such spirits, and this form of possession as a cultural institution. An additional complication is that singular and plural forms of nouns are the same in the Malagasy language. To avoid confusion I will distinguish between *tromba* mediums and *tromba* spirits. The term *tromba* alone refers to the institution as a whole.

5 In 1987 I estimated that nearly half of all women in Ambanja – with a population of 27,000 – were possessed by these popular spirits. (For more information see Sharp 1993: 154–65, and Sharp 1995).

6 As will be described in more detail below, the Merina are generally assumed to be the dominant ethnic group of Malagasy speakers in Madagascar. They comprise approximately 26.1 per cent of the national population (Covell 1987: 12).

7 Translation: 'On these plains the grass is abundant throughout the seasons. [In the Sambirano one finds] magnificent pastures that nourish the most beautiful and numerous herds that exist [in the region] from Mahajanga to the Sambirano. The cattle are superb and they give 100–150 kilos of meat [a piece]; one can sell them on the spot for up to 20 francs. ... This region of the Sambirano is very rich [in other ways as well]. [The river] empties out into the sea, [producing] the large bay of Passandava. It is convenient[ly placed] and [it lends itself well] to the easy construction of a route [inland].

8 This was among the few regions in Madagascar where the French created reserves for indigenous people. The fact that this occurred underscores the richness of the soil – and thus the value of the land – in the Sambirano Valley, in contrast to the poorer quality of soils found throughout much of Madagascar and tropical mainland Africa.

9 Normally, it is taboo (*fady*) to utter the name that a ruler carried when he or she was alive; instead, one uses the praise name (*fitahina*), which is the same name that the ruler's *tromba* spirit bears. In the Sambirano, however, the Bemazava generally do not follow this rule in everyday discussions about history for reasons that will become clear below.

10 For example, British missionaries in 1863 reported outbreaks of 'dancing mania' or *Ramanenjana*, where hundreds of people in the highlands became possessed by the dead Merina Queen Ranavalona I. Dancers often approached Europeans, knocking off their hats and assaulting them in other ways as well (see Davidson 1889; Sharp 1985).

11 When I first re-visited the Sambirano in 1993 it was clear that such fears were well-founded. The traffic through town had increased dramatically, as had the local population (a census was in progress to determine by just how much). The town of Ambanja had four new hotels, two built to serve the needs of seasonal labour migrants, while the other two catered to the growing influx of European and South African tourists who now passed through on their way to other destinations. Significant concerns voiced by the town's inhabitants included the effects of an over-taxed sewage system and the increase in crime in the area.

12 For an interesting contrast compare Feeley-Harnik's (1991) account: 'Sakalava to the south in the Analalava region see themselves as people who do move. This statement is made in reference to two practices: first, the movement in each generation of Sakalava royalty as they seek to establish a new palace (and, potentially, dynasty); and peasants' movements from countryside to town, since their survival is rooted partially in their ability to acquire wage labour'.

13 *Fady* are an important aspect of Malagasy culture regardless of the region or ethnic group. They include, for example, taboos placed on foods, days of the week, and locations. Visitors and travellers are expected to inquire about local *fady* and thus tourist guidebooks typically list the more important ones for a given region.

14 By mid-1993 Zafy Albert, the new president of Madagascar, had declared that the country would revert to French as the official language used for teaching in state schools. This decision was made in response to a common sentiment expressed throughout the island that the inability to speak fluently a more international language has led to the cultural and political isolation of this country. Furthermore, many feel that malagasization in the schools failed because the majority of non-Merina students and teachers struggled with official Malagasy, while the elite escaped such problems by sending their children to private French schools. These education issues define the focus for current research activities, with data drawn from fieldwork conducted from 1993 to 1995. See, for example, Sharp (1996).

15 In spite of the trend towards privatization under President Zafy, and continued by Ratsiraka in the 1990s, Merina and other highly elite have remained in place as the directors of the majority of the Sambirano's enterprises.

16 This also is a highly unusual event: Sakalava rulers should only approach the royal tombs when it is time for their bodies to be placed there. Tsiaraso Victor III explained that as a Catholic he felt comfortable in breaking from tradition.

References

Apter, Andrew (1992) *Black Critics and Kings: The Hermeneutics of Power in Yoruba Society*, Chicago: University of Chicago Press.

Baré, Jean-François (1980) *Sable Rouge: Une Monarchie du Nord-ouest Malgache dans l'Histoire*, Paris: Editions L'Harmattan.

Bloch, Maurice (1971) *Placing the Dead: Tombs, Ancestral Villages, and Kinship Organization in Madagascar*, New York: Seminar Press.

Boddy, Janice (1989) *Wombs and Alien Spirits: Women, Men, and the Zar Cult in Northern Sudan*, Madison: University of Wisconsin Press.

Brown, Karen McCarthy (1991) *Mama Lola: A Vodou Priestess in Brooklyn*, Berkeley: University of California Press.

Comaroff, Jean (1985) *Body of Power, Spirit of Resistance. The Culture and History of a South African People*, Chicago: University of Chicago Press.

Comaroff, Jean & John Comaroff, (1991) *Of Revelation and Revolution: Christianity, Colonialism, and Consciousness in South Africa*, Chicago: Chicago University Press.

—— (eds) (1993) *Modernity and its Malcontents: Ritual and Power in Postcolonial Africa*, Chicago: University of Chicago Press.

Covell, Maureen (1987) *Madagascar: Politics, Economics and Society*, London: Frances Pinter.

Crapanzano, Vincent (1973) *The Hamadsha: A Study in Moroccan Ethnopsychiatry*, Berkeley: University of California Press.

—— (1983) *Tuhami: Portraits of a Moroccan*, Chicago: University of Chicago Press.

Davidson, Andrew (1889) *The Ramanenjana or Dancing Mania of Madagascar*, Antananarivo Annual and Madagascar Review 4, 8: 19–27.

Dury, S. V. (1897) 'De Tsaratanana à Nossi-Be', *Notes, Reconnaissances et Explorations*, vol. 2., semestre 2 (November), 413–45.

Feeley-Harnik, Gillian (1982) 'The king's men in Madagascar: slavery, citizenship and Sakalava monarchy', *Africa* 52, 2: 31–50.

—— (1991) *A Green Estate: Restoring Independence in Madagascar*, Washington, DC: Smithsonian Press.

Foster, Stephen (1988) *The Past is Another Country*, Berkeley,: University of California Press.

Galliéni, J. S. (1900) *La Pacification de Madagascar (Operations d'Octobre 1896 à Mars 1899)*, Paris: Librairie Militaire R. Chapelot et Cie.

—— (1908) *Neuf Ans à Madagascar*, Paris: Librairie Hachette et Cie.

Giles, Linda L. (1987) 'Possession cults on the Swahili coast: a re-examination of theories of marginality', *Africa* 57, 2: 234–58.

Gow, Bonar A. (1979) *Madagascar and the Protestant Impact. The Work of the British Missions, 1818–1895*, New York: Africana Publishing Company.

Graeber, David (1995) 'Dancing with corpses reconsidered: an interpretation of *famadihana* (in Arivonimamo, Madagascar)', *American Ethnologist* 22, 2: 258–78.

Kehoe, Alice B., & Dody A. Giletti (1981) 'Women's preponderance in possession cults: The calcium-deficiency hypothesis extended', *American Anthropologist* 83, 3: 549–61.

Kendall, Laurel (1988) *The Life and Hard Times of a Korean Shaman: Of Tales and the Telling of Tales*, Honolulu: University of Hawaii Press.

Kent, Raymond K. (1968) 'Madagascar and Africa: Part II. The Sakalava, Moroserana, Dady and Tromba before 1700', *Journal of African History* 9, 4: 517–46.

Lan, David (1985) *Guns and Rain: Guerillas and Spirit Mediums in Zimbabwe*. Berkeley: University of California Press.

Lewis, I. M. (1966) 'Spirit possession and deprivation cults', *Man* 1, 3: 307–29.

—— (1971) *Ecstatic Religion: An Anthropological Study of Spirit Possession and Shamanism*, Baltimore: Penguin Books.

—— (1986) *Religion in Context: Cults and Charisma*, Cambridge: Cambridge University Press.

Lewis, I. M., Ahmed Al-Safi, & Sayyid Hurreiz, eds. (1991) *Women's Medicine: The Zar-Bori Cult in Africa and Beyond*, Edinburgh: Edinburgh University Press for the International African Institute.

Linton, Ralph (1927) 'Rice, a Malagasy tradition', *American Anthropologist* 29: 654–60.

Morsy, Soheir (1978) 'Sex roles, power and illness in an Egyptian village', *American Ethnologist* 5: 137–50.

Mutibwa, P. M. (1974) *The Malagasy and the Europeans: Madagascar's Foreign Relations 1861–1985*, Atlantic Highlands, NJ: Humanities Press.

Nash, June (1979) *We Eat the Mines and the Mines Eat Us: Dependence and Exploitation in Bolivian Tin Mines*, New York: Columbia University Press.

Ong, Aihwa (1987) *Spirits of Resistance and Capitalist Discipline: Factory Women in Malaysia*, Albany: State University of New York Press.

—— (1988) 'The production of possession: spirits and the multinational corporation in Malaysia'. *American Ethnologist* 15, 1: 28–42.

Ortner, Sherry (1974) 'Is female to male as nature is to culture?', *Women, Culture, and Society*, Michelle Z. Rosaldo and Louise Lamphere (eds) 67–87. Stanford: Stanford University Press.

Pred, Allan, & Michael J. Watts (1992) *Reworking Modernity: Capitalisms and Symbolic Discontent*, New Brunswick, NJ: Rutgers University Press.

Rabinow, Paul (1989) *French Modern: Norms and Forms of the Social Environment*, Cambridge, MA: MIT Press.

Ramamonjisoa, Suzy Andrée (1984) 'Symbolique des rapports entre les femmes et les hommes dans les cultes de possession de type Tromba à Madagascar', *Bulletin Academie Malgache* 63, 1–2: 99–110.

Raybeck, D., J. Shoobe and J. Grauberg (1989) 'Women, stress, and participation in possession cults: a re-examination of the calcium deficiency hypothesis', *Medical Anthropology Quarterly* 3, 2: 139–61.

Reiter, Rayna (ed) (1975) *Toward an Anthropology of Women*, New York: Monthly Review Press.

Rosaldo, Michelle Z. (1974) 'Woman, Culture, and Society: A Theoretical Overview', *Woman, Culture, and Society*, Rosaldo, Michelle Z. & Louise Lamphere, (eds) 17–43, Stanford: Stanford University Press.

Rosaldo, Michelle Z. & Louise Lamphere (1974) 'Introduction', *Woman, Culture, and Society*, Rosaldo, Michelle Z. & Louise Lamphere (eds) 1–16. Stanford: Stanford University Press.

Sharp, Lesley A. (1985) 'Social change, social protest: the 'dancing mania' in nineteenth century Madagascar', paper presented at the annual meetings of the American Anthropological Association, Washington, DC.

—— (1990) 'Possessed and dispossessed youth: spirit possession of school children in northwest Madagascar', *Culture, Medicine and Psychiatry* 14: 339–64.

—— (1993) *The Possessed and the Dispossessed: Spirits, Identity, and Power in a Madagascar Migrant Town*, Berkeley: University of California Press.

—— (1994) 'Exorcists, psychiatrists, and the problems of possession in northwest Madagascar', *The Journal of Social Science and Medicine* 38, 4: 525–42.

—— (1995) 'Playboy princely spirits of Madagascar: possession as youthful commentary and social critique', *The Anthropological Quarterly* 68, 2: 75–88.

—— (1996) 'Adolescents' understandings of history in Madagascar: contemporary de- and reconstructions of the colonized mind', paper delivered at the annual meetings of the American Anthropological Association, San Francisco.

—— (1997) 'Royal difficulties: a question of succession in an urbanized Sakalava kingdom'. *The Journal of Religion in Africa*, 27, 3: 270–307 special volume on Madagascar, K. Middleton ed.

Shkilnyk, Anastasia M. (1985) *A Poison Stronger than Love: The Destruction of an Ojibwa Community*, New Haven: Yale University Press.

Taussig, Michael T. (1977) 'The genesis of capitalism amongst a South American peasantry: devil's labor and the baptism of money', *Comparative Studies in Society and History*, 19: 130–55.

—— (1987) *Shamanism, Colonialism, and the Wild Man. A Study in Terror and Healing*, Chicago: Chicago University Press.

Thompson, Virginia & Richard Adloff (1965) *The Malagasy Republic: Madagascar Today*, Stanford: Stanford University Press.

Wafer, James (1991) *The Taste of Blood: Spirit Possession in Brazilian Candomblé*, Philadelphia: University of Pennsylvania Press.

The World Bank (1980) *Madagascar: Recent Economic Developments and Future Prospects*, Washington, DC: The World Bank.

Zola, Irving (1978) 'Medicine as an institution of social control', *The Cultural Crisis of Modern Medicine*, J. Ehrenreich (ed.) 80–100. New York: Monthly Review Press.

2

Power to Heal, Power to Kill

Spirit Possession & War in Northern Uganda (1986–1994)

Heike Behrend

Postcolonial times have seen a growing number of wars in Africa, for instance, in Angola, Mozambique, Somalia, Liberia, Rwanda, Sudan, Zaïre and Uganda.[1] Rather reluctantly, anthropologists have taken notice of this disturbing fact.

The works of J. Bazin and E. Terray (1982), T. Ranger (1985, 1992), D. Lan (1987), C. Geffray (1990), J. Haas (1990), C. Meillassoux (1990), N. Kriger (1992), K.F. Otterbein (1994), S.P. Reyna and R.E. Downs (1994) and S.E. Hutchinson (1996) mark the beginning of a development towards an anthropology of war which not only deals with 'traditional' warfare but, above all, tries to understand the recent modern or postmodern wars in their global and local contexts.

As Ranger and, most important of all, Lan have shown in their works on the liberation war in Zimbabwe, spirit mediums not only played a substantial role in establishing a relationship between the guerillas and the local peasant population but also in legitimizing their fight.[2] Furthermore, some more recent anthropological works (Roesch 1992; Wilson 1992) have demonstrated that spirit mediums were also used in the liberation war in Mozambique by RENAMO and by another new movement, the so-called NAPRAMA-Movement, which emerged at the beginning of the nineties as a cult of counter-violence (Wilson 1992), assisting FRELIMO in its fight against RENAMO. The leader of this movement, a man named Manuel Antonio, was possessed by various Christian spirits, who – in local perspective – took part in the fight against RENAMO. Thus, in Mozambique the war between FRELIMO and RENAMO also developed into a war of spirits (Wilson 1992: 49).

In many societies, even in precolonial times, war was related to spirits and spirit mediums. Before a war could take place, spirit mediums would be consulted and asked for their advice. While they would sometimes only give spiritual support, at other times they would even take part in the actual fighting as war leaders (for example Lamphear and Webster 1971: 33; Jacobs 1965: 77). Although these spirit mediums were normally empowered by their spirits to guarantee the well-being and fertility of the land and the people, they also could use their power to kill. It is this ambivalence in the concept of the spirits' power, their oscillation between healing and killing, between peace and war, which I will address from an historical perspective in this chapter.

In Acholi, in Northern Uganda, a series of prophets, possessed by various spirits, emerged to organize resistance against the government of the National Resistance Army (NRA) of Yoweri Museveni.[3] In 1985, a young woman named Alice Auma, from Gulu in Acholi, was possessed by a previously unknown Christian spirit named Lakwena.[4] His mission was 'to help as a doctor'. Under the guidance of this spirit, Alice established herself as a spirit medium and built up a new cult of affliction, working as a healer and diviner.[5] In August 1986, in a situation of internal and external crisis (Behrend 1992), she started to organize the 'Holy Spirit Mobile Forces' (HSMF) and to wage war against the government, against witches and against impure soldiers. She recruited many former soldiers into her movement. After the first military successes against the NRA, other segments of the population joined her. She created a complex initiation and purification ritual in which she freed the 'Holy Spirit soldiers' of witchcraft and evil spirits. She promised her soldiers magical protection against the enemy's bullets and invented the so-called 'Holy Spirit Tactics', a way of warfare in which she combined modern war techniques and magical practices. Under the leadership of various spirits, Alice marched with 7,000 to 10,000 men and women towards Kampala, the capital of Uganda. Near Jinja, some 30 miles from Kampala, she and her soldiers were defeated by government troops. Many of her soldiers died or were injured. She crossed into Kenya, where she remains to this day.[6]

Even after the HSMF had suffered the decisive defeat of October 1987, the spirit Lakwena took possession of Alice's father, Saverino Lukoya, who continued to fight with the rest of her soldiers until 1989, and Joseph Kony, a young cousin of Alice's, who has continued the struggle in Northern Uganda. In fact, there were not just three but, at times, even five different Holy Spirit movements. With the exception of Alice, all the other leaders were men. She marked the beginning of a series of prophets, and it was the discourse and practice she 'invented' which the others, with some variations, took over.

In the first part of this chapter, I will reconstruct a history of spirits and spirit possession in Acholi, Northern Uganda, with special reference to the ambivalence of healing and killing inherent in the various discourses on power. I will attempt to unfold the inner logic of alternate cults and movements in a limited diachronic perspective. A cult or a movement as a unit of analysis, seen in isolation, ignores and obscures the fact that cults and movements develop in relation to each other, sometimes in opposition to each other, and that they borrow from each other. Thus, it is the analysis of religious pluralism (Fabian 1985) in the context of power struggles which opens up new ways of understanding the construction of difference.

In the second part of the chapter, I will present the political situation which gave rise to the different Holy Spirit Movements; in the third and last section I will come back to the construction of difference concerning spirit possession, this time dealing with the 'minor' differences between three 'Holy Spirit Movements' (HSM), the movement of Alice, her father, and Joseph Kony, all of which shared more or less the same Christian discourse created by Alice. In addition, I will try to establish a correlation between the more or less local or global character of spirits emerging in the movements and the movements' different political and social contexts.

Reconstruction of the history of religions in Acholi

Central to the religions in Northern Uganda was and still is the term *jok*, any of a variety of forces, powers or spirits which can take possession of people, especially women, animals and things, gifting them with a particular power or strength.

The power of the *jogi* (pl. of *jok*) has been deeply ambivalent. It could be used for good and bad purposes, for healing, and for killing. Thus, in precolonial times, the chief of one of about 30 chiefdoms (which, during colonial times, became Acholi) would use the power of the chiefdom *jok* to advance the well-being and fertility of the land and its people. However, he would also use the same power to wage a war against a neighbouring chiefdom.[7] The chiefdom *jogi* were guardians of the moral order. A more or less immoral state of society would make them angry and would result in their sending social or natural catastrophes. Thus the *jogi* were held responsible for misfortune and catastrophes which hit the chiefdom and, at the same time, were a power against them.

It appears that in the middle of the last century, at the time of slave raiding and slave-ivory trade, a paradigm shift occurred in the discourse of the spirits. During this time of external (and internal) threat, a wave of new spirits called free *jogi* arrived from the outside world. While the chiefdom-*jogi* were bound to locality, to mountains, trees or caves of a chiefdom, the free *jogi* as alien spirits were much more global in character, bringing the threats from the outside world and, simultaneously, acting as an instrument against these threats. Their spirit mediums, in Acholi called *ajwaka*, formed centres of various cults of affliction. While the chiefdom *jogi* were primarily responsible for the collective good of the chiefdom, the free *jogi* healed individual suffering and, in a way, became 'agents of modernity', appropriating into their cults Western commodities. However, the healing by a free *jok* (or the *ajwaka* of a free *jok*) was deeply ambiguous because it included an act of retaliation against the aggressor who had caused the suffering. Thus, from the aggressor's point of view the *jok*'s power was used to harm or even kill him or her.

When Christian missionaries, from the Church Missionary Society and the Catholic Comboni Mission, came to Acholi at the beginning of the twentieth century, a complex process of mutual influence began, a reorganization and reformulation of religious discourses. In this process, the Acholi religion was not only Christianized but the Christian teachings were also 'Acholicized'. In this process, the ambivalence inherent in the Acholi concept of *jok* was split into a moral dualism. While the Christian god, given the name *Jok Rubanga*,[8] became the absolute goodness, the other *jogi*, as lesser spirits, were equated with Satan, then became known as *jogi setani* and were thought of as evil in themselves. The missionaries thus produced a hegemonic discourse in which a large number of evil spirits lost their ambiguity and were increasingly suspected of being used mainly for witchcraft and sorcery, or more precisely for killing. Besides demonization and diabolization, these spirits now were subdued under the one Christian God. Comparable to the canonists, bishops and inquisitors in Europe, who substantially molded the dominant ideas of witches (Ginzburg 1990), the missionaries in Acholi also produced what they were actually seeking to fight.

While the Christian religion, supported by the colonial power, gradually

advanced to central cults, the pagan cults of affliction were increasingly marginalized and discriminated against. Also, since some of the mediums became commer-
cialized and profit-oriented, they were sometimes suspected of being witches
themselves.

Through the mediation of a fundamentalist Christian movement, the Balokole, in
the forties, the Christian discourses became more and more detached from their
colonial heritage. The Balokole not only vehemently criticized the immorality of the
established churches but also furthered the Acholization of the Christian messages.
In this process, the Christian Holy Spirit, leaving God the Father and Son behind,
gained increasing importance and finally, split – like *jok* – into a plurality of holy
spirits. When, at the beginning of the seventies, under Idi Amin Dada, many Acholi
lost their lives or were forced into exile to Tanzania, a few Christian holy, unam-
biguously morally good spirits – for example the spirit of the Virgin Mary or the
spirit of Jesus – appeared for the first time in Acholi. A renewed change of
paradigms in the world of spirits then took place. These new spirits opposed the *free
jogi* as being pagan, criticizing their corruption and greediness for money. They no
longer called themselves *jogi* but *tipu maleng*, 'pure ancestor', a term the Catholic
missionaries, especially the Verona Fathers in Gulu, had used to translate the Christian concept of the Holy Spirit. To mark the opposition to the pagan spirit mediums,
the Christian spirit mediums took over the name *nabi* or *nebbi*, from *nabi* ('prophet'
in the Old Testament). In contrast to the pagan spirit mediums who not only healed
but also tried to harm and even kill the aggressor who had caused the affliction, the
Christian spirit mediums would only heal and purify from witchcraft without
bewitching the witch. Thus, the chains of retaliatory bewitching which had previously never ceased in Acholi, were put to an end.

However, these Christian spirit mediums remained in a marginal position until
Alice Lakwena took over the new Christian discourse and spread it in the North of
Uganda.

Political history

After the Uganda National Liberation Army (UNLA) with the help of Tanzanian
troops had ousted Idi Amin and Obote had regained power, allegedly by means of
a rigged election, a brutal civil war began in Uganda in which Acholi, for the most
part, fought on the side of the government army (UNLA) against Museveni's NRA.
During this civil war in which many Acholi fell, the spirit Lakwena appeared. On 2
January 1985, he took possession of Alice Auma and ordered her to heal the sick and
the wounded with holy water. Rivalries within the UNLA – Acholi soldiers suspected Obote of sacrificing them senselessly in the war – led to a coup. Headed by
an Acholi, Bazilio Okello, soldiers, mostly Acholi, marched on Kampala and ousted
Obote in July 1985. Tito Okello, also an Acholi, became the new State President. By
now, a group of Acholi took state power for the first time in the history of Uganda.
They used this power, as had others before them, to gain wealth and to retaliate, for
instance, against people from the West Nile and the Langi. However, after this victory, the UNLA disintegrated into a number of marauding groups which divided up
Kampala between them and went on a plundering rampage.

Although the Okellos concluded a peace agreement with the NRA in December 1985, the NRA marched on Kampala in January, and since the UNLA was no longer capable of mounting effective resistance, the Okellos were ousted by the NRA on 26 January 1986. Thousands of Acholi soldiers fled to the North, into their home villages or into Sudan. They hid their weapons in the villages and attempted to lead a peasant life, but only a few were successful. During the civil war, they had lived from plundering and had become contemptuous of peasant life. They had become 'internal strangers' (Werbner 1989: 239) and their return caused disturbances and violence. They began to plunder in the villages and terrorize anyone they did not like. The elders tried to exercise their authority over the soldiers, often through recourse to 'Acholi traditions', but they were unable to gain the upper hand.

Even after the NRA had established itself as an occupying power in Gulu and Kitgum, the tensions, conflicts, denunciations and acts of revenge among the Acholi continued. Already during the civil war, death in war had been interpreted in terms of witchcraft. The enemy's bullet that killed an Acholi was not seen to be the true cause of death. Often – from a local perspective – a relative or neighbour with whom the deceased had been in conflict had bewitched him to ensure that the enemy's bullet would hit him and no one else. The war against an exterior, alien enemy, the NRA, was thus turned inward, increasing tensions and conflicts among the Acholi that may otherwise have remained latent. In this situation of inner discord, the first AIDS deaths occurred at the beginning of 1986. In Acholi, AIDS was and is interpreted in the idiom of witchcraft.[9] This also further escalated the inner conflicts in Acholi.

Then, a new battalion of the NRA was stationed in Acholi, consisting of former FEDEMO soldiers who had fought against the Acholi during the civil war, especially in Luwero. When these soldiers took the opportunity to take revenge on the local people by plundering, torturing, murdering and raping, some former Acholi soldiers took their weapons from hiding and joined the Uganda Peoples Democratic Army (UPDA), which had meanwhile been founded in Sudan. When the NRA ordered the general disarming of the Acholi and carried out 'operations', in the course of which Acholi were tortured or disappeared in so-called 'politicization camps' – similar to concentration camps – more and more soldiers joined the UPDA. But the UPDA soldiers also began to terrorize the civilian population. In this situation of extreme interior and exterior threat, the spirit Lakwena ordered his medium Alice to stop healing, which had become senseless anyway, and to build up the HSMF instead, in order to bring down the government, to purify the world of sin and to build up a new world in which humans and nature would be reconciled (Behrend 1995a).

Let me isolate some of the causes that led to the HSM's war:

1 The loss of state power – consequently the HSM's war can be seen as an attempt to regain the power of the centre.
2 The threat of the NRA to take revenge and kill the Acholi. Actually it was much more than a threat. After the NRA had conquered Acholi in March 1986 and stationed battalions in Gulu and Kitgum, former soldiers and civilians were arrested and detained in military camps. Some of them never returned, others were tortured. In addition, property was looted by NRA soldiers, especially cars and cattle. Furthermore, Acholi in senior positions in government and

companies were dismissed and evicted from their official residences. Matters were made worse by the official propaganda in the media, radio and newspapers against the people of the North, the Acholi in particular, holding them responsible for all the sufferings Ugandans had undergone (Ocan 1996).

3   The desperate situation of a group of soldiers who, having been defeated, lost their jobs and fled as 'loosers' and 'cowards' back to their homes. There they were seen as 'internal strangers' (Werbner 1989) (because they had become unclean by killing and thus were bringing *cen*, the spirits of the killed)and, as many of them opposed the demands of the elders to undergo cleansing rituals as unpure persons they were responsible for the misfortune that hit Acholi.

4   A situation of internal terror (Lonsdale 1992: 355) in Acholi caused by internal conflicts between elders and young men (soldiers), rich and poor people and between men and women, but actualized and reinforced by a discourse on sorcery and witchcraft. As Lonsdale remarked in relation to the comparable situation of Mau Mau in Kenya, enmities multiplied (ibid. 441) and turned parts of the north into a mood of moral panic (ibid. 388).

The Holy Spirit Mobile Forces of Alice Lakwena

In August 1986, Alice started recruiting former UNLA and UPDA soldiers to build up the HSMF. In strong opposition to the UPDA,[10] as well as to the NRA, she stressed the moral rehabilitation of the soldiers. Indeed, she was successful in disciplining and reintegrating the soldiers using the indigenized Christian discourse she had taken over from other Christian spirit mediums and which she had developed further. However, from a local perspective, it was not her but the spirits of the movement who decided which words were to be spoken and which actions taken. Beside Holy Spirit soldiers and parts of animate and inanimate nature (Behrend 1995a), there were 140,000 spirits fighting in the HSMF. These spirits were 'heavenly spirits', who formed the 'spiritual forces' of the movement. During fighting, they protected the soldiers as 'guardian spirits'. Should a soldier die in battle, after a short stay in purgatory, his spirit would rejoin the movement and continue fighting with the living soldiers. Thus, the HSM created a sort of ancestor cult, not based on descent but on membership of a corporate unit, the HSMF. Most of these spirits were without names. However, there were a few, the most important ones, who had names and who, in a complex process of mutual affirmation between medium and the public – the soldiers – developed into social persons.

These spirits formed a hierarchy. At their head was Lakwena, an Italian spirit whose discourse was one of Christian morality. He was the chairman and commander in chief of the HSMF. Then, following him, came an American spirit called Wrong Element who had a trickster-like character. When the Holy Spirit soldiers did not obey the Holy Spirit Safety Precautions (Behrend 1991), some twenty rules governing Christian behaviour, he would change sides and fight with the government troops to punish his soldiers. He was also responsible for the intelligence service. Franko was a spirit from Zaïre; he was called *Mzee*, meaning old man in Kiswahili, and was well respected. He took possession of Alice only rarely and was responsible for the supply of food and other necessities. Ching Poh was a spirit from Korea.

He was responsible for the supply of weapons and transport. He also organized the production of the so-called stone grenades. While Lakwena was the overall commander of the HSMF, Wrong Element, Franko and Ching Poh were leading one of the three companies of the army, named A, B, and C company. Another spirit called Jeremiah made his appearance infrequently. He worked as a nurse and healed wounds and diseases. Besides these spirits, there were a number of Islamic or Arabic fighter spirits in the HSMF who were mainly responsible for the fight against the government troops. They were called Kassim, Mohammed, Miriam, Medina and Ali Shila. In addition to the female spirits Miriam and Medina, there was one other female spirit working in the HSMF. This spirit was called Nyaker, and came from Acholi. Nyaker was the only indigenous spirit while all the other spirits were alien spirits. Nyaker means daughter of a chief in Acholi. The daughter of a chief in precolonial times could not be married to a commoner but had to marry the chief of another chiefdom. By this alliance, peace between the two chiefdoms would be ensured. The spirit Nyaker worked as a nurse in the HSM, healing the wounded and sick. She specialized in exorcism, chasing away bad spirits who possessed the Holy Spirit soldiers. Thus, the opposition between healing and killing was again reproduced in the spirits' division of labour. While Jeremiah and Nyaker were responsible for healing, the duty of the Arabic spirits was to kill.

Before a military action began, the spirit Lakwena took possession of his spirit medium Alice. She and her soldiers then stayed in the yard, the public ritual centre of the defence. She sat on a stool, like a chief, and wore a white *kanzu*, male Islamic dress, with a rosary around her neck. The spirits took possession of her during the morning parade and during the seven o'clock evening parade. The chief clerk of Lakwena, the secretary, stood beside her to translate and write down what the spirits said.

While the various cults of affliction in Acholi – pagan as well as Christian – could be described as democratic or egalitarian in the sense that everybody was free to be possessed by a spirit and then establish a cult of affliction, Alice monopolized the spirits of the HSM. She alone was their medium. Should other people be possessed by spirits, these were then, by definition, bad spirits which had to be exorcized. Thus, by monopolizing the good spirits, Alice expressed her claim to the powers of a new centre (Behrend 1995b). She succeeded in establishing the discourse of her movement as the dominant discourse, at least for a short time, not only in the HSMF but also in some of the 'liberated' areas such as Kitgum and Apac. However, although Alice had originally appropriated the good, holy Christian spirits for healing, she now used them to wage war, that is, for killing. In order to heal society, she had to use violence, the power to kill. Thus, despite her intense opposition to pagan *jogi*, she reactivated the ambivalence inherent in the concept of *jok* by using her spirits for healing as well as for killing. By fighting witchcraft and sorcery, she used the means of a witch since she used the power of the spirits to kill. Thus, it is no surprise that after her defeat she was accused of being a witch by many of her former followers.

The spirits of Severino Lukoya

After the defeat of Alice's HSMF in October 1987 and her flight to Kenya, many of her soldiers who had survived the last battles tried to retreat to Acholi again. Some joined the Uganda Peoples' Army (UPA), a resistance movement operating in Teso.

Others became members of the UPDA, another movement fighting the government and operating mainly in Acholi. Some soldiers gave up fighting entirely and went home to work on their farms, while others changed sides completely and joined the former enemy, the government forces, thus fighting their former allies. And yet still others joined Alice's father, Severino Lukoya, who after his daughter's defeat, decided to continue the fight.

In 1958, Alice's father, Severino Lukoya, had had a vision. He fell from the top of a roof (according to another version, his wife beat him up), so that he became unconscious and went straight to heaven, where God told him that one of his children was the chosen child. God also filled him with many spirits. When, in 1985, his daughter Alice was possessed by Lakwena and became very sick, he looked after her. Being a former catechist of the Church of Uganda, his religious education seems to have had a strong influence on Alice. However, shortly before the spirit Lakwena took possession of her, she converted to Catholicism, thus marking a breach and a separation from her father's teachings. When Alice was already waging war and leading the HSMF, her father came and tried to participate in her movement; however, the spirit Lakwena immediately took possession of Alice and explained that there was no need for Severino to join the movement. Thus, Severino did not take part in his daughter's HSMF, and remained in Kitgum, in the northern part of the Acholi district. Only after Alice's defeat did he succeed in gathering a following of about 2,000 men and women. Like Alice, he established ritual centres, called 'yards', where praying took place and people were purified and healed. Like Alice, he trained some ritual experts called 'technicians', who did the ritual work in the yards. He succeeded in establishing some 200 ritual centres. People in Kitgum would leave the established churches and come to pray in the yards. It seems that a millenarian and eschatological enthusiasm increased among the people of Kitgum at this time.[11] Like Alice, Severino condemned witchcraft and forced the *ajwakas*, the pagan spirit mediums, to leave their 'satanic' work, even killing a few of them. It seems that he was rather successful. Some people from Kitgum told me that even notorious witches burned their medicines and joined the new established *yards*.

While Alice was leading a strongly centralized army, the movement of Severino, called the Lord's Army , was much more decentralized. It was organized into three departments: a military, a medical and a religious department. The military department was led by the chief of forces who operated quite independently from the other departments. Severino himself did not fight but sent some spirits who did. He also gave his soldiers spiritual support, cleansed them and, by praying for them, gave them magical protection.

Although Severino continued the war, the healing and cleansing of people – not only soldiers but also civilians – became more important in his movement than in Alice's. This may have been due to the total breakdown of health care in Northern Uganda. During the war, the health centres and hospitals were destroyed or were closed by government forces. Thus, the spirits were busy giving out recipes for medicines, for various 'Holy Spirit drugs', which would be locally produced to heal all sorts of trouble, including AIDS.

Following the example of his daughter, Severino took over some of Alice's spirits. He expressed continuity by harbouring the spirits Lakwena, Wrong Element, Nyaker, Miriam, Mohammed and Ali Shaban. Only Ching Poh refused to join. In addition to these spirits, a number of new spirits appeared called Oyite Ojok,

Ojukwu, Dr Ambrosoli and Bernhard. These new spirits were the spirits of historical persons who had lived in Acholi and, in one way or another, had influenced the
recent history of the north: Oyite Ojok was the spirit of a high UNLA officer from
Lango who died in an air crash on 2 December 1983 during the civil war. There were
rumours that he was killed by an act of sabotage by Obote because he had become
too powerful. Ojukwu was the spirit of the commander of the seventieth and
ninetieth battalions of the UPDA, Stephen Odyek, nicknamed Ojukwu.[12] He originally came from Kitgum and had already served under Idi Amin in the Uganda
Army. He then changed and became a member of the UNLA. In November 1986, he
gave Alice 150 of his soldiers to build up the HSMF, refusing to fight under her
command himself. In May 1987, some Karimojong cattle rustlers shot him and he
died, supposedly the way the spirit Lakwena had prophesied. Dr Ambrosoli was
the spirit of an Italian doctor. He came from an Italian family from Milan that had
become rich with the production of sweets. In 1955, he was ordained as a priest and
joined the Verona Fathers. Since 1956, he had worked in the Kalongo Hospital in
Kitgum. In March 1987, the government closed the hospital – fearing collaboration
between the HSM and the Catholic Verona Fathers who, without doubt, had sympathy for the HSMs. Dr Ambrosoli and his patients were forced to go to Lira, where
the doctor died of a heart attack on 27 March 1987. Bernhard was the spirit of an
American brother who taught in the Alokulum seminary and died there.

While the spirits of Alice's HSM, as well as the ones her father took over from her,
were 'international', more global in character, and formed more or less abstract
images which could not be related to a locality and to biographies of concrete living
persons, these new spirits of Severino were the spirits of persons who had lived
very recently among the Acholi. Although they had come from the outside – with
the exception of Ojukwu – they were well-known in Acholi and had taken part in
one way or another in the struggle against the government. They were bound to the
locality of Kitgum and used to construct a common local discourse in opposition to
the government. However, due to the moral element which was attached to these
spirits, and being the spirits of concrete historical persons who had become victims
of the government forces in one way or another, it is also possible that the Catholic
concept of saints and martyrs was appropriated and reformulated in the context of
spirit possession in Severino's movement.

There is something ironic about the way the biography of a historical person like
Ojukwu was reinvented when he became a spirit. Although in real life, as I mentioned above, he assisted Alice by giving her 150 soldiers to start her fight, he per-
sistently refused to fight under her command. Only after his death, after becoming
a spirit, did he finally fulfil the demand and became a spiritual member of the HSM.
Thus, in the idiom of spirit possession, a narrative is told and turned – as in wish
fulfillment – into a success story.

While Alice monopolized the good, holy, Christian spirits, Severino did not. His
movement was much more egalitarian in character. Everybody could be possessed
by a good Christian spirit. However, being possessed by a spirit was interpreted as
being a sign of being chosen to fight. Thus, although Severino used the power of his
spirits to heal afflictions, in general, spirit possession in his movement involved the
duty to kill. While in Alice's movement, with the exception of herself, exorcism was
practised, in Severino's movement, adorcism (de Heusch) took place, the proliferation of spirits in his movement not being confined by their monopolization. This

development gives evidence that the monopolization of spirits in a region with a long history of various democratic cults of affliction is difficult to retain. The claims to power expressed in the idiom of spirit possession give rise to a new pluralism, to new spirits and new mediums who will not accept the monopoly of others and try themselves to establish new centres.

The Lord's Resistance Army of Joseph Kony

The proliferation of spirits was even further developed in the third HSM, the movement of Joseph Kony. In contrast to the movements of Alice and her father, which only lasted a short time, Kony's movement has had a longer history, beginning in about 1987. Since then, the character of his movement has substantially changed. Unfortunately, I can reconstruct its history only in fragments.

Joseph Kony, a young man from Gulu, a school dropout, claimed to be the cousin of Alice (a claim she sometimes denied). According to one version, he became a soldier of the UPDA. According to another, he joined Alice's forces. Then, he himself became possessed by the spirit Lakwena; or according to another version, by the spirit Juma Oris, a spirit of a former minister under Idi Amin, who in 1993 formed the West Nile Bank Front in Sudan, another movement fighting the NRA. Following the orders of the spirit, he started building up his own HSM. While Alice operated in the Kitgum District and then marched towards Kampala, he mainly recruited his soldiers from Gulu. He offered Alice an alliance of their forces against the common enemy, but Alice's Lakwena refused, rendering Kony ridiculous. This he never forgot. To take revenge, he started cutting the food supply for Alice's forces and killed some of her soldiers. The rivalry escalated to such an extent that both groups started fighting against one another.

When Alice was defeated, some of her soldiers joined Kony's movement. After 1988 he also recruited soldiers from the UPDA (who nicknamed the HSMF Holy Spirit Devil Forces), especially those who wanted neither to accept the government's amnesty offer nor to stop fighting. Although he was a rival of Alice's, he nonetheless adopted the discourse and practices she had invented. Following her, he established a complex initiation and cleansing ritual. In addition, he issued rules of behaviour, the so-called Holy Spirit Safety Precautions and, like Alice, he fought witchcraft and killed pagan spirit mediums, the *ajwakas*. He also took over the so-called Holy Spirit Tactics, a way of fighting combining modern Western military techniques with ritual practices. Kony's movement was organized in three divisions, each of which had three departments called *won*, the father; *wod*, the son; and *tipu maleng*, the Holy Spirit. Before a battle took place, the soldiers were ritually loaded with *malaika*, the Swahili word for angel, to protect them against the enemy's bullets.

In contrast to Severino, who took over most of the spirits of Alice's movement, Kony was possessed by completely new spirits. After his quarrel with Alice, he never again became possessed by Lakwena (if he ever was). Thus, he marked his own claim to power in terms of discontinuity. The spirit of Juma Oris became chairman and commander of forces. A female spirit called Silli Silindi (Saint Cecilia) from Sudan became operation commander. She also led the Mary company, uniting the female soldiers of the movement. Ing Chu came from China or Korea. According to one version, he controlled the government forces' bullets and caused them to hit only sinful Holy Spirit soldiers. According to another version, he had the job of a jeep commander and made the NRA, the government forces, see jeeps coming towards them. El Wel Best was another Chinese or Korean spirit who planned military actions. Silver Koni was a spirit from Zaïre. He too controlled the bullets of the NRA. According to another version, he was commander in the *yard*. King Bruce came from the USA. He led the support unit and was responsible for the exploding of stone grenades (I suppose that he owes his name to Bruce Lee, the hero of Kung Fu films). Major Bianca was another female spirit from the USA. She was responsible for the *yard*. According to another version, she worked for the intelligence. Jim Brickey also came from the USA. He led the intelligence service. Like Wrong Element, he had trickster-like qualities and would change sides when the Holy Spirit soldiers had not followed the Holy Spirit Safety Precautions. In addition, there were the spirits Dr Salam or Saline, the chief medical officer, and two other spirits called Ali and Jacobo, about whom I have no further information.

Although Kony's spirits had new names, they strongly resembled Alice's with respect to their functions and characteristics. All these spirits would speak through Kony alone. He was their medium. Like Alice, he would sit in the *yard*, dressed in a white kanzu, and then the spirits would come, possess him and deliver their messages. Although Kony, like Alice, monopolized these spirits, he nevertheless allowed other mediums to join his movement and have their own spirits. Thus, a man called Nelson Odora, who was possessed by a spirit of the angel Gabriel, joined Kony's movement and preached, healed and prophesied for the soldiers. In addition, a woman called Poline Angom, possessed by twelve spirits, joined Kony's movement, in 1987 (Lukermoi 1990). She, like other women, was allowed to work as a spirit medium, to divine and heal soldiers.

In contrast to Alice, who led a big army and transcended ethnic boundaries, Kony was only able to fight a guerilla war, operating in more or less independent small fighting groups in Northern Uganda and Southern Sudan. Although he centralized the power by monopolizing the main spirits, other guerilla groups were allowed to have their own spirit mediums working at the periphery. Thus, in a way, we have here a compromise between the strong centralization of Alice's spirit-organization and the democratic organization of her father, Kony, combining the two principles.

While the spirits which were monopolized by Kony more or less shared the abstract character of Alice's spirits, the spirits of his spirit mediums were, like the new spirits of Severino, much more concrete and locally bound. They were either the spirits of historical persons known in Acholi, such as the spirits of Bishop Hannington and Bishop Luwum, or the spirits of biblical persons like Luka, Noah, Sarah and Marc, to name just a few examples. The local properties of these spirits corresponded to the ethnic and locally-confined character of Kony's (and Severino's) movement, while the more abstract character of Alice's spirits may correspond to the supra-ethnic nature of her movement. It seems that to an even stronger extent, Kony's mediums tried to integrate the Christian biblical discourse to mark opposition to the pagan mediums.

Like Alice, Kony used his spirits to heal and to kill. Thus, although in a Christian discourse, he reactivated the ambivalence inherent in the concept of *jok*. However, in May 1988, the government and some parts of the UPDA signed a peace treaty.

The rest of the UPDA joined Kony's movement and its leader, Odong Latek, became quite influential in shaping the movement. A process of secularization took place: Holy Spirit tactics were replaced by guerilla tactics, and the name of the movement was changed to the Uganda Peoples Democratic Christian Army (UPDCA). The religious discourse retreated into the background, though it did not disappear completely. However, when Odong Latek was killed, Kony changed the name of his movement again to Lord's Resistance Army (LRA); and it seems that he reinforced the religious discourse.

After 1990, the war in Northern Uganda gained an international dimension. The LRA found new allies. Kony cemented relations with the Sudanese government, which provided his soldiers with weapons and means of transportation, since the Ugandan government supported the SPLA. Beyond this, Kony also fought in cooperation with the West Nile Bank Front (WNBF), a movement, as already mentioned, born in 1993 in the West Nile Region under the leadership of Juma Oris. Idi Amin is also said to stand in close contact with the WNBF. However, in 1997 this movement was crushed by the joint forces of NRA (now called Uganda Defence Forces), SPLA and Kabila's Alliance of Forces for Democracy and Liberation in Congo Zaïre (personal communication from Mark Leopold).

Since the war has now lasted for more than ten years, it has become a system of production and has created a form of life, 'normalizing' and banalizing violence and brutality and blurring the distinction between war and peace. For most of the soldiers, whether they fight on the side of the government or its opponents, war has become business and is more profitable than peace. They have thus developed an essential interest in keeping the war going or extending it to other terrains, for example Rwanda (compare Behrend and Meillassoux 1994) or Zaïre.

While on the one hand, new international support allowed Kony to enter the international media stage – his publicity agent in Nairobi published the movement's programme on the Internet – he on the other hand, increasingly lost the support of the local population. His soldiers, forming small desparate groups, lived mainly from stealing, plundering local peasants, kidnapping young girls and boys and making attacks and laying ambushes here and there. They were only tolerated in some parts of Acholi because the government soldiers behaved in an even worse manner.

As the history of the three HSMs shows, caught in the desperate cycle of violence and counter-violence, the initially pure aims inevitably became soiled. While at its beginning Alice's HSM tried to heal society and to reconstitute the moral order, the following movements at the end became groups of killers forcing the ambivalence inherent in the concept of *jok* to one extreme: killing. Thus, the Christian spirits' attempt to create a new moral space without witchcraft and sorcery failed.

Notes

1   The end of the socialist governments in Eastern Europe, an increasing trade in weapons, the politics of the IMF (International Monetary Fund) and the World Bank imposing processes of so-called democratization, the existence of predatory states and the emergence of likewise predatory resistance movements could be given as some of the reasons for the recent increase in wars in Africa.

32   Heike Behrend

2   Although I agree with Kriger in her critique of Lan neglecting too much coercion and violence by the guerillas to mobilize the peasants, I think that she herself underestimates the importance of the guerillas fighting witchcraft to legitimate their fight and their claim for political power.
3   In 1987, I began work on the war of the Holy Spirit Movements in Northern Uganda. The University of Bayreuth's *Special Research Programme* (SFB) allowed me to work in Uganda, especially in Kampala and Gulu for some sixteen months from 1987 to 1995. I would like to thank the SFB and the *German Research Foundation* for their kind support. In addition, I want to thank Mike Ocan for his kind assistance and the permission to quote from his paper (Ocan 1996).
4   Lakwena means messenger and apostle in Acholi.
5   In the following, I will keep to the local perspective representing the spirits as the actors and not Alice.
6   For a more detailed analysis of the war in Northern Uganda see Behrend (1993).
7   There existed, however, a moral confinement. The *jogi* were said to be helpful only if the war waged was a rightful war, if, for example, the war could be interpreted as an act of retaliation. I am grateful to Zeru D. O. Abukha for this remark.
8   To choose Jok Rubanga for a translation of the Christian God was indeed a very unfortunate choice of the missionaries, since in Acholi *Jok Rubanga* was responsible for bringing tuberculosis of the spine (Okot p'Bitek 1980: 41ff).
9   The discourse on witchcraft was one of a few alternate discourses which were used to explain death by AIDS. Ancestor spirits or the Christian God were also made responsible for bringing AIDS as a punishment for transgressions of the moral order.
10 Different versions exist about the relationship between the HSMF and the UPDA. According to one version, Alice, at the beginning, was fighting under the leadership of the UPDA, more or less a puppet in the hand of a small group of UPDA soldiers. Only later did she gain independence from the UPDA and, toward the end, even started fighting some UPDA battalions. According to another version, after having taken over 150 soldiers from the UPDA, she never really relied on this movement.
11 Unfortunately, due to problems of security, I have not visited Kitgum to do further research on regional differences with respect to the various resistance movements.
12 He called himself Ojukwu after the Southern Nigerian leader of Biafra in the Nigerian civil war, because he had a beard like the real Ojukwu.

References

Bayart, J.-F. (1989) *L'Etat en Afrique: La Politique du Ventre*, Paris, Fayard.
Bazin, J. & E. Terray (eds) (1982) *Guerres de lignages et guerres d'états en Afrique*, Paris: Archives Contemporaines.
Behrend, H. (1991) 'Is Alice Lakwena a witch? The Holy-Spirit-Movement and its fight against evil in the north of Uganda', *Changing Uganda* H.B. Hansen & M. Twaddle, (eds). London: James Currey.
—— (1992) 'Violence dans le nord de l'Ouganda', *Politique Africaine*, 48: 103–15.
—— (1993) *Alice und die Geister. Krieg im Norden Ugandas*, München: Trickster. (French edition, Paris: Harmattan, 1997; English edition, Oxford: James Currey, forthcoming).
—— (1995a) 'The Holy Spirit Movement and the forces of nature in the north of Uganda 1985–87', in *Religion and Politics in East Africa*, M. Twaddle & H.B. Hansen (eds). London: James Currey.
—— (1995b) 'Power and women as spirit mediums', *Gender and Identity in Africa*, M. Reh & G. Ludwar-Ene (eds) Münster/Hamburg: Lit Verlag. 51–9.
Behrend, H. & C. Meilassoux (1994) 'Krieg in Ruanda', in *Lettre* 26, 5: 12–15.
Fabian J. (1985) 'Religious pluralism', *Theoretical Explorations in African Religion*, van Binzbergen & M. Schoffeleers (eds). London: KPI.
Geffray, C. (1990) *La cause des armes au Mozambique*, Paris: Karthala.
Ginzburg, Carl (1990) *Hexensabbat*, Berlin: Verlag Klaus Wagenbach.
Haas, J. (ed.) (1990) *The Anthropology of War*, Cambridge: Cambridge University Press.
Hutchinson, S.E. (1996) *Nuer Dilemmas: Coping with Money, War, and the State*, Berkeley, Los Angeles, London: University of California Press.

Jacobs, A.H. (1965) 'The traditional political organisation of the pastoral Maasai', unpublished PhD thesis. Oxford.

Kriger, N. (1992) *Zimbabwe's Guerilla War*, Cambridge: Cambridge University Press.

Lamphear, J.E. & Webster, J.B. (1971) 'The Jie-Acholi War', *Uganda Journal*, 35: 23–42.

Lan, David (1987) *Guns and Rain: Guerillas and Spirit Mediums in Zimbabwe*, London/Berkeley: James Currey/University of California Press.

Lonsdale, J. (1992) 'The moral economy of Mau Mau', *Unhappy Valley*, Bruce Berman & John Lonsdale (eds), London: James Currey.

Lukermoi, A. (1990) 'The effects of the Holy Spirit Movement on the Christian Church', MA thesis, Makerere University, Kampala, Uganda.

Meillassoux, C. (1990) 'Poissons a brûler', paper given at the International Conference on Starving and Society, Madrid.

Ocan, M. (1996) 'The war currently taking place in Northern Uganda', paper presented to the Sessional Committee on Defence and Internal Affairs, Parliament House, Kampala, Uganda.

Otterbein, K.F. (1994) 'Feuding and Warfare' in *War and Society*, vol I, Amsterdam: Gordon & Breach Science Publishers.

P'Bitek O. (1980) *Religion of the Central Luo*, Kampala: East African Literature Bureau.

Ranger, T. (1985) *Peasant Consciousness and Guerrilla War in Zimbabwe*, London: James Currey.

—— (1992) 'War, violence and healing in Zimbabwe', *Journal of Southern African Studies*, 18.

Reyna, S.P. and R.E.Downs (eds) (1994) 'Studying War, Anthropological Perspectives', *War and Society*, vol. 2, Amsterdam: Gordon & Breach Scientific Publishers.

Roesch, O. (1992) 'RENAMO and the peasantry in Southern Mozambique', in *Canadian Journal of African Studies*, 26, 3.

Werbner, R.P. (1989) *Ritual Passage, Sacred Journey*, Manchester: Manchester University Press.

Wilson, K.B. (1992) 'Cults of violence and counter-violence', *Journal of Southern African Studies*, 18, 3: 527–82.

3

The Invention
of Anti-Tradition
Dodo Spirits
in Southern Niger

Adeline Masquelier

novelty is no less novel for being able to dress up as antiquity
Eric Hobsbawm, *The Invention of Tradition*

Negotiating tradition and modernity in spirit possession

Forms of resistance to Western custom and commodities in postcolonial Africa have been richly documented by scholars eager to demonstrate the creative, if not successful, ways in which the marginal and the dispossessed struggle to defuse colonial institutions, reroute the flow of market goods and reconfigure exploitative systems of production. According to David Lan (1989), Shona mediums in Zimbabwe resisted their incorporation into capitalist economy by rejecting products that could only be obtained with cash. For the Beng of Ivory Coast, Alma Gottlieb (1992) tells us, this reluctance to enter the world of mass-produced goods and mechanized transportation takes the form of a repulsion for cigarette smoke and gasoline fumes which have become apt symbols of the elusive, yet expansive, power of Western consumerism. Among the Tshidi Zionists of South Africa described by Jean Comaroff (1985), reversing the destructive impact of proletarianization has meant ritually washing all purchased objects whose commodity status threatens the integrity of church members seeking to remain free from the polluting influence of the global market culture. Whether such avoidance centres on noxious smells or Coca Cola bottles, motorized vehicles or imported goods, the various sets of ritual prohibitions followed by Africans across the continent are often grounded in a notion of pollution, or rather of the polluting effects of commodities which so tangibly objectify the estranging world that has produced them.

In Arewa, the Hausaphone region of the Niger republic where I conducted field-work in 1988 and 1989, resistance to modern technology and market goods is neither couched in the idiom of pollution, nor systematically and homogeneously carried out by people determined to lay out the basis of a new moral order. Rather it takes the form of a highly personalized etiquette which the mediums of certain spirits by the name of Dodo struggle to enforce against all odds. Dodo devotees rarely belong to a possession troupe and keep their affairs separate from the sphere of *bori*, the better known and more amply documented social structure through which mediums as well as other people communicate and interact with spirits (Monfouga-Nicolas 1972; Besmer 1983; Tremearne 1914; Lewis 1991; Lewis, Al-Safi and Hurreiz 1991; Masquelier 1993a; Echard 1989, 1991). They operate strictly on their own, guided only by the spirits to whom they regularly lend their bodies so that these amorphous creatures may for a brief moment be endowed with corporeality. Thus, while Dodo mediums might be possessed by *bori* spirits – who also make demands upon their human devotees – and even attend *bori* rituals if it is appropriate, they will never be possessed by a Dodo while participating in a *bori wasa* ('play'; i.e., ceremony). When they are possessed by their Dodo, no *bori* spirits are allowed to enter the ritual arena by mounting their devotees. One might say that the Dodo are loners who do not require the company of fellow spirits to productively interact with humans.

In contrast to the mediums of the *bori* whose practices are motivated by an urgency to appropriate novel modes of generating value, and to objectify their control over moral and material economies, Dodo mediums shun certain imported commodities, motor transportation and literacy so as to restore a semblance of 'tradition' in communities which they see as spoiled by the influx of Western goods and customs. In an attempt to distinguish themselves from those who have turned healing practices into profitable ventures, they draw from the past to relocate themselves in a present that stands – at times resolutely and at times not so – opposed to things 'modern'.

Before I go on, let me locate this invention of tradition – which is itself the contestation of another tradition, that of *bori* – in the historical and social context in which it emerges. For many Hausa-speaking Mawri villagers, even among those who have wholeheartedly embraced the teachings of the Qur'an in what is now a predominantly Muslim country, *bori* is synonymous with 'traditional'. In the eyes of many Mawri, especially women – for whom the continued support of spirits is essential to the affirmation and realization of their fertility (Masquelier 1995) – the *bori* helps preserve a local heritage (*gado*) whose continued viability is threatened by modernity and the encroachment of Islamic rites and values on Mawri communities (Masquelier 1993b, 1994). For *bori* is above all concerned with maintaining, or at times mending, the symbiotic relationship between spirits and humans upon which the health and prosperity of individuals, households and communities are contingent.

Such a view is shared not only by illiterate peasants, who paradoxically openly disapprove of spirit possession, but also by members of the educated elite – regardless of their professed religious allegiances – who no longer fear that attending rituals of possession will earn them the label 'backward' that is generally pinned on spirit devotees by those who follow the paths of Allah. Because through their education and occupations, they stand safely in the secular realm of modern, bureaucratic practices, Mawri civil-servants, teachers and engineers can claim the *bori* back as part of their cultural identity if only to illuminate how modern and progressive they have become in contrast to other villagers. Thus for them, *bori* is useful as an authentic relic of Mawri 'traditions' and as a foil against which to reassert one's identity while investing more 'modern' practices with renewed prestige. Besides amounting to 'traditional culture' for the educated elite, *bori* is seen as an important source of healing power for many civil-servants who feel acutely the sting of competition and the fear of unemployment. When Qur'anic medicines and prayers seem to lose their efficacy, teachers and bureaucrats will seek the services of a *bori* healer to insure their protection and prosperity in a ruthless world where one's inability to hold on to a salaried position, or simply to manoeuvre within one's professional sphere is often attributed to the evil schemes of a competitor or a jealous colleague.

For the Muslim majority who clings to the prestige awarded by the status of follower of the Prophet in a region where Qur'anic principles have only recently become the norm, *bori* also stands for tradition and community, but it is at the same time synonymous with backwardness and superstition because it competes with, and contradicts, Islamic values and conventions. As a pre-Islamic religious practice which has long endured the criticisms and attacks of Islam, *bori* has now become a marginal cult disowned by prosperous Muslim traders and prominent officials, and predominantly attracting women.

But not everyone sees the possession cult as a well of tradition. For the old *bori* guard who has witnessed the takeover of *bori* institutions by an increasing number of alleged healers who set up shop to sell medicines and services, the practices surrounding spirit possession have become an immoral business (Masquelier 1993a). The ambitious young men who openly compete with each other and steal their master's medicines and clientele have corrupted the *bori* cult to such an extent that it is now a religion of facade and pretence run by eager entrepreneurs who have little knowledge of medicinal plants, charge exorbitant prices and show no commitment to their patients. Whether or not *bori* healers used to be the disinterested and upright individuals some claim they once were in an increasingly distant, yet oddly prominent, past, it remains that the cult offers today a fan of opportunities to aspiring mediums eager to acquire money, recognition and easy gratification.

It is against this backdrop of alleged corruption, materialism and competition that the Dodo spirits emerged, demanding commitment, sincerity and integrity from their mediums. Refusing to take part in the frenzied search for money that threatened to diminish the quality and efficacy of healing practices at the hands of both Muslim and *bori* practitioners, Dodo spirits did not compromise. If their mediums behaved inappropriately, showed signs of immorality or greed, or simply did not live up to their Dodo's expectations, the spirits would simply leave them. Overnight, mediums would find out that they no longer had the capacity to invite their spirits to take possession of their corporeal shell. With the spirit gone, so would all the extraordinary curing and divinatory powers that compelled the sick to travel huge distances to experience the force of their healing touch. In this chapter, I want to describe some of the facets of Dodo mediumship in an attempt to explicate how some Mawri villagers have capitalized on the notion of tradition to reconfigure an order of value which, because it remained anchored in people's relationships to spirits, was threatened by the Mawri's growing lack of commitment to *bori* deities.

Though they appeal to an idealized notion of the *traditional* – that stands resolutely opposed to the 'tradition' of *bori* – to counter the nefarious evils of modernity, the ritualized attempts to reform personal disciplines and spiritual selfhoods I will discuss below clearly defy simplistic oppositions between the meaningful order of the past and the material economy of the present, between the morality extolled in 'traditional' creeds and the selfish interests that govern modern life. As others have argued elsewhere (Comaroff and Comaroff 1993), such synthetic distinctions between tradition and modernity only obscure the complex dialectics of change and continuity which are brought to the fore through the innovative schemes of ritual bricoleurs like the Dodo mediums of Arewa. They are also misleading in that they presuppose that ritual critiques and contestations can only be meaningfully explicated as attempts to deal with cultural 'disintegration'.

This is not to say that we can or should disregard people's own understandings of global history and local transformations. To be sure, for all their lack of 'objectivity' and linearity, and their poetic contrasts (Comaroff and Comaroff 1987; Bonte and Echard 1976; Tonkin 1992), indigenous histories should be carefully situated and analysed with the understanding that such interpretations of the gloomy present are necessarily constructed against the backdrop of a beautified, almost commoditized, 'tradition'. Modernity here is an imagined, yet hardly static, category of experience that often serves to contextualize and authorize newly nuanced conceptions of evil, affliction and economic hardship. Thus, rather than argue about whether to label the experimental practices of Dodo devotees as inventions of tradition, inversions of tradition or even, following the title of this paper, as inventions of anti-tradition, I wish to locate these practices in the local field of moral and material relations in which they have emerged. Like other ritualized movements the world over which seek to redefine bodies, technologies and communities, the conventions of Dodo mediums constitute an imaginative, yet no less pragmatic, effort to regain control over a moral order whose viability hinges on the strength of spiritual bonds rather than on the power of market relations.

Elusive spirits and fragile bonds

While anyone may theoretically become the mount of a Dodo, it is clear that the spirit chooses carefully the person whom he wants to endow with the gift of healing. Villagers generally find out that they have a Dodo as they would any other spirit: they become sick and no conventional treatment seems to be effective. It is often after they have unsuccessfully tried various cures that they are finally diagnosed as being plagued by a spirit. Only by placating this superhuman force and agreeing to his/her request will they see their condition improve. One of my neighbours, whom I shall refer to as Amadou, recounted for me how he had met his Dodo:

> When I was first caught by Dodo, I spent six months in bed without going out. I only drunk milk and water with medicine [to sustain myself]. I was travelling in the bush and I met a young student. The student was really Dodo who had taken on a human appearance. Then, he changed himself into a dog who followed me wherever I went for three months. It is only after [this period] that Dodo possessed me and told [me] to hold ceremonies [on a regular basis] so those who needed him could come and be healed. After that Dodo possessed me and people came from all over to see me. I healed everyone, except if it was a disease that could not be cured.

This is a common account of what happens to someone who falls prey to a spirit's attention. Perhaps the main visible difference between having a *bori* spirit and having a Dodo spirit lies in the kinds of commitment mediums must make toward their respective deities. While the initiated *'yan bori* ('son of *bori*,' i.e., member of the cult) are not expected to hold a *wasa* (ceremony) more than once a year – and in fact

38 Adeline Masquelier

rarely have the finances to do so – to satisfy their spirits, the mediums of Dodo, who are not initiated, have to invite their spirit to a *wasa* once, twice and even three times a week. The ceremony is held neither to thank one's spirits for their benevolence nor to acknowledge one's devotion to them, but rather to enable the spirit to dispense his healing powers over the afflicted. This means that mediums must associate themselves with a band of musicians who will play the songs of the spirits each time a *wasa* is held.

Individuals who become recognized as the new mediums of Dodo spirits will more than likely see their reputation enhanced overnight as people start coming to them in the hope that they will provide them with the medicine that will heal their ailments and ensure continued prosperity. The healing and divinatory powers of Dodo horses[1] (*doki*) are far superior, I was told, to the already impressive capacities of some of the more prominent figures of *bori*. As one Dodo medium put it, 'Dodo is like a chief and other spirits are afraid of him'. The long lines of clients patiently awaiting their turn during the weekly, bi-weekly or daily possession ceremonies attest to the renown Dodo mediums earn while the spirits are 'on their heads'.[2] Dodo spirits are most efficient at divining the future because they have four eyes, two in front and two in the back. Seeing, here, is not about vision in the conventional sense. It is a question of erudition as well as discernment and moral fortitude, a set of qualities which dedicated *bori* mediums can also technically acquire through an initiatory ritual which 'opens the medium's eyes'.[3]

Partly because they see things no one else sees, Dodo devotees may see their reputation spread like fire. Such fame, however, rarely lasts. For 'Dodo spirits are like the wind', people say. They come and they go without warning and there is no use trying to regain one of these deities' attachment if he has decided that his horse has behaved improperly or selfishly. My neighbour Amadou, whose Dodo had rendered him so sick at first, had held ceremonies for his spirit three days a week for five months when the deity allegedly decided to leave him. Though he felt that his healing powers had not totally evaporated – after all, he had succeeded in curing a woman who was infertile – he knew, after several failed attempts, that there was no point in inviting the spirit to possess him. The Dodo was gone. 'He was fooling around', a spirit devotee volunteered about Amadou's problem, 'and Dodo spirits don't forgive'. The man was alluding to the fact that, in contrast to Dodo spirits who do not give their mediums a second opportunity if they ruin their first chance, spirits of the *bori* pantheon usually send their horses a warning in the form of an affliction (or misfortune) when they have been offended. If the devotees make amends, placate the spirits with an offering and promise to respect them in the future, the deities will forgive them, at least in principle. Though I heard of a few cases of villagers who lost their *bori* spirits, or worse their lives, as retribution for having committed a particularly grave offence, such cases are considered exceptional.[4] By contrast, leaving their horse after a few months or years to find another, more suitable mount seems to be the rule rather than the exception for Dodo spirits.

The well-known elusiveness and instability of these deities[5] was aptly captured in a man's comparison of Dodo to a donkey. 'Dodo spirits are like donkeys,' he explained to me, 'because if one finds a donkey who belongs to someone else, one only has to feed him millet regularly to win his attachment. He will soon leave his former master to stay with the person who gives him food.' Dodo spirits thus exhibit a proclivity for abandoning their current mediums to look for new and morally superior ones when they are dissatisfied with their current relationships to humans. It is not that they are disloyal because they can be a medium's best ally, but rather they, like other spirits of the past, only have dealings with honest and dedicated healing practitioners. Such a commentary indirectly casts a negative light on the enterprise of *bori* which for many is now synonymous with business, and even dishonest business. *Bori* has become part of the consumer culture it so often attempts to mediate and as we shall see below, this is one of the major dimensions of conventional spirit possession which Dodo mediums have reacted against in their embattled relationship with modernity.

Partly as a result of the Dodo's uncompromising principles, there is a pervasive fear, among Dodo mediums, that their fruitful relationship with these deities will soon come to an end. 'To keep a [Dodo] spirit, one needs to be frank and honest. Otherwise, the spirit will leave his mount to find someone else to possess,' one *bori* devotee had explained to me. It is to avoid such unfavourable prospects that mediums adopt a whole set of prohibitions and recast their existence with an orientation towards the past, even if only an invented one. In one of the first villages I visited during my fieldwork, I attended one of the possession ceremonies an elder Dodo medium held every Sunday at twilight. Once possessed by his spirit, the man I shall call Baidou simply handed the handful of sand he had just picked off the ground to those who requested medicine. In exchange, the patients gave him 25 francs CFA (10 US cents), knowing that once they experienced a major improvement in their conditions, they would have to reward him more substantially.

Here we can already appreciate a substantial difference in the way Dodo and *bori* healers commoditize their services. As I pointed out earlier, a growing number of *bori* practitioners charge a fixed price for their services and expect to be paid before the treatment begins, regardless of the outcome. Dodo mediums pride themselves in their disinterested commitment to healing the sick and comforting the wretched. They only accept a token payment – the equivalent of 5 or 10 US cents, which anyone can afford – for the healing touch or consolation they provide. They put pressure on no one to send gifts as tokens of gratitude once their situation or health has improved. They recognize that health cannot be expressed in monetary terms and that their spirits did not endow them with the capacity to heal in order to commoditize it but rather to provide comfort and solace to those who desperately need them.

And it is as if the potency of their healing is superior precisely because their gift of medicines has not been mediated by a mandatory return 'gift' of money. Raw and unmediated, the medicine acts directly on the afflicted person. The possessed devotee is a repository of Dodo's condensed powers. Anything s/he touches can become a channel for her/his healing capacity. This is why even the handful of sand that the possessed medium grabs off the ground to give to a patient is often more effective than the pounded mixture of carefully gathered roots, barks and leaves a *bori* practitioner might sell to his clientele. The fact that Dodo mediums charge almost nothing for their consultations is only proof that they have close ties to a powerful superhuman agency. It implicitly conveys the message that devotees need not worry about how to make a living, but that they should concentrate on restoring people to health. The Dodo are there to make sure that neither they nor their dependents shall ever want.

When I went to greet Baidou the day after the possession ceremony he had held for his Dodo, he was cordial and offered me a kola nut,[6] but he systematically evaded my questions about his spirit and his activities as a medium. I later found out from one of his friends that he was very afraid that I had come to steal his spirit. Knowing that as a 'rich' Westerner, I possessed some of the nice things that his Dodo was perhaps coveting – here we become aware of the contradictions that emerge out of these mediums' discourses when they stress the Dodo's aversion for commodities while simultaneously implying that these spirits want 'modern' things – he had steadfastly refused to engage in any conversation that might alert the spirit to the tempting alternative that I represented for a deity in search of another medium. I also learnt that Baidou had already chased away some Europeans who had allegedly come to take the Dodo away from him.

As I became more involved in the study of Dodo mediumship, I was told several times that some people come from very far away to steal someone's Dodo in order to make money because such spirits make their horses rich and famous. This fear of spirit theft is very real because losing one's Dodo implies not only losing the benefits associated with such extraordinary mediumship, but also allowing the subversion of Dodo's productive capacities to serve the interests of the materialism these spirits are precisely reacting against through their injunctions to avoid commodities.

The statement above also captures a bitter irony: in their attempts to recreate an ideal community impervious to the selfish designs of market entrepreneurs and budding capitalists, Dodo spirits have turned themselves into coveted commodities which can only be acquired through theft. For if true and truthful Dodo mediums only charge a minimum fee of 25 or 50 francs CFA for their services just as their spirit told them, those who wish to channel the powers of the Dodo to serve their own selfish interests command much higher prices when they heal the sick. A young man whom I will refer to as Tahirou even boasted about the 50,000 francs ($2,000) he had just received from an anxious husband whose wife was suffering from a spirit-induced case of madness. By charging high rates for their services because they want to make money, they only succeed in betraying the trust the Dodo have put in them because these spirits 'take care of everything so their devotees never want'. This disregard for the spirits' recommendation that patients be charged but a nominal fee is not only a sign of unhealthy greed, but also a symptom of the selfish desires to which the *bori* has already succumbed and against which Dodo spirits are currently reacting. Thus if Amadou occasionally found someone willing to pay his price, he was nonetheless regarded with suspicion by the majority of *bori* devotees who felt that he was a 'fake'[7] and a charlatan.

Prohibitions and discipline: recasting a moral order

To return to the case of Baidou, the medium who feared I might steal his Dodo, it is not the deity who makes the rules here but the medium who decides whom to talk to and whom to avoid, what to adopt and what to reject. In an effort to enforce what he described as his spirit's moral precepts and purity rules, Baidou had also changed what used to be a daily ritual to a weekly one: quotidian possession ceremonies had brought to his hamlet a string of prostitutes attracted by the prospects of a stable clientele. Because they bring together men and women without any of the social, spatial and moral constraints that are enforced in other public settings, spirit possession ceremonies encourage prostitution, a practice in which a large number of women engage off and on to make a living in between marriage or supplement their personal income.[8] Reluctant to foster promiscuity and encourage the selling of sexual services, Dodo had allegedly ordered his medium to cut down on the number of rituals held so as to discourage the prostitutes from establishing permanent residence in the proximity of the ritual grounds where the healing sessions took place. From then on, the tiny hamlet's tranquility was only disturbed on Sunday evenings with the cries of the violin and the clacking of the calabash drums whose melodious sounds induced Dodo to take possession of his human vessel.

Though Dodo mediums often stressed the importance of marital fidelity and the dangers of sexual promiscuity, none, save for Baidou, actually took pains in enforcing strict rules of morality and sociality in the settings of their ceremonies. Another Dodo medium told me that soon after he started becoming possessed, he stopped having sex with his two wives on the ground that it was what the spirit had ordered him to do. He had built a special house for his spirit where he slept alone and had informed his wives that they could not come in because the Dodo forbade it. This was a rather unusual interpretation of the Dodo's general injunction against sexual promiscuity. Though I met female *bori* devotees whose 'marriage' to a spirit meant they had to stop engaging in sex with their human spouse because the spiritual husband would forbid or prevent it, most Dodo mediums never voluntarily went to this extreme to achieve the desired state of purity that would insure the success of their careers as vessels of Dodo potency.

Some villagers possessed by a Dodo spirit end up refusing to go to school. Mahammadou with whom I discussed Dodo matters, before attending his *wasa*, told me he was a very good and motivated student until the day that he became 'caught' by Dodo. From then on, every time he attended school, he would see two teachers in the classroom; one was the 'real' teacher, the other was the spirit who, he said, 'told me everything so I had no need of learning from the 'real' teacher'. No one else in the class saw the spirit/teacher and though he enjoyed Dodo's presence, Mahammadou felt very much disturbed by what was happening. He started missing school a lot, and by the end of the year, was rarely seen attending classes. 'I passed my exams because the spirit had taught me everything,' Mahammadou said, 'but then the spirit made me so crazy that I could not go to school.' Here, a devotee is encouraged to learn, though not through the established channels and it is clear that by substituting himself to the human teacher, Dodo is expressing his distaste for French-style education.

Literacy here is seen as a dangerous tool that leads those who have been shaped by it to be cut away from the moral community to which they belong. Literacy is about power, but not the right kind when it serves as a bureaucratic instrument of domination and secrecy. For many Mawri villagers who have learned to associate literacy with modernity, Muslim hegemony and the legacies of colonialism, learning how to write is not necessarily a good thing.[9] This much emerges from *bori* practices which seek to prevent mediums from attending Qur'anic school while at the same time encouraging them to learn the Arabic script at the hand of their spirits. Literacy, if it is at all permitted by Dodo spirits (devotees often claim to write what they have been taught in dreams or they say that an invisible force is guiding their hands), should become a tool for healing or an instrument of divination instead of serving to insert the educated in a modern economy of production and exchange that alienates them from their moral community. It is perhaps in a defiant gesture of opposition to Muslim healers who wield the pen – a symbol of sophistication and worldly powers – to inscribe Qur'anic verses with ink that will be washed off and administered to patients as *rubutu* (writing) that some Dodo mediums view the word with suspicion and simply hand a handful of sand to those who come to be healed.

Dodo mediums may exhibit distrust of, and resistance to, certain Islamic practices but paradoxically, they sometimes also appropriate other Muslim customs. Recall how Dodo mediums customarily hand out sand to their patients rather than provide them with herbal medicine. Such a healing technique is reminiscent of the Islamic custom of removing sand from the grave of an exemplary Muslim so that his *baraka* (power) can be spread to others. Dodo mediums encourage their clients to drink the sand mixed in water or to wash themselves with it rather than wear it in a pouch on their bodies as devout Muslims would after accomplishing a pilgrimage to the tomb of a holy man. Nonetheless, both practices are based on the same principle that the healing capacities of exemplary individuals are contagious and can be spread via certain mundane media such as sand, of which there is plenty in the Sahelian belt. The Dodo mediums' response to the established hegemony of Islam is therefore not overt rejection but rather a complex and enduring process of opposing and accommodating the dominant order whose symbols, values and practices may, at times, be reinterpreted and put to useful ends.

Aside from literacy, most of the prohibitions I encountered centred around the avoidance of mechanical and modern things. One woman who was periodically possessed by Dodo refused to wear the mass-produced rubber sandals so many Nigeriens have adopted over leather ones because of their low cost and durability. Another medium I visited said to me right away that he could not allow the use of a tape recorder because his spirit forbade it – most *bori* mediums while perhaps hesitant at first, never actually forbid me to tape their conversation. While we were conversing, someone came to warn my interlocutor that a man, who had fallen sick, needed his services in the next village. Knowing from experience that healers derived much satisfaction and prestige from private automobile transportation, I offered him a ride in my Peugeot. To my surprise, he refused explaining that his spirit disapproved of cars and other road engines, and that he would walk to the ailing man's hamlet.

The Dodo medium I met in the small town of Matankari also strictly avoided motorized transportation after his spirit made it clear that he needed to reform his personal habits if he was to be worthy of receiving the gift of healing. Once, he told me, he had been asked to find and dig up potent evil medicines (*biso*) that had been buried in the centre of a small village. Several healers had been sent by the *chef de canton* (customary chief) to remove the bad medicine but the place was so hot[10] that they could not get close to the charm, much less pull it out of the ground. A member of the *bori* who had attempted unsuccessfully to extirpate the bad medicine with a horn, came to visit our man to convince him that he, the devotee of Dodo, was the only hope the villagers had of getting rid of the *biso* that threatened the prosperity of their small community. Upon accepting the task, the horse of Dodo first waited for his spirit to possess him before attempting to retrieve the noxious charm. The ground around which the charm was buried had become extremely hot but the medium, protected as he was by his ties to an omnipotent spirit, felt no heat, only coolness as he dug deeper into the earth.

When he finally retrieved the *biso*, the charm was 'screaming,' as he put it, and all the leaves of the nearby trees allegedly fell to the ground – presumably from the effect of the tremendous heat exuded by the malevolent object. The devotee put the noxious bundle of medicine in a calabash, covered it with straw and set it on fire. The envoy of the *chef de canton* that had been dispatched to witness the procedure, rushed back to his chief to announce that the medicine had been successfully destroyed. He soon returned to offer the horse of Dodo a ride in the chief's Land Rover as he had been ordered. The *chef de canton* wanted to see the medium in person and have him rid his house of the malignant charms he suspected his enemies to have planted to harm his family. But the spirit, who was still mounted on his devotee when the envoy came back, said he would walk, and that he never rode in cars. Besides attesting to the extraordinary potency of Dodo mediums (they can successfully annihilate dangerous forces when no one else can), the incident was narrated to me in such a way as to leave no doubt as to the source of this potency: the medium had the energy, skill and the protection needed to retrieve the noxious medicine *because* he followed closely a set of moral rules, one of which prescribed that he should not ride automobiles.

Is there a logic to the mediums' selective avoidance of commodities?

This resistance to technology and consumer culture is a strategy through which Dodo mediums stress the power of their alliances with their spirits and reaffirm the legitimacy of their invented traditions. By resolutely shunning certain commodities, they also create the very power that differentiates them from the mediums of *bori* spirits whose abilities to diagnose an illness, to heal and to predict the future are said to have diminished in direct proportion to the fading of their commitment to cult deities and their growing desires to acquire consumer goods. Everyone involved with spirits knows the corrosive effects of money which only eats away the ties woven long ago between spirits and people.[11] And though they enjoy the mobility afforded by motorized transportation, *bori* devotees like others are very much aware of the dangers associated with roads and their unmediated, uncontrolled traffic of goods, people and substances (Masquelier 1992). By warning against the destructive impact of consumer goods and motorized transport, Dodo spirits only reiterate a message rural Mawri have heard often, though in a different form, namely that the widespread hunger for wealth and things 'modern' has compelled the adoption of new moral values irrespective of the cost to heritage and 'tradition'.

At this point, it seems helpful to make a parallel between Islam and Dodo mediumship in their mutually antagonistic relations to *bori*. As I have pointed out earlier, both use the *bori* cult as a foil against which to reaffirm their own conceptions of morality, power and creativity. Both have attempted to distance themselves from the cult to reassert some fundamental truths about the nature of the relationship between humanity and divinity. For Muslims who construct their social identity in contrast to the provincial and rustic *yan bori* (members of *bori*), the cult becomes a convenient foil against which to re-define one's own worthiness and prestige. For Dodo mediums whose ethics and standards of purity have also developed in direct opposition to what they see as the corrupt, unhealthy practices of local mediumship, *bori* is also taken as a foil against which to reaffirm a sense of closeness with the spiritual world that has long been lacking in mainstream spirit possession. Though both Islam and Dodo mediumship tend to locate themselves in opposition to the *bori* on the local map of ritualized practices, they stand opposed in one respect: while Islamization represented (and still represents) a marked shift away from what it constructed as a parochial past, Dodo mediumship symbolizes a reactionary return to lost 'traditions' that are ostensibly contrasted to the spectre of modernity. And thus, while Islam paved the way for commerce and commoditization by providing a religious rationalization to economic motivations and success, Dodo mediumship rejects commodities because they embody an 'order of circulating media' (Weiss 1992: 548) that subverts the productive relations and processes upon which spirit possession is based. Let me add that the different notions of person and body to which Muslims and Dodo mediums subscribe have also important implications for the ways that they each separately locate themselves within local economies of power and exchange. The followers of the Prophet generally strive to dampen the fire of their emotions. Hence Muslim practices aim at producing self-contained, cool individuals who are not easily de-stabilized by the forces of their local environment and who value the notions of private property, material accumulation and impersonal transactions so essential to a capitalist world view. In contrast, Dodo mediums are enjoined to let external forces impinge upon their selfhood and renew partially severed ties to a reality the Muslims are only too anxious to forget in their ambitious march toward modernity. The result is that while Muslims have taken over the reins of commerce, Dodo mediums have insulated themselves from the market to avoid participating in the circulation of commodities whose easy convertibility and rapid movement threatens other essential connections. *Bori* stands uneasily between these two extreme positions. *Bori* devotees' claim to fame and authority is the power they derive from their association with spiritual forces. Hence, they loudly denounce the practices of Islam which have led people to forget their responsibilities towards the spirits. Paradoxically, ever since they became estranged from the local centres of economic and political power, they have attempted – at times successfully – to renegotiate their place in the local economy. By symbolically appropriating what they have identified as Islam's techniques for producing and reproducing value, they show how eager they are to create their own circuits of wealth and to reap some of the benefits currently associated with a Muslim identity (Masquelier 1993b, 1994).

Against the perceived excesses of *bori* devotees who are willing to compromise themselves for the sake of monetary gains, Dodo mediums shun those practices – such as prostitution – and goods – such as tape recorders – which for them emblematize the grizzly world of consumers and commodities. At the same time, they make ample use of other foreign objects that have perhaps inserted themselves more insidiously in their cultural landscape. They, for instance, eat their daily meals out of brightly coloured enamel ware imported from Czechoslovakia; some of them enjoy a morning cup of instant Nescafé, and yet others have no qualms about sporting a watch assembled in Taiwan or lighting their compound with a kerosene lamp made in China, once darkness has set in. Thus, their refusal to ride in cars or to encourage prostitution is not an unconditional resistance to entering the world of mass-production and consumption. Rather like the Beng who shun gasoline smells but drink Coca Cola (Gottlieb 1992), Dodo mediums selectively reject certain goods while adopting others, all in an effort to insert themselves firmly into the 'space between old and new commodities' (Comaroff and Comaroff 1990: 212). As Lan (1989) suggests in his analysis of why Shona mediums find Coca Cola dangerous but money inoffensive, resistance to certain commodities co-exists with acceptance of others.

The seeming contradictions and the lack of consensus that emerge out of some Mawri villagers' encounter with, and response to, things modern is evidenced by the spirits' own reluctance to take a firm stand when it comes to banning Western commodities: recall how Baidou's Dodo vigorously opposed the commoditization of sexual services while being more ambivalent about taking a stance toward other 'things' he might after all enjoy having and using. It is difficult to trace an overall logic governing Dodo mediums' selective avoidance of certain commodities because, as I pointed out earlier, mediums listen to the voice of their own spirits when it comes to establishing a moral code and they operate independently of each other. What seems clear, though, is that it is not all commodity forms, per se, that are deemed dangerous and must therefore be avoided. For two of the mediums I encountered, it was automobiles that were included in the category of 'things to be avoided' because they conjured up an ominous order of circulating commodities through their association with roads – themselves an apt metonym for the uncontrolled and often unproductive flows that link rural Nigerien – and other African – communities to transnational centres. For others, it is a pair of plastic sandals that embodies the capitalist circuits and processes one must stay away from in order to preserve other generative activities that hinge upon one's unconditional commitment to one's own moral and spiritual environment.

Before concluding, it seems pertinent to muse briefly on the implicit connection between cars and plastic sandals, two of the items rejected by Dodo devotees in their anxious efforts to insulate themselves from the exploitative world of capitalism. For a great many Dogondoutchi villagers, capitalism finds its aptest expression in the asphalt roads that unfurl along the arid landscape of Niger. In much of Africa, roads and their associated signs and processes provide a symbolic framework for addressing the paradoxes and possibilities of modernity (Auslander 1990b; Bastian 1991; Weiss 1993; White 1993). While for many aspiring taxi-drivers and traders, they are avenues to wealth and prestige through their role in transport, trade and labour migration, for the older generation, roads conversely evoke painful memories of forced labour and white supremacy during the colonial period (Cary 1969; Masquelier 1992). If we take people's mixed feelings of fascination with, and fear of, roads as indicative of their concerns with modernity, refusing to ride in a car and shunning plastic sandals both appear to have the same aim: namely to reject the easily gained, but often uncontrolled mobility associated with motor transportation and the wide circulation of mass-produced commodities. Though *bori* healers may travel widely to attend ceremonies in neighbouring villages or to find new markets for their medicinal goods, Dodo healers are enjoined to stay home and to wait there for prospective clients. Dodo spirits may travel as fast and far as the wind, but it is essential that their mediums remain grounded if they want to postpone the hasty departure of their spiritual hosts for as long as possible. Mediums are nothing but anchors for the wandering spirits and channels for their extraordinary powers. By rejecting two obvious symbols of mobility, Dodo mediums are thus repelling from their moral order the threatening processes of modernity that cars and plastic sandals so vividly objectify. Dodo devotees' refusal to enjoy the convenience of motorized transport may also be rooted in the equestrian imagery so prevalent in spirit possession. Recall that mediums are said to be the horses of the spirits who mount them to take control of their corporeal shell during the act of possession. Though no medium ever suggested it, the association of mediums with horses may prove antithetical to the act of riding an automobile – where the medium becomes the rider rather than the ridden – for certain mediums who struggle to enforce symbols and images of what they conceive as threatened tradition. Though only an elite minority can afford to replace horses and donkeys with cars or trucks, motorized transport has become an inescapable reality even in the remotest villages of Arewa. Rejecting the efficiency and comfort of motor transportation might be a way for certain mediums to concretely reassert the primacy of their roles as horses periodically ridden by the elusive spirits to whom they owe their fame as healers filled with special powers.

Conclusion

In their efforts to mediate the collision between Western and indigenous realities, Dodo mediums construct the present by pitting the spectre of modernity against a constantly recreated tradition anchored in a mythical past. What makes their message powerful and meaningful is that unlike the *bori* deities whose past accomplishments and glorious histories live only in the memories and as representations of pastness severed from an increasingly secular present, these spirits and their mediums live their exploits in the present and as representations of the present. In order to resist, if not reverse, the tide of modernity, these human receptacles of the forces of tradition construct a moral community for envisioning the world of today through the lens of an idealized memory of the past – creating a world where past and present fuse and where automobiles, factory-made sandals and commoditized health services are noticeably absent.

Although spirit possession tends to create a discursive space in which humans may comment on the cost and contradictions of modernity, we cannot reduce the practices surrounding Dodo mediumship to a critical commentary of post-colonial progress framed in a 'symbolic' or 'cultural' idiom. Through their rejection of commodities or consumer culture, Dodo mediums are also re-weaving and reviving the ties that once united people and spirits. In so doing, they re-create a safe network of socio-moral relations that insulates them from what they see as dangerous forms of productivity and power that have begun to de-stabilize their local worlds of experience.

In briefly sketching out the codes of conduct elaborated by Dodo spirits (or their mediums), I have tried to point out how varied and personalized the mediums' responses to their current predicament have been. By variously mediating the rising tide of imported goods and practices which threaten to erode their social land-scape, the devotees of these potent spirits are recasting the past as both the source and the instrument of their power. Though Dodo mediums can undoubtedly be cast among the 'malcontents of modernity' (Comaroff and Comaroff 1993), this does not imply that their efforts to defuse the elusive effects of transnational forces can be understood as a pre-capitalist hold over that indiscriminately denounces the pitfalls and disenchantment of modernity. Instead, their re-evaluation and rejection of various commodities and practices that have become fetishized signifiers of the modern become a tool of empowerment at the same time that it enables them to regain control over a world run amok.

Acknowledgements

Fieldwork in the Republic of Niger was carried out in 1988–9 thanks to a research fellowship from the National Institute of Mental Health, a dissertation grant from the National Science Foundation, and a grant for anthropological research from the Wenner-Gren Foundation. Further research during the summer of 1994 was made possible by a fellowship from Tulane University's Committee on Research. A prior version of this article was presented to the 1993 American Anthropological Association Meeting in Washington DC, and I thank those who gave me comments at the time. I am particularly grateful to Misty Bastian and Janice Boddy for their insightful suggestions. The present form of the essay is naturally my own responsibility.

Notes

1 The equestrian theme, prevalent in many possession cults (Matory 1993; Boddy 1989; Deren 1991), is a potent metaphor for making sense of the act of possession in which a medium is mounted *(hau)* by an ethereal creature who takes the reins of control. Interconnected with the horse/rider imagery is the idea that possession is a sexual act: the devotee is mounted by the spirit as s/he surrenders to the penetrating/controlling action of that spirit. This is why the initiate in a *bori* ritual is called a bride *(amarya)*.
2 People say they are 'caught' by a spirit when they first suffer from a spirit-induced affliction that can only be treated successfully if they appeal to the spirit(s) suspected to have sent the illness. Once the relationship between the spirit and her/his human host has been 'normalized' through the initiation ceremony which officially identifies the medium as a member of the *bori* cult, the spirit is said to be on this individual's head. By mentioning the head, which is the seat of consciousness, Mawri villagers refer to the state of possession in which the spirit temporarily replaces the medium's awareness with his own.
3 Initiated members of *bori* may achieve prominence by undergoing a ceremony by the name of *shan ice. Shan ice* literally means 'to drink from the tree,' a reference to the many tree barks that are used to make the potent medicine the initiate will have to drink for the whole duration of the ritual. The *shan ice* effects a transition from an ordinary condition to a more refined state of being and knowing which is comparable to that of a chief. As repositories of the powers of the bush (ingested through the tree bark medicine), they see what normal human beings cannot see and are credited with the ability to channel mysterious and invisible forces.
4 Being initiated into the *bori* is comparable to being married, save for the fact that two people who marry each other can also divorce each other, while mediums cannot 'divorce' their spirits. They are 'married' to them for life.
5 A woman who had been the horse of a Dodo for over three years told me that she had not built a house for her spirit – something mediums of important *bori* deities do in order to anchor their

spirits in the local landscape and legitimize their dealings as healers – because she knew that these deities never stayed long in one place. As she put it: '[Dodo] comes and goes. He changes mounts. Even if he asked me to make him a house, I would not build one. Once he has been on a person's head for a while, he goes away.'

6   Kola nuts are a popular and inexpensive stimulant which villagers regularly share among, or give to, each other as a gesture of generosity and sociality.

7   The fear that some mediums might actually fake their possession performance is very real and the object of intense debates. Especially among the older generation, there is a sense that young people only become possessed to take advantage of someone or something, or to attract attention when it is convenient to do so. A seasoned *bori* practitioner can recognize at once those who only pretend to be in trance.

8   Despite the *bori* cult's prohibitions against sexual promiscuity for spirit mediums, many *bori* devotees are prostitutes who use the arena of spirit possession to market their sexual services (see Masquelier 1996). Though not all prostitutes are cult devotees (many only attend ceremonies to find customers), the relationship between possession and prostitution is so self-evident for Muslim Mawri that they assume that any woman who engages in *bori* is, by definition, a prostitute.

9   A few villagers considered French-style schools as 'dens of vice' which produced unwanted pregnancies rather than training young girls to be good housewives and mothers. There is also a sense, especially for women, that too much instruction is dangerous and deleterious because they no longer fear their husbands and act respectfully.

10 Here, the heat emanating from the object is the symptom and the source of danger. There is a sense that those who are unprotected against this destructive kind of heat would die if they were to be touched by it. Even proximity to the source of heat might have a deleterious effect on a person. Fire is a complex element which has multiple referents, some positive, some negative. Hence, it is said that the life-taking capacities of witches are a function of their excessive and uncontrolled heat. Similarly, it is the heat contained in the thunder stones allegedly thrown by the fearful spirits of rain which kill those who are struck by a lightning bolt.

11 Mawri legends and tales are replete with explicit allusions as to how human greed and selfishness have progressively destroyed the fruitful symbiosis that existed between people and spirits. The past is often constructed as an idyllic world where no one was wanting because the spirits took care of everyone's need so long as people trusted them and took care of them.

References

Auslander, Mark (1990b) 'Enemies within: secrecy, witchcraft and state power at eastern Zambian roadblocks', paper presented at the African Studies Association Meeting, Baltimore.

Bastian, Misty (1991) 'Blood and petrol: the dangerous eroticism of roads and transport in southeast Nigeria', paper presented at the African Studies Association Annual Meeting, Baltimore.

Besmer, Fremont (1983) *Horses, Musicians and Gods: The Hausa Cult of Possession-Trance*, South Hadley, Massachusetts: Bergin & Garvey.

Boddy, Janice (1989) *Wombs and Alien Spirits: Women, Men, and the Zar Cult in Northern Sudan*, Madison: University of Wisconsin Press.

Bonte, Pierre & Nicole Echard (1976) 'Histoire et histoires: conception du passe chez les Hausa et les Tuaregs Kel Gress de l'Ader (Republique du Niger)', *Cahiers d'Etudes Africaines* 62: 237–96.

Cary, Joyce (1969) *Mister Johnson*, New York: Time Incorporated.

Comaroff, Jean (1985) *Body of Power, Spirit of Resistance: The Culture and History of a South African People*, Chicago: University of Chicago Press.

Comaroff, Jean & John Comaroff (1990) 'Goodly beasts, beastly goods: cattle and commodities in a South African context', *American Ethnologist* 17: 195–216.

—— (1993) 'Introduction' *Modernity and its Malcontents: Ritual and Power in Post-Colonial Africa*, Jean Comaroff & John Comaroff (eds), xi–xxxvii. Chicago: University of Chicago Press.

Comaroff, John L. & Jean Comaroff (1987) 'The madman and the migrant: work, labor in the historical consciousness of a South African people', *American Ethnologist* 14: 191–209.

Deren, Maya (1991) *Divine Horsemen: The Living Gods of Haiti*, New York: McPherson and Company.

Echard, Nicole (1989) *Bori: Genies d'un Culte de Possession Hausa de l'Ader et du Kurfey (Niger)*, Paris: Institut d'Ethnologie.
—— (1991) 'Gender relationships and religion: women in the Hausa Bori of Ader, Niger', *Hausa Women in the Twentieth Century*, Catherine Coles and Beverly Mack (eds) 207–20, Madison: University of Wisconsin Press.
Gottlieb, Alma (1992) *Under the Kapok Tree: Identity and Difference in Beng Thought*, Bloomington: Indiana University Press.
Lan, David (1989) 'Resistance to the present by the past: mediums and money in Zimbabwe', *Money and the Morality of Exchange*, J. Parry and M. Bloch (eds), 191–208, New York: Cambridge University Press.
Lewis, I. M. (1991) *Ecstatic Religion: An Anthropological Study of Spirit Possession and Shamanism*, New York: Routledge.
Lewis, I. M., Ahmed Al-Safi & Sayyid Hurreiz (eds) (1991) *Women's Medicine: The* Zar-Bori *Cult in Africa and Beyond*, Edinburgh: Edinburgh University Press.
Masquelier, Adeline (1992) 'Encounter with a road siren: machines, bodies and commodities in the imagination of a Mawri healer', *Visual Anthropology Review* 8: 56–69.
——(1993a) 'Ritual economies, historical mediations: the poetics and power of *Bori* among the Mawri of Niger', PhD dissertation, University of Chicago.
——(1993b) 'Narratives of power, images of wealth: the ritual economy of *Bori* in the market', *Modernity and its Malcontents: Ritual and Power in Post-Colonial Africa*, Jean Comaroff & John Comaroff (eds) 3–33. Chicago: University of Chicago Press.
——(1994) 'Lightning, death and the avenging spirits: *Bori* values in a Muslim world', *Journal of Religion in Africa* 24: 2–51.
——(1995) 'Consumption, prostitution and reproduction: the poetics of sweetness in *Bori*,' *American Ethnologist* 22: 883–906.
—— (1996) 'Mediating threads: clothing and the texture of spirit/medium relations in *Bori* (Southern Niger)', *Clothing and Difference: Embodied Identities in Colonial and Postcolonial Africa*, Hildi Hendrickson (ed.), 66–93, Durham & London: Duke University Press.
Matory, James Lorand (1993) 'Government by seduction: history and the tropes of 'mounting' in Oyo-Yoruba religion', *Modernity and its Malcontents: Ritual and Power in Post-Colonial Africa*, Jean Comaroff & John Comaroff (eds) 58–85. Chicago: University of Chicago Press.
Monfouga-Nicolas, Jacqueline (1972) *Ambivalence et Culte de Possession: Contribution à l'Etude du Bori Hausa*, Paris: Anthropos.
Tonkin, Elizabeth (1992) *Narrating our Past: The Social Construction of Oral History*, New York: Cambridge University Press.
Tremearne, A.J.N. (1914) *The Ban of the* Bori: *Demons and Demon Dancing in West and North Africa*, London: Heath, Cranton & Ouseley.
Weiss, Brad (1992) 'Plastic teeth extraction: the iconography of Haya gastro-sexual affliction', *American Ethnologist* 19: 538–52.
—— (1993) 'Buying her grave': money, movement and AIDS in northwest Tanzania', *Africa* 63: 19–35.
White, Luise (1993) 'Cars out of place: vampires, technology, and labor in east and central Africa', *Representations* 43: 27–50.

II

Complexities
& Proliferation
of Spirit Possession

4

On History
& Language of the
'European' *Bori* Spirits
Kano, Nigeria

Matthias Krings

This chapter focuses on a group of 'European' spirits, who are part of the spirit pantheon worshipped in the *bori* cult of spirit possession widespread among the Hausa speaking populations of Nigeria and Niger.[1] First, drawing on personal experience and data collected in the northern Nigerian city of Kano, I outline my research methods and portray the *iskokin Turawa* ('European' spirits) as they manifested themselves during public and private occasions in 1992–3. I then go on to give a representation of their language comprising certain linguistic modifications of the Hausa language as well as English and French derived lexical items. To elucidate the usage of French-derived lexical items I then follow up the history of the 'European' spirits in colonial Niger, Ghana and Nigeria, relying on the extensive literature already published. Drawing from the cult's mythology recounted by *bori* adepts, cult musicians and the spirits themselves, I finally depict the process of the 'European' spirits' integration into, and their transformation within the *bori* of Kano. Throughout the text, the spirits mounted on their mediums are treated as acting subjects differing from, though not independent of, their mediums.

To study the language and mythology of the *Turawa* spirits I decided to conduct tape-recorded interviews with the spirits themselves. Therefore the spirit mediums were visited at their homes, as is the common practice for private consultations with the spirits. Usually such a consultation would start with the payment of the *gwiwan bori*, which consists of a certain amount of money for the services of the medium and of gifts to the spirit in expectation. In the case of the *Turawa* spirits cigarettes of a certain brand were given as a gift. Having received the *gwiwan bori* the medium would start to silently recite certain praise formulae directed to the spirit world, which were sometimes accompanied by the inhalation of incense, in order to attract the spirit's attention. Following the summoning of the spirit, the *jan gora*,[2] comprising a series of ritualized physical actions, indicated the spirit's mounting of his medium. Having taken the body of his medium the spirit would stand up and call, or rather shout the names of his spirit relatives. Then followed the mutual greeting and the announcement of my proposed interview. The uncustomary wish to consult a spirit only to conduct an interview without having a concrete personal problem was usually accepted by the spirits as *neman ilimi*, a European's quest for knowledge. The interviews which were usually conducted in the presence of a *bori-*

initiate lasted an hour on average. At the end the spirit would bid us farewell and leave the body of his medium in a process similar to that of the *jan gora*. The final departure of the spirit was always marked by the medium sneezing three times.

In the interviews the spirits not only related to me their genealogical backgrounds and their mythical stories which connect them with other spirits of the *bori* pantheon, they also talked about topics concerning the local *bori* community – politics, religion and society. The interviews with the spirits were complemented by interviews and conversations with spirit mediums, cult musicians and regular clients of the spirits. The mythical stories related by the spirits themselves corresponded to a large extent to the stories told of the spirits by their regular clients, spirit mediums and cult musicians. The spirits, however, seemed to have a higher extent of historical knowledge concerning their genealogies and origin than their mediums.

Turawa spirits of contemporary Kano

The *Turawa* spirits *(sg. Bature)* are also frequently referred to as *'yan Babule (sg. Babule)* or *'yan Mushe (sg. Mushe)*. *Babule*, a term of unknown etymology, is usually translated as 'spirit of the fire'. *Mushe* (/mùushee/) deriving from the French word *Monsieur*, is listed by Bargery (1957[1934]) denoting 'Mister' or 'a Frenchman'. Today the term has lost its original semantic value; *bori* adepts are indefinite in translating it. *'Yan Mushe* could be merely translated as 'followers (lit. children) of *Mushe*', where *Mushe* could stand for 'Europeanness'.[3] The majority of the *Turawa* spirits are characterized as male soldiers. They are related to each other according to their military rank, thus constituting a group of commanding and command–receiving spirits. At publicly held *bori* dances *Komanda mugu* (the wicked commander), *Kafaran Salma*, *Kafaran gadi* (corporal), *Mai yak'i* (lit. owner of war), *Barkono* (pepper) and *Lokotoro* among others, under the leadership of *Gwamnan bataliya* (governor of the batallion) transform the dance ground into a military drill ground. The spirit with the highest rank at the time not only commands his fellow 'European' spirits, but sometimes even the spectators or onlooking *bori* adepts to perform all kinds of military-like drills.[4] Most of the *Turawa* spirits wear military-style uniforms red in colour, some of them green or khaki coloured uniforms. The colour red can be traced also in the gifts given to, and the animals sacrificed for these spirits: they prefer cigarettes of a brand with a red package and animals with red hair or feathers. The paraphernalia of the *Turawa* consists of sunglasses, thunderer whistles, whips, toy guns, cigarettes and alcohol, as well as ballpens and notebooks. At public *bori* dances the performance of a 'European' spirit usually ended with a demonstration of his invulnerability to fire. Therefore the spirit would remove parts of his uniform, wash the upper part of his body and his legs and arms with kerosene, in order to stroke his body with a burning torch.

The language of the *Turawa* spirits

Apart from the group of the *Turawa* spirits, other groups of 'foreign' spirits are an integral part of the *bori* pantheon. Like the *Turawa* spirits they are considered by the *bori* adepts as having originated from several foreign, non-Hausa speaking societies. Each group of foreign spirits uses its own language, consisting of a certain manner of Hausa particular to them. According to the language background attributed to each group of foreign spirits, linguistic interferences of the spirits' 'mother-tongues' occur in the Hausa that is spoken by them.

The Hausa spoken by *Buzaye* spirits (Tuareg serfs) resembles in intonation and phonology some northern dialects of Hausa, which are spoken in areas where the Tuareg live. Furthermore it contains some phrases, which *bori* adepts identify as *Tamashaq*, the language spoken by Tuareg. *Fulani* spirits speak Hausa with a large amount of *Fulfulde* vocabulary. Their pronunciation of Hausa is similar to that of *Fulfulde* mother-tongue speakers who speak Hausa as a second language. Hausa used by *Gwarawa* spirits, 'pagan' spirits who are said to have come from the Middle-Belt region of Nigeria, is characterized by the alteration of certain consonantal phonemes and the frequent use of vulgar expressions.

The language of the *Turawa* spirits will now be examined in more detail. Similar to the 'languages' of the other foreign spirits mentioned above, it exhibits lexical, phonetical and grammatical modifications in contrast to standard Hausa.[5]

Lexical modifications

Apart from Hausa vocabulary the lexicon of the *Turawa* spirits' language contains vocabulary derived from English and French. The following examples may serve to illustrate the lexical characteristics:

'Mai yak'i ɔfən zi maus ... a bæg, a bæg Mai yak'is, afɔ̃) ...'[6]
 H   E   E   E   E   H   F
Mai yak'i open the mouth ... I beg, I beg Mai yak'i, à bon ...
Mai yak'i, speak ! ... Please, please Mai yak'i, okay ...

In this example the semantic content of the English- and French-derived expressions changes slightly in contrast to the meaning they have in English or French. The expressions [ɔfən zi maus] and [a bæg] are used according to the semantic content they have in the Nigerian version of Pidgin English. [afɔ̃] derives from the French 'à bon', which in French is used as a speaker's spontaneous exclamation in reference to a statement by someone else, that either slightly surprises him, meaning 'I see!', or that he approves, meaning 'okay'. *Turawa* spirits frequently use [afɔ̃] to endorse their own statements – an uncommon usage of the exclamation 'à bon' in French.

'a si: akwai ma:mɔnsi, afɔ̃, akwai bɽɔda nasi ...'
 E   H   E   H F   H   E   H
I say akwai mama-nshi, à bon, akwai brother nashi ...
Look, there is his mother, okay, there is his brother

In this example the English based expression 'I say', as in Nigerian Pidgin English, is used as an exclamation for emphasis at the beginning of a sentence. The semantic content of the English derived terms [ma:mɔ] and [bɽɔda], remains unchanged. [ma:mɔnsi] is a compound form of the English term 'mama' and the Hausa possessive pronoun (3.p./m./sg.) *shi*, which in Hausa is attached to masculine nouns with the linker -*n*-.

^ʔi sei ya yi *farti* da ita … *"ai wɔn go farti ju hauz!"'*
<u>E</u>   <u>H</u>   <u>F</u>   <u>H</u>   <u>E</u>   <u>E</u>   <u>F</u>   <u>E</u>
He say ya yi partir da ita … 'I want go partir you house'
He said he would leave with her … 'I want to take you home'

[*farti*] derived from the French *partir* is part of the standard vocabulary used by the *Turawa* spirits. It is also commonly employed if a 'European' spirit announces that he is going to dismount his medium. Thus a spirit says: 'Zan yi *farti*' (I will *leave*). The second part of the example above shows how 'broken' English is used in the language of the *Turawa*; in this case also including the French derived [*farti*].

Apart from French- and English-derived vocabulary with unchanged and slightly changed semantic content, some expressions are to be found, having a new meaning:

<u>bandʒu savai trɛ bjẽ</u>   <u>savai bandʒu</u>   <u>sa va</u>
F   F   F
<u>*bon jour ça va très bien*</u>   <u>*ça va bon jour*</u>   *ça va*
that's it   *that's it*   *okay*

These are fixed phrases composed of phonetically modified French expressions. They are frequently used in the *Turawa* spirits' language as expressions of approval, meaning 'that's it', 'very well' or 'okay'.

Further expressions of uncertain etymology, that seem to be lexical innovations are to be found:

"Ba na <u>dùŋgùɽa dùŋgùɽa</u>:"   *"hasi Mai yak'i …"*   *"A gaya wa dègusi: nawa ..*
I am not <u>praying</u>   *Come on Mai yak'i*   *One should tell my <u>medium</u>*

Whole passages of speech imitating French or English without any identifiable meaning can also be heard. Though versed in the language of the *Turawa* spirits, these passages are not understood by the *bori* adepts and the *'yan k'warya*, a group of non-initiated persons who are serving the spirits in various ways and who also act as translators and mediators between the spirits and their clients. Such passages are understood as utterances in the 'mother tongue' of the spirits. As the *Turawa* spirits often declare, they use the Hausa language only so that they can be understood by their clients.

Phonetic modifications

Hausa vocabulary in use by the *Turawa* spirits exhibits, in contrast to standard Hausa, several phonetic modifications, which will be illustrated in the following examples. Some phonetically altered words of standard Hausa belong to the fixed lexical inventory of the *Turawa* spirits' language:

Standard Hausa:	/gàskiyaa/;	/laafiyàa/;	/sabòodà/
Turawa language:	[gàskuma:];	[la:fuʷà:];	[sabajà:dà]
	truth	*health*	*because of*

The majority of phonetic modifications consist of the substitution of one phone by another. Thus the consonants /sh/, /c/ and /z/ are substituted by [s]: e.g., *tashi*, *lokaci* and *yanzu* of standard Hausa become *tasi*, *lokasi* and *yansu* in the language of the

Turawa. The consonant /b/ is substituted by [f], the consonant /j/ by [z]: e.g., *bangare* and *gaji* in standard Hausa become *fangare* and *gazi* in the language of the *Turawa*. In some words the initial consonants are substituted by [m] or [mʷ], e.g.:

St.H.:	/ʔauree/;	/hausa/;	/ʔidòo/;	/wani/;	/suunaa/
T.L.	[mauɽe:];	[mausa];	[mʷidò:];	[mʷani];	[mʷu:na:]
	marriage	Hausa	eye	someone	name

The vowel /a/ of standard Hausa, if occurring as the final sound of a word, is sometimes substituted in the language of the *Turawa* spirits by the nasalized vowel [ɔ]. (Likewise /aa/ is substituted by [ɔ̃:]):

St.H.:	/kumaa/;	/gàlàdiimàa/;	/bà......ba/;	/gàba/
T.L.	[kumɔ̃:];	[gàlàdi:mɔ̃:]	[bà......bɔ̃];	[gàbɔ̃]
	also	trad. Title	neg. marker	ahead

This phenomenon can be interpreted as reflecting French vowels, which frequently occur as nasalized vowels in terminal positions.

Another phenomenon can be best described as a tendency to substitute as many vowels as possible standing in final position of a word by the vowel [i], or to attach the apparently meaningless syllable [si] to the final sound of a given word:

St.H.:	/bìl ʔadamà/;	/baabù/;	/kafaran/;	/'dan màama/
T.L.	[bìl ʔadamì];	[ba:bì];	[kafaɽansi];	[ɗam mà:mansi]
	mankind	there is none	Kafaran	'Dan mama

In accordance with the above mentioned consonantal substitutions whole phrases are formed in which the syllable [si] occurs frequently:

'a si si Mai yak'i, – e – isi kana so – e – si na yare – si anisi nawa ne,...'
E   H   H   F?   H   H   H   H
I say shi Mai yak'i – e –, ici, kana so – e – shi na yare – shi ainihi nawa ne, ...
I say he Mai yak'i - e – do you want (it) here – e – in (the) tongue, that is my original one .

Further modifications

The fact that *Turawa* spirits do not distinguish natural gender in their language constitutes a modification of Hausa grammar; women are addressed and referred to as men. Usually only the masculine forms of the person/aspect markers, object pronouns and possessive pronouns 2./3.p./sg. (of which standard Hausa has two distinct forms referring to each gender) are used by the *Turawa* spirits.[8] It is perhaps significant that French and English, the languages attributed to the spirits as their mother-tongues, do not distinguish gender in 2.p./sg. pronouns. This lack of distinction may well be transferred to the spirits' use of Hausa, where it also influences the use of the pronouns 3.p./sg.

In everyday language, speakers of Hausa employ certain oaths to endorse a statement. *'Na rantse da Allah'* and *'Na rantse da manzon Allah'* are frequently heard oaths, evoking Allah and his Prophet Mohammed. In contrast when *Turawa* spirits make an oath, they evoke their mother, the sun or a certain mythical rock:

'Na rantse da mɔmi nawa.'   'Na rantse da dutsen Takwarkwasi.'
I swear by my <u>mother</u>;   *I swear by the rock of Takwarkwashi*

By using such oaths, *Turawa* spirits emphasize the fact that they are not of the Islamic faith.

Ideolect and sociolect

The linguistic alterations of standard Hausa outlined above can be understood as part of a body of alteration rules that constitutes the language of the *Turawa* spirits. These 'rules' are not strict and far from being without exception. Exceptions are likely to occur even in the speech of a single spirit possessing one of his mediums. For example, the substitution of the consonant /sh/ by [s] may take place virtually always; however, in some cases – independent of the phonetical environment – /sh/ may remain unaltered. Nevertheless, the relatively frequent occurence of substitution allows the use of the term 'rule'.

The language of the *Turawa* spirits, and likewise the language of any other group of foreign spirits, can be best termed a sociolect of Hausa constituted by a set of 'ideal-type' rules. These are realized to a varying extent in the ideolects of the spirits, having mounted their mediums. The realization of the sociolect in a spirit's ideolect is linked to the quality of the language teaching that takes place during a neophyte's initiation into the cult when a spirit manifests himself for the first time in his new medium. If the persons initiating the neophyte do not devote enough time to the spirit's acquirement of language, he will never speak a proper version of the *Turawa* spirits' sociolect. *Bori* adepts say: *'aljani yaro ne kan sabon kai'* – a spirit on a new medium (lit head) is like a small child (who has to be taught everything).[9]

In order to be recognized as a 'European' spirit, every 'European' spirit has to adopt at least some of the characteristics of the *Turawa* spirits' sociolect in his ideolect. In the interviews and in communication with their clients and cult members, all the *Turawa* spirits used the exclamation [afɔ], English and French derived expressions to a varying extent and at least some of the above mentioned consonantal substitutions. The indefinite use of masculine and feminine pronouns was also common to all. The remainder of the above described alterations of standard Hausa were used to a varying extent. The frequency of the use of French or English derived expressions in the ideolect of a spirit correlated to the French or English language competence of his medium. As *bori* adepts say, a medium's character and capability influence the character and capability of a spirit that takes possession of the medium's body. Nevertheless, cult members and clients of the spirits also reported on spirits speaking in languages their mediums never learned.

Reconstructing the history of the *Turawa* spirits

The phenomenon of English vocabulary used in the sociolect of 'European' spirits in Northern Nigeria, a former British colony, is not difficult to account for. One would expect the *Turawa* spirits – being mimetical interpretations (Kramer 1987: 243) of the British colonialists – to speak at least fragments of English. But why also French? The use of French or French-derived vocabulary can be accounted for by a reconstruction of the *Turawa* spirits' history. Some of the popular 'European' spirits of contemporary

Kano can be traced back by name to the birth of the *Hauka* movement[10] in 1925. Around this time a group of foreign spirits hitherto unknown to the members of the local cults of spirit possession manifested themselves for the first time during a public dance of young adults held in a small village of Filingue district in the western part of what later became the Republic of Niger.[11] The spirits introduced themselves as *Hauka* spirits,[12] claimed to have come from the Red Sea and to be guests of the spirit *Dongo* (the spirit of thunder worshipped in the *holey* cult of spirit possession of the *Songhay* speaking people). They said they had come to the district of Filingue together with a Hausa pilgrim who had returned to Niger from Mecca (Rouch 1960: 73). Among the *Hauka* who introduced themselves under the leadership of *Gomno Malia* (Governor of the Red Sea) were *Mayak'i* (Warrior), *Kapral gardi* (Caporal de garde) and *Babule* (the blacksmith). Peculiar to their appearance was their military-like behaviour, salutations and drills, similar to those of the French military, and the use of burning torches with which they stroked their bodies unharmed.

The French colonial administration, alarmed by the indigenous local chiefs who had been either established or sanctioned by the French, considered the *Hauka* spirits and their mediums to be hostile to the newly-established political and social order. Sixty adepts of the *Hauka* were brought to Niamey and imprisoned. Upon their release the district commissioner Major Crochichia brutally forced them to publicly admit the non-existence of the *Hauka*, after which they were dismissed and went back to their villages. After a short period of time a new spirit emerged among the *Hauka*: *Komanda mugu*, the 'wicked commander' whose personal name was *Krosisya* or *Korsasi* (Rouch 1960: 74; 1978: 1007). Cult leaders and members of the local cults of spirit possession, *holey* and *bori*, rejected the *Hauka* and their adepts. It is likely that they felt their ritual status threatened by these new, obviously powerful spirits and their adepts. Therefore the *Hauka* spirits, who were called *Babule* (spirits of the fire) by the Hausa speaking people and *Zondom* (malicious madmen) by the Songhay speaking people, were neither integrated into the pantheon of the *bori*, nor into that of the *holey* cult. These factors led to the development of an independent *Hauka* movement in about 1926, which spread first through the Songhay and Hausa speaking areas of western Niger. *Hauka* adepts, mostly young adults in their early twenties, founded new settlements where they started to organize resistance to the French colonial administration and the indigenous local chiefs. The French colonial administration soon reacted by banning the *Hauka* movement. The main leaders were imprisoned or exiled to Upper Volta and to Ivory Coast (Fuglestad 1975: 205; Echard 1991: 71).

In the early 1930s the *Hauka* cult was brought to colonial Ghana by seasonal migrants in search of work. Jean Rouch calls colonial Ghana the 'Mecca' of the *Hauka*. There new spirits emerged and the pantheon rapidly began to grow: among others were *Kafaran Salma* – possessing the name of the first district commisioner of Niamey, Lieutenant Salaman, *Kafaran kot* - Corporal of the coast, and *Lokotoro* the doctor,[13] to mention but a few (Rouch 1953/54; 1956: 151; 1978: 1007). Similar to their mostly Songhay speaking mediums the spirits began to acquire the Pidgin English of colonial Ghana. Thus the language of the spirits became 'a glossolaliac melange of broken French and English' (DeBouzek 1989: 308). Together with their adepts, most of whom were returning to Niger on a yearly basis, the *Hauka* went back to Niger, where the process of their integration into the *holey* cult of the Songhay-speaking population started at the latest during the 1940s. The *holey* spirits and their mediums accepted them as '*Dongo's* younger brothers'. But as late as 1947 the older generation among the cult members were still resentful of the *Hauka*. Rouch reports on a *sorko* (praise singer) who angrily shouted out 'That's not true!' during a *holey* dance as the spirit *Dongo* was about to introduce several *Hauka* spirits who had taken the bodies of their mediums to other *holey* spirits and onlookers [Rouch 1960: 76]. In the following two decades the *Hauka* spirits were fully integrated into the *holey* cult, now constituting the sixth spirit family of the *holey* pantheon. Today they play an important role in the struggle against witchcraft [Stoller 1984: 178; 1989].

How were the *Hauka* spirits integrated into the *bori* cult of the Hausa speaking population? On the basis of the literature concerning the *bori* before decolonization it is difficult to make any definitive statement. One of the earliest references to a 'European' spirit in a *bori* context is to be found in an issue of *West African Review* that was published in 1957 in Ghana. A photograph shows a spirit called *Soja* (soldier) having taken the body of a medium. The article dates back to a *bori* dance the author witnessed in Accra, Ghana in February 1956.[14] Clothing and attributes of this spirit resemble those of the *Hauka* spirits who were filmed by Jean Rouch near Accra in the early 1950s (see Rouch 1953/54).

At this time a huge Hausa-speaking population lived in Accra and other Ghanaian cities. Hausa served as lingua franca between the immigrants who came from the northern savanna regions of colonial Niger, Nigeria, Mali and Upper Volta (Rouch 1956: 137). Thus contact between adepts of the *Hauka* and adepts of the *bori* cult seems conceivable.[15] Paul Stoller comments on the adepts of the *Hauka* in postcolonial Niger, that '... they have come from a variety of ethnic groups ... [they] are Songhay, Zerma, Peul, Bella, Hausa and Kanuri in ethnic origin ...' (Stoller 1984: 186). The same applies to members of the recent *bori* cult of Zinder in southern Niger. In addition, the boundaries between *holey* and *bori* seem to be fluid, as can be seen from the following fact: during a public *bori* dance held in 1993 in Zinder the *holey* spirit *Dongo* took possession of a *holey*-initiated medium who was a visitor from Niamey. Soon after *Dongo's* arrival several *Turawa* spirits took the bodies of their local, *bori*-initiated, mediums.[16]

Contact between *bori* adepts across the Nigeria–Niger border is a common practice in recent times and is likely to have existed before independence. For example, some years ago a group of Nigerian *bori* musicians and cult members under the leadership of the *garaya*[17] player Adamu Makaho of Zaria, Nigeria, toured throughout Niger for nine months.[18] Personal contacts of *bori* adepts with Niger, Nigeria and Ghana can be also traced in the biographies of prominent members of contemporary Kano *bori*.[19]

The first reference to 'European' spirits in Northern Nigeria is to be found in the biography of 'Baba of Karo'. She describes the arrival of 'European' spirits in 1943, when she moved to a village called *Sabon giwa* near Zaria.[20] Literature from research conducted during the early 1960s refers to 'European' spirits with the general term *Babule* or *Bature*.[21] Kurt Krieger who did fieldwork in Anka, North-western Nigeria in 1952–3 and again in 1961–2 mentions a spirit called *Mai yak'i* and the spirit called *Babule*, who was reported to be an English speaking madman burning his body with fire and beating himself with a stick (Krieger 1967: 99). The spirit praise songs recorded by A.V. King in 1964 in Katsina include a praise song to a spirit called *Bature* (King 1967: 132f). Ludger Reuke who worked in the same year with Hausa speaking *Maguzawa* ('pagans') of Katsina province gives a more detailed description of the *Turawa* spirits popular during that time (Reuke 1969). Among the twelve

'European' spirits he lists, *Mai yak'i*, *Soja* and *Gwabna* (who are reported to speak English) are also to be found. Altogether seven of the spirits are still popular in the Kano *bori* of recent times.[22] A spirit called *Mushe* is described by Reuke as 'torch-bearer'. Reuke's informants stated that the *Turawa* spirits manifested themselves for the first time approximately twenty years ago, i.e., around 1944.[23] Ralph Faulking-ham who did fieldwork in a village called Tudu near Madaoua, Southern Niger in 1968, describes two exclusive cults existing at the same time. The *'yan bori* (adepts of *bori*) were concerned with the cult of the traditional, 'inheritable' *bori* spirits, whereas the *'yan Mushe* served the 'European' spirits, called *Mushe*. The *Mushe* spirits 'danced military-like' and used 'French commands' (Faulkingham 1975: 40). Among the thirteen *Mushe* spirits listed by Faulkingham, three of the early *Hauka* spirits can be found: *Komandan*, *Kabran sakitar* and *Mai yak'i* (see Rouch 1960: 75; 1953/54).

In the interviews of 1993 some of the spirits recalled their origin and also certain historical events. Thus the spirit *Mai yak'i* when asked for the history of the *Turawa* spirits said: ' Then we went out of *France*, and came into your Nigeria.'[24] World Wars One and Two as experienced by many Africans both overseas and in Africa are also reflected in the stories told by the 'European' spirits: 'At the time when you had trouble in your cities, when you had your uproar, well, we took it (as if it were) our uproar.'[25] The frequently mentioned *yak'i na boda* (war of the border) could either refer to acts of war overseas or those in Africa during World War Two, where the Allies and the Free French opposed the French Vichy regime.[26] Following the older generation of 'European' spirits who appeared in the context of colonial Niger and Ghana, further 'European' spirits emerged in colonial and postcolonial Nigeria. One of them who appeared in recent times presumably in Nigeria is *Jamus* – *'bata k'asa* (lit. Germany – destroyer of land).[27] The phrase *Jamus 'bata k'asa* is the first line of an anti-German war slogan that was spread by the British colonial administration in Nigeria during World War Two.[28] Like the other *Turawa* spirits, *Jamus* is character-ized as a soldier. His praise epithet expresses his soldierly qualities:

Jamus 'bata k'asa – bindiga cike da mugunta – wuta gasa baya
Jamus destroyer of land – gun full of wickedness – fire that roasts the back

In an interview *Jamus* explained that he would use an aircraft to travel back and forth between places he frequently visits, including *Jamus*, *India*, *Ghana*, *Mara'di* (in Niger) and Nigeria. He is of the Christian faith and visits the church in *birnin Rum* (Rome) every Sunday. Besides his profession as a soldier he is also concerned with road construction. *Jamus* explained his name as follows: before he is able to build roads he has to destroy the land (also earth), in order to level it. Therefore he also employs heavy tools: 'then I will use a caterpillar … that is going ahead with me to plane the earth – it pushes (the earth) and deposits it.'[29]

That it is *Jamus* among all the *Turawa* spirits who is concerned with road con-struction seems to be no coincidence: some of the companies building roads in Nigeria are German.

Integration and transformation of the *Turawa* spirits

How were the *Turawa* spirits finally integrated into the pantheon of the *bori* cult?

Even in 1969, one author writes that the status of the 'European' spirits in the 'hierarchy' of the *bori* pantheon '... was never properly established' [Onwuejeogwu
1969: 292]. In the two decades that have passed since that time, the *Turawa* spirits
have lost their ambiguous status and have been integrated into the social network
of the *bori* pantheon by various means.

Each spirit of the *bori* pantheon is characterized by his mythical deeds and mythical events that relate him to other spirits. Cult members and the spirits themselves
report on those mythical events. When not taking possession of their mediums,
spirits are said to live in the mythical city called *Jangare*. There, according to their
descent, craft or ethnic background, they inhabit several 'houses' (sg. *gida* or *zaure*).
The houses of the spirits are interrelated by a social network constituted by relations
of marriage or descent among their inhabitants (also Besmer 1973; 1983). Through
the constitution of a new house of spirits the *Turawa* spirits were integrated into the
social network of *Jangare*.

Turawa spirits have an affinity to the blacksmiths of *Jangare*: both are dealing with
fire. Head of the house of the blacksmiths is the spirit *Batoyi* ('The one who sets fire
on purpose'), who was previously mentioned by Tremearne (1968 [1914]). In recent
times *Batoyi* became the classificatory father of the 'European' spirits and is therefore also called *uban Turawa* (father of the Europeans). His daughter *Ladi mayya* (Ladi
the witch) is frequently referred to by the *Turawa* spirits as their classificatory
mother.

Turawa spirits are also classified as *arna* or *kafirai* ('pagans' or non-Muslims). They
do not observe Islamic customs, they smoke, drink alcohol and eat meat of animals
who are either forbidden by, or not slaughtered according to Islamic customs (also
Rouch 1978: 1007). The same non-Muslim behaviour is attributed to the 'pagan'
Gwarawa spirits who are also called *arna* or *kafirai*. In *bori* mythology and in praise
songs addressed to *Gwarawa* spirits they are characterized by their eating of dog
meat and their breaking of the incest taboo. When they have taken the bodies of
their mediums they stagger around as drunkards and smoke two or three cigarettes
at the same time.

Besmer's informants (1983) reported the houses of *Turawa* and *Gwarawa* spirits to
be interrelated through marriage. Five sisters of *Sarkin Gwari* (head of the *Gwarawa*
spirits) married 'European' spirits and are living in the house of the *Turawa* spirits.
The offspring of these marriages were adopted by their mother's brother *Sarkin
Gwari* and are living with him in the house of the *Gwarawa*. In return *Sarkin Gwari*
gave some of his children as wives or adopted sons to the 'European' spirits (Besmer
1983: 104).

Through the female spirit *Halima* the *Turawa* spirits are related to the house of the
Buzaye spirits (Tuareg serfs) from whom *Halima* descends. The marriage of *Halima*
and one of the 'European' spirits obliges the *Turawa* to pay respect to their classificatory parents in law: the group of the *Buzaye* spirits. Out of respect for the *Buzaye*,
the *Turawa* salute and bow down to the *Buzaye* if members of both groups are present at *bori* dances. *Halima* is characterized by her praise song as follows:

Sannu Halima 'yar Buzaye, sannu Halima 'yar Turawa,
Greetings *Halima* daughter of Tuareg serfs, greetings *Halima* daughter of Europeans,
sannu Halima matar Mushe, sai suka san ba ta da wayo,
greetings *Halima* wife of *Mushe*, because they knew she was not cunning,

sai suka ba ta naman jaki, sai suka ce na 'dan akuya ne.[30]
they gave her donkey meat and said it was goat meat.

Her naivety about food is typical for the *Turawa* spirits, who do not observe Islamic customs concerning food (also Besmer 1983: 108). The identity of *Halima's* husband remains obscure. Depending on the person or spirit asked, different answers were given: either *'Dan mama, Kafaran Salma*, or *Mai yak'i*. Her name *matar Turawa* (wife of Europeans) indicates that she has relationships to several 'European' spirits. Besmer explains it with a story, which I did not hear in 1993: 'She is reported to entertain men (for a price) when her husband is away fighting and has organized this into a business of which she is the "Madam".' (Besmer 1983: 108). This is why she is also called *Madam*. *Halima's* son *Small boy* is the youngest among the *Turawa* spirits. He is the *'dan auta*, the last born and spoiled child similar to those of other families of 'foreign' spirits.

One of the mythical stories involving the *Turawa* recounts how the spirit *Sarkin rafi*[31] became the 'driver' (*direba*) of the 'European' spirits. One day *Halima* had disappeared from the house of the *Turawa*. In their search for *Halima* the 'European' spirits met *Sarkin rafi*, who told them that his brother *'Dan galadima* had abducted *Halima*. Because *Sarkin rafi* knew the place where his brother had brought *Halima* he agreed to help them. When they finally found her, she was standing on the opposite bank of a river. *Sarkin rafi* crossed the river and brought *Halima* back to the *Turawa* who were waiting for them at the bank of the river. Since that time *Sarkin rafi* became the *direban Turawa* (driver of the Europeans) who escorts the *Turawa* spirits on their mythical warfare and assists them in crossing the water. Thus *Sarkin rafi* enters the floods of a river, leading the *Turawa* who are following one by one.[32]

Relations between *Fulani* spirits and *Turawa* spirits are marked by ritual animosity. A myth recounts the origin of this dislike. One day the female *Fulani* spirit *Bak'ar doguwa* kidnapped *Small boy* because she liked him. *Kafaran* and *Komanda mugu* searched for him, and when they found *Small boy* together with *Bak'ar doguwa*, *Kafaran* started to wrestle with her while *Komanda mugu* took the child. While they were wrestling *Bak'ar doguwa* broke the lower right leg of *Kafaran*. That is why *Kafaran* has to balance his weight on the left leg, whenever he takes possession of one of his mediums.[33] The animosity of *Turawa* and *Fulani* spirits is expressed by ritualized provocations of the *Fulani* by the *Turawa* spirits and the former fearing the latter if they happen to be on the same dance ground.

In contemporary Kano *bori*, genealogies of 'European' spirits are undergoing a process of transformation. Whereas the *Turawa* spirits of the oldest generation, *Mai yak'i, 'Dan mama, Kafaran, Umaru, et al.* do not have a clearly defined descent in Besmer's representation (1983) dating back to data collected in 1972–3, these very spirits are ascribed *Fulani* or *Gwarawa* descent by present-day Kano cult members and spirits alike.[34] Most of the spirits called *Turawa* are no longer spirits of European descent, but those with African genealogies, who adopted the military drill and 'European' customs in 'European' military barracks built on African soil, thus becoming ambiguous 'European Africans'. A myth recounts how *'Dan mama*, having *Gwarawa* ancestry, became a 'European' spirit: *'Dan mama* started to work as a cook in the barracks of the *Turawa* spirits. The *Turawa* gave him biscuits and eggs and he became used to the 'European' way of living to such an extent that he adopted it.[35] Similar to *'Dan mama* other 'European' spirits of 'African' descent gave up their cultural heritage (*gado*) in favour of the 'European' alternative. The transformation of the genealogies of *Turawa* spirits cannot only be understood as referring to historical events that took place during the colonial period, but also as a further means of integration built on a theme not uncommon in *bori* mythology. The loss of cultural heritage acquired by birth can also be traced in myths relating to other *bori* spirits. For example, *Mai gizo* who is of *Fulani* descent is said to have adopted the way of living of his friend *Sarkin arna* (chief of the 'pagans') in such a way that he is now smoking, drinking alcohol and womanizing and has moved from the house of the *Fulani* spirits to that of the *Maguzawa* ('pagan') spirits.

Mimesis, ritual representation of a foreign culture, and the *Turawa* spirits

The history of the 'European' spirits of the *bori* cult can be read as a history of the perception of a 'European' culture by an 'African' culture. Writing on possession by foreign spirits Fritz Kramer employs the concept of mimesis. In the process of cultural contact members of the societies involved are confronted with each other's mutually unfamiliar ways of living. The strangeness of the other can 'overwhelm' and 'force' to mimesis: a *gestalt* emerges that interprets the other through mimesis (Kramer 1987: 243). The early *Hauka* spirits emerged at a time when the influence of the colonial French administration on the local societies had grown strong. The *Hauka* and later on the *Turawa* as well, ritually adapted and represented the colonial French and British culture as perceived by the members of the local societies. Within the characterization of the *Hauka* and *Turawa* spirits, certain features of colonial French and British culture were emphasized, others neglected. Tobias Wendl (1991:312) describes the principle underlying the ritual representation of a given 'reference culture' as a synecdochical one, in which 'parts represent the whole'. The same applies to the *Turawa* spirits of the *bori* cult. The European 'reference culture' is split up in several synecdochical fields. The one which is stressed most is the power and military force of the 'European' reference culture, symbolically represented by the *Turawa* spirits' handling of fire, their military-style uniforms, paraphernalia and behaviour. Another synecdochical field comprises the consumption customs of the 'European' reference culture, illustrated by cigarettes, alcohol, bottled soft drinks, eggs and the eating of meat prohibited by Islamic law. Language, too, constitutes an important synecdochical field: similar to the colonial Europeans the *Turawa* spirits' 'mother tongues' are foreign to the Hausa language. If they speak Hausa to communicate with their clients, it is grammatically and phonetically altered: they pronounce it incorrectly, they are often unsure of words or they simply switch into their 'mother tongue' in the middle of a sentence.

During the process of the *Turawa* spirits' integration into the *bori* pantheon the cult's mythology expanded. New myths developed, interrelating the 'European' spirits with the 'traditional' *bori* spirits in various ways. In recent times the genealogical backgrounds of the spirits are undergoing a process of transformation: they are becoming spirits of African descent who have adopted European manners and customs. Thus the *gestalt* of the *Turawa* spirits today combines the mimetical interpretation of the *other*, the 'European' culture, with the reflection on the *self*, the Northern-Nigerian culture and its later history.

Notes

1 For a general account of *bori* practices the reader is referred to Tremearne (1966 [1914]), Mon-fouga-Nicolas (1972) and Besmer (1983).
2 *Jan gora* (lit. dragging of a cane): metaphor that relates to a blind man led by someone with a cane. Here it is the spirit who leads his medium.
3 J. Broustra-Monfouga writing on *bori* in Birnin Konni/Niger mentions a 'European' spirit named *Jan mouche* the name of whom is translated as 'Monsieur rouge' (1973: 204). (Europeans are called 'red skinned' [ja] in Hausa language.)
4 Military-like parade (*fareti*), press-ups, 'frog-walk', etc. See also Krings (1997) and (1998).
5 Syntactical modifications and alterations in tone, though existing, will not be considered in the present chapter.
6 Underlined expressions of the spirits' language are written in a broad phonetic transcription; non-underlined expressions are written orthographically. The abreviations E (English), F (French) and H (Hausa) refer to the linguistic origin of the marked expressions.
7 In the following examples oblique brackets /.../ denote a phonemic-, square brackets [...] a broad phonetic transcription.
8 One of the interviewed spirits, while possessing a particular medium, was using the feminine forms of the 2.p/sg. pronouns to address masculine persons.
9 The process during which a spirit is taught his behaviour, dance style, language etc., is called *koyemi* (imitation). Thus a person or a spirit of the same spirit family acts, dances and speaks next to the spirit having taken the body of his new medium, trying to 'imitate' his teacher. For a general account on initiation see Besmer (1977).
10 See Stoller (1984; 1995) and Olivier de Sardan (1993). Also refered to as *Babule*-movement (Echard 1992: 96).
11 In this region of Niger, Hausa- and Songhay-speaking people settled in close proximity.
12 *Hauka* is a Hausa term denoting 'madness', 'folly'.
13 In Songhay language European doctors are called *lokotoro* (Stoller 1989: 204).
14 'The male participant 'Soja' (soldier) dances. He is beating himself with supple twigs and is quite insensible to the pain.' (Price 1957: 22.)
15 Though Rouch reports an animosity among Songhay-speaking immigrants towards the Hausa (1956: 133). *Hauka* dances publicly held in Songhay-speaking communities of Ghanaian cities in the 1980s were also attended by Hausa people (personal communication with Yahaya Ahmed Becker, Darmstadt).
16 Personal observation of the author of this chapter.
17 *Garaya*: a two-stringed plucked lute used in the *bori* cult of Northern Nigeria.
18 Personal communication with Adamu Makaho, Zaria and Saminu 'dan Jan Dutse, Tudun Wada.
19 The late *sarkin bori* (cult leader) of Kano, Alhaji Inusa mai Badosa who died during a visit to Ghana in 1992 was born and brought up in Magariya, Niger where his brother holds the title of *sarkin bori*. *Dokta* Mohammadu Moni, who holds the title of '*shugaban 'yan mushe*' (Leader of the mediums of 'European' spirits) of the Kano branch of the Nigerian Association of Medical Herbalists, spent his youth in Niger.
20 'When we moved here to New Giwa the spirits filled the town, the European spirits began to come too.' (Smith 1964: 209). Note that Harris (1930) and Greenberg (1966 [1946]) do not mention any 'European' spirit.
21 Whether those spirits also had personal names remains obscure.
22 These are the spirits *Gwabna*, his wife *Mami*, *Umaru*, *Mai yak'i*, *'Dan Auta*, *Halima* and *Barkono* (Reuke 1969: 123).
23 Although one informant said that the spirits manifested themselves for the first time 'exactly 32 years ago' (1931) (Reuke 1969: 72).
24 '*sai mun fito Faranse, sai mun shigo Najeriya naku.*' *Mai yak'i* (#1) 14.5.1993. Kurna/Kano. 'Faranse' (France) in everyday language is used as a synonym for Niger.

25 'ko da wani lokasi kamar yanda gari naku kuna trobis nasi, kuna yi riguma naku, afo, mu, muna 'dauka shi rigima namu.' *Mai yak'i* (#1) 14.5.1993. Kurna, Kano.

26 Rouch mentions that Ousmane Fode, *zima* (ritual priest) of the *Hauka* cult in Ghana from 1929 to 1943, fought with the British army in World War One (Rouch 1956: 40). The leader of the *'yan mushe* of Tudu, Abdu 'dan Umma fought with the Free French in North Africa during World War Two' (Faulkingham 1975: 40).

27 Besmer (1983) and Reuke (1969) do not mention *Jamus*.

28 Personal communication with Aminu Shariff Baffa, Kano and Yahaya Ahmed Becker, Darmstadt. Up to the present day the phrase *'Jamus-'bata k'asa'* is a spontaneous reaction of Hausa speakers, young and old alike, at the mention of 'Germany'.

29 'Zan sa katafila ... wanda za ta ci gaba da ni gyara 'kasa – ta tura shi, ta ajiye.' *Jamus* (#1) 6.5.1993 Gadan Tamburawa/Kano.

30 Sung by Idi na Ladi mai daddawa, 8.12.1992 Wudil, Kano. In other versions 'donkey meat' is substituted by 'cadaver of a donkey' /*muushèn jàakii*/. (Also Reuke 1969: 130).

31 *Sarkin rafi* (chief of the stream) is related to water and farming on irrigated plots, also called *'rafi'*. (Tremearne 1968 [1914]; Greenberg 1966 [1946]; Besmer 1983).

32 Interview with *Kafaran Salma* (#4) 6.5.1993 Gadan Tamburawa, Kano. Similar versions were told by other spirits and cult members.

33 Interview with *Kafaran Salma* (#1) 10.5.1993 'Dambare, Kano. Rouch recounts a myth on *Bak'ar doguwa* and the Hauka fighting each other (1960: 75).

34 Statements varied depending on person or spirit asked. The ritual animosity of *Turawa* and *Fulani* spirits that seems to oppose a *Fulani* descent of the *Turawa* was explained by referring to locally differing initiation practices.

35 Interview with *Mai yak'i* (#1) 14.5.1993 Kurna, Kano.

References

Bargery, G. P. (1957) [1934] *A Hausa–English Dictionary; and English–Hausa Vocabulary*, London: Oxford University Press.

Besmer, Fremont E. (1973) 'Avoidance and joking relationships between Hausa supernatural spirits', in *Studies in Nigerian Culture* 1,1: 25–51.

—— (1977) 'Initiation into the *bori* cult: a case study in Ningi town', in *Africa* 47,1: 1–13.

—— (1983) *Horses, Musicians and Gods*, South Hadley, Mass.: Bergin & Garvey.

Broustra-Monfouga, Jacqueline (1973) 'Approche ethnopsychiatrique du phénomène de possession. Le *bori* de Konni (Niger), étude comparative' in *Journal de la Société des Africanistes* 43: 197–220.

DeBouzek, Jeanette (1989) 'The 'ethnographic surrealism' of Jean Rouch', in *Visual Anthropology* 2, 3–4: 301–15.

Echard, Nicole (1991) 'The Hausa *bori* possession cult in the Ader region of Niger: its origins and present-day function', in *Women's medicine. The* Zar-Bori *Cult in Africa and Beyond*, I.M. Lewis *et al.*, (eds) 64–80. Edinburgh: International African Institute.

(1992) 'Cultes et possession et changement social. L'exemple du *bori* Hausa de l'Ader et du Kurfey', (Niger)', in *Archives de Sciences Sociales des Religions* 79, 3: 87–100.

Faulkingham, Ralph (1975) *The Spirits and their Cousins. Some Aspects of Belief, Ritual and Social Organization in a Rural Hausa Village in Niger*, Amherst: University of Massachusetts, Department of Anthropology.

Fuglestad, Finn (1975) 'Les *Hauka*: une interprétation historique', in *Cahiers d'Études africaines* 58: 203–16.

Greenberg, Joseph (1966) [1946] *The Influence of Islam on a Sudanese Religion*, Seattle & London: University of Washington Press.

Harris, P. G. (1930) 'Notes on Yauri (Sokoto province), Nigeria', In *Journal of the Royal Anthropological Society* 60: 283–334.

King, A. V. (1967) *A Bòorìi Liturgy from Katsina*. (Supplement to *African Language Studies*, 7). London: School of Oriental and African Studies, University of London.

Kramer, Fritz W. (1987) *Der rote Fes. Über Besessenheit und Kunst in Afrika*, Frankfurt a.M.: Athenäum.

Krieger, Kurt (1967) 'Notizen zur Religion der Hausa', in *Paideuma* 13: 96–121.

Krings, Matthias (1997) *Feuer, Alkohol und Zigaretten: Die Europäergeister im bori-Kult der Hausa* (working papers on African societies 9), Berlin: Das Arabische Buch.

—— (1998) *Geister des Feuers: zur Imagination des Fremden im Bori-Kult der Hausa,* Hamburg: Lit Verlag.

Monfouga-Nicolas, Jacqueline (1972) *Ambivalence et culte de possession,* Paris: Éditions Anthropos.

Olivier de Sardan, Jean-Pierre (1993) 'La surinterprétation politique: les cultes de possession *hawka* du Niger', in *Religion et modernité politique en Afrique noire: Dieu pour tous et chacun pour soi.* Bayart, Jean François (ed.) 163–213. Paris: Karthala.

Onwuejeogwu, Michael (1969) 'The cult of the *Bori*-spirits among the Hausa', in *Man in Africa,* M. Douglas & P. M. Kaberry (eds) 279–305, London: Tavistock.

Price, J. H. (1957) 'A *Bori* dance in Accra', in *West African Review* 57, 1: 20–24.

Reuke, Ludger (1969) *Die Maguzawa in Nordnigeria: Ethnographische Darstellung und Analyse des beginnenden Religionswandels zum Katholizismus,* Bielefeld: Bertelsmann.

Rouch, Jean (1953/54) *Les mâitres fous,* Paris: Comitée du Film Ethnographique.

—— (1956) *Migrations au Ghana,* Paris: Société des Africanistes.

—— (1960) *La religion et la magie Songhay,* Paris: Presses Universitaires de France.

—— (1978) 'Jean Rouch talks about his films to John Marshall and John W. Adams', in *American Anthropologist* 80: 1005–22.

Smith, Mary (1964) *Baba of Karo,* New York: Praeger.

Stoller, Paul (1984) 'Horrific comedy: cultural resistance and the *Hauka* movement in Niger', in *Ethos* 12, 2: 163–88.

—— (1989) *Fusion of the Worlds. An Ethnography of Possession among the Songhay of Niger,* Chicago & London: The University of Chicago Press.

—— (1995) *Embodying Colonial Memories. Spirit Possession, Power and the Hauka in West Africa,* New York & London: Routledge.

Tremearne, A. J. N. (1968) [1914]) *The Ban of the Bori,* London: Frank Cass.

Wendl, Tobias (1991) *Mami Wata. Oder ein Kult zwischen den Kulturen,* Münster & Hamburg: Lit Verlag.

5

Horse, Hunter
& Messenger
The Possessed Men
of the Nya Cult in Mali

Jean-Paul Colleyn

Introduction

Spirit possession stands at the crossroads of such disciplines as psychology, sociology, medicine, history, anthropology, and even performance art theory, to each of which it poses many questions. For some years a rich literature illustrated the theme of what Roger Gomm called 'bargaining of weakness' (Gomm 1975; Lewis 1971, 1996; Monfouga-Nicolas 1972; Echard 1989; Messing 1958; Boddy 1989; Stoller 1989; Rouch 1948, 1954, 1972). In addition, according to another well received theory in African studies, possession is related to a historical crisis and is seen as a product of acculturation. Possession cults are considered as marginal appearing beside dominant religions such as Islam and Christianity and are supposed to decline as soon as they receive official recognition. Against these approaches, I here try to use the polemic properties of a Malian possession cult, the cult of *Nya*, in order to enlarge the scope of structural variances in the comparative studies of spirit possession. The *Nya* cult actually presents many features that contradict the above-mentioned theoretical approaches: it is a rural cult; possession is the privilege of a minority of male members of a society into which they have been initiated; possessed men still belong to powerful lineages; their careers never begin as an illness; trance has no therapeutical value; possession confirms a dedication to a specific localized deity; spirit possession is related to divination, a means of expression of a superior 'voice' and a shamanistic technique. Moreover, far from flourishing at the margins of dominant Islam, the *Nya* cult loses its influence whereas Islam is spreading. My information is based on fieldwork, carried out since 1971 in Mali, amongst people classified in the colonial literature as 'Minyanka', but who now call themselves 'Myanka' or more often 'Bamana'.[1]

The *Nya* cult

There are *Nya* sanctuaries in nearly every village in the south-east of Mali, in an area corresponding roughly to the Segu administrative region in the south of the Bani river and in the Sikasso region in the north of the Banifing. On the eastern side, *Nya* has spread in many villages of Burkina Faso. Two main languages are spoken in this area, a Mande language, bamana (noted as b) and a northern Senufo one, myanka-mamara (noted as m). *Nya* sanctuaries co-exist with hundreds of other sanctuaries and shrines related to better known socio-religious institutions of Mande origin, such as *Komo, Kono, Korè, Namakoro, Tyi-wara* and many others. Until very recently, all those cults were articulating the entire religious life. Fifteen years ago, possession cults of *Nya* and Nankon still occupied the centre of the stage as major institutions. We do not know anything about the context of their creation but today social instability, far from favouring them, tends to diminish their influence. With the development of a market economy, of state judicial institutions, of education, and of Islam, *Nya* sanctuaries lose their prestige and their political power.

The vital structure of this society of subsistence cultivators was based on patrilineal kin groups organized as communities, but since the end of the sixties, these have split up under the pressure of cotton cultivation and a monetary economy. In the absence of both central political institutions and segmentary organization, authority is divided between village chiefs, family heads, imams, marabouts, and animist fraternities. Social order depends on a balance between them. The population is composed of lineages of diverse origins, but, although there is no central chart embodying a mythically codified vision of the world, the culture is relatively homogeneous. Reality is conceived through a network of varied secret symbols. The supreme and unforgotten creator, called Allah by the Muslims, Ngala or Klè by the animists, is responsible for good and evil. But he is said to be distant and hardly preoccupied with details of individual life. These matters are the concern for imams and marabouts on the one side and for a multitude of intermediary mystical powers without hierarchical structure, on the other. I call these powers 'deities' rather than spirits, because people ask them for life, health, fecundity, rain, harvests and wealth. People have little interest in defining them with precision but hundreds of sanctuaries still exist in the country. The cults dedicated to them are focused on sacred objects called *boliw* (b) or *yaperle* (m), each of which corresponds to a secret knowledge. Among these deities, one distinguishes those who express themselves verbally and those who have to be interpreted by mechanical divination. The first are said to 'take a mouth' (b: *da minè*, m: *nyu co*) through incarnation into a masked dancer or a possessed person. In consequence, among tens of deities, only a few 'take' human beings into trance and possession. The most well known are *Nya* (or Wara) and Nankon, the former being the most important. Possession is thus a particuliar form, among others, of communication with the divine world.

In possession cults, accredited men are invaded by a deity and speak in her or his name. *Nya* is believed to control rainfall, to favour fertility and to play a protective role against witches (b: *suba-mogow*, m: *sikan-fè*). People congregate at the shrine to consult *Nya* (through its human mount) for advice on matters of domestic life and diagnoses after repeated misfortunes. *Nya* receives bi-annual sacrifices of dogs and chickens in exchange for forgiveness and blessing.

Twice a year, a ceremony stages a raid of *Nya* into the bush, from where all kinds of knowledge come. In the turmoil of a noisy crowd and of a band of musicians, a procession takes form around the two or three accredited possessed men. One of them opens the sanctuary and carries the three bags containing the sacred altars, in order to 'go into the bush'. The destination is actually a special permanent enclosure called *Nya*'s wood (Nya-*tu*), where sacrifices have to take place. During the trip, the musicians sing the praises of *Nya*, saying, for instance:

> Your exploits, they cannot be described, *Nya*; your exploits, they cannot be described, Venerable!
> (m: *Hé mu kale wa jo mè Nya, mu kale wa se jo yè Lègho*).
> If a foolish witch gets up to attack you, show him, and you will deserve your name
> (*Sikanfo sicèr-fèghè mè yiri ma kana ma na li shyè u na na ma yè ta*)
> All the creatures, he (*Nya*) is able to kill them, all the creatures, him, the superior one
> (*Yara gbo na gbale yara ka yeghele-folo*)
> This big guy got up to betray *Nya*, but the betrayer is in the power of *Nya*.
> (b: *Yèrè ba wulila u shyè Nya kOrObO, kOrObO-ba de ye a bolo*).

At *Nya*'s wood, while the possessed persons are 'set free' by *Nya*, the altars are taken from the bags and placed in large pots on top of which dogs and chicken are sacrified. As a diurnal inhabitant of the village, the dog is viewed as a substitutive victim replacing the hyena, wild and nocturnal animal of the bush, considered as expert in witchcraft. 'To nourish *Nya*' the altars are covered with sacrificial blood, while the meat is transported to the village in order to be cooked and eaten by the initiates. In the evening, the musicians go back to their instruments and start to sing *Nya*'s praises while the deity mounts her or his 'horses' again 'to go home and take rest'. In the weak light of a straw fire, at the door of the sanctuary, with his hands resting on the altars bags, the specially accreditated possessed man called *Nya*'s mouth (Nya *da*) or messenger (m: *tutumo*), pronounces oracles, foretells, gives advice, threatens the malevolent witches, answers the supplications and mediates in the conflicts between villagers.

Hundreds of *Nya* sanctuaries, with their corresponding fraternities and their own set of traditions, are to be found throughout the country. Only those with common roots or who have concluded a friendship pact maintain close contacts and invite each other to their respective festivities. Some sanctuaries are famous and attract a large public, others do not go beyond the limits of the village. Famous *Nya* 'have daughters' : people of other villages have bought the sacred altars (*boliw* or *yaperle*) and learned the secrets in order to establish a new sanctuary at their place. Related societies always participate in each other's ceremonials, which take place after the harvests and before the sowing.

A 'society of *Nya*' (Nya *ton*) is always based on the alliance of several families. 'The ways of *Nya* are threefold' one says: one is the owner of the altars, another the possessed person and the third is the smith, who is often the witness (*sere*) of the possessed man. Of great importance are also the singers (*cèlè*) without whom *Nya* would never receive enough 'heat to warm up' the possessed man. Each of these categories expresses a particular knowledge. The officiants are consulted as social and medical advisers. The owner of the altars is the chief of the cult (b: Nya-*tigi*; m: Nya-*folo*), the medium incarnates periodically the deity, the smith, as witness repeats his words, mediates in case of conflict and sacrifies the animals. Elsewhere in Africa, possession cults belong very often to what Max Gluckman called rituals of rebellion: the possessed transgresses, blasphemes, mocks, adopts obscene behaviour. Here, this function is not performed by the possessed man, but by ritual buffoons (*kordubala*) who have a cathartic joking relationship with everybody. All these offices are hereditary, in a loose manner, but sufficiently to maintain from one generation to another a certain stability in the college directing the cult. The seances perform a ritual communication act between the world of living people and those who have departed to the 'village of the dead'.

An ideal (more often proclaimed than fulfilled) is that the possessed, the smith and the chief should be of different lineages in order to increase the credibility of a cult which is supposed to be above all particular interests: with a medium acting as an impartial arbitrator.

I propose to analyze this cult, using five criteria which present interesting aspects for a comparative study. This framework will show how the usual spectrum of possession cults should be enlarged.

Some atypical features

The relation to Islam

In the course of history in Mali, many lineages have probably gone to Islam and returned to 'animism', adopting after their migration the language, customs and beliefs of the place where they settled. In 1910, the missionary Joseph Henry observed that the mass of inhabitants of Segu Circle were 'fetishists'. When I first arrived in the field in 1971, people identified by Maurice Delafosse as Bambara, Dyonka, Minyanka, Senufo, Bobo and Bwa were still said to be '*Bamana*' in the sense of non-Muslims. The number of Muslim people was estimated to be about twenty per cent – even if that kind of estimation is rather imprecise – the cult of *Nya* was largely dominant. Today, the proportion is reversed, and for the majority, the social status of possessed people is no longer honored. Progressively the role of the possessed is shifting from high status to something shameful. A few years ago, the possessed man was a sort of village 'star' and was said to be a *kamalemba* : a very strong, proud and powerful person.

Since the early sixties, conversions to Islam have been massive, but the process has been peaceful and discreet. By the hundreds, young people have abandoned the old practices. When they move to the cities during the dry season to find a temporary job, not only do they miss important rituals, but also, they are ashamed to be different if they do not pray to Allah. Islam offers prestige, new sets of solidarity and a way to escape from the elders' authority. Even prominent elders, like traditional priests or diviners, try to maintain their influence on the young generations through conversion to Islam. Retaining the knowledge related to the most powerful 'animist' cults, like *Komo* and *Nya*, they become Muslim and even 'marabouts' to increase their power. Having learned some prayers and verses of the Koran from travelling proselytes, it is as if they have progressed in esoteric knowledge. Moreover, the political and judicial functions that *Komo*, *Kono*, *Nya* and other cults used to fulfil are not tolerated any more by the government and the sanctuaries have lost much of their prestige. (See below).

Spirit possession is a specific form of divination and the possessed persons, besides their direct inspiration, are actually experts in geomancy. But the marabouts are as well. The system is the same, though with different vocabularies, different symbols and, of course, different ritual prescriptions. But 'animism' and Islam have been so much under mutual influence that divination cannot be qualified as purely 'animist' or 'Muslim'. With a bitter irony, the priests of *Nya* cults say that they meet the marabouts in the middle of the night, searching for the roots of the same tree in order to prepare 'medicines'. Actually, the Muslims do not say that *Nya* or *Komo* do not exist; they only say that the power of God is stronger. They do not deny the belief in witchcraft; they pretend to be better equipped to fight against it. However, if Muslims are often accused of detaining some hidden fetish objects (*boliw*), the idea of spirit possession is strongly rejected by them. This is a totally different pattern than in other West African contexts such as these of the Songhay *Holey*, the Hausa *Bori*, the *Zar* of East Africa, and the Hamadsha brotherhood of Morocco, which are tolerated and legitimized by the fact that *jinn* are mentioned in the Koran. Anyway, we can observe in this case that the success of possession is inversely proportional to that of Islam and that the cultural crisis does not favour this possession cult.

The gender paradigm

I have here to state that my ethnography has a limited dimension as most of my fieldwork concentrated on the male side. Descriptions unavoidably reflect the male domain of experience, and a full version is still to be developed. Nevertheless, the contrast with other West African cults, even Malian ones is complete. The vast majority of possession cults studied by I.M. Lewis concern women marginalized in male-dominated Muslim societies who exert mystical pressures on men by the means of peripheral cults in dynamic relation with Islam. This scheme is also true in Western Mali for the *Jine-don* studied by Gibbal or the cults curing *jine-bana* (the sickness of the spirit) in Beledugu. All these religious associations have probably succeeded getting a certain recognition by Islam because they are, in many respects, powerful counterhegemonic feminine societies which cannot be dismissed. But the pattern of the Bamana cults is quite different: the so-called 'traditional' religious associations are completely dominated by men, and *Nya* societies do not deviate from that fact. *Nya* services are dominated by elderly men. Women assist as faithfuls but are excluded from secret knowledge, from possession and from the direction of the cult. Only a wife of the chief's family is tolerated as the housewife of the sanctuary. This type of possession cult thus differs strikingly from those where, through possession, women protest against a male dominant orthodoxy. Here, on the contrary, possession expresses men's domination in a defensive ideology arguing that witchcraft is mainly a female malevolent power against which they have to defend themselves.

The status of the Nya society chief

Nya, a religious but not personified power, is reputed to be an androgynous, dominantly female divinity. Verbally, *Nya* is referred to as 'she' or 'he' following the metaphors or the allegories which are employed. A man who builds a new *Nya* sanctuary 'contracts a marriage' and becomes metaphorically the 'husband of *Nya*' (Nya-*polo*). During his trance, the possessed man acting as *Nya*'s mouth calls the chief 'my husband'. The chief is in relation with *Nya* by the way of dreams and personal rituals including fumigations and sacrifices. He is the owner of the sacred objects, while the possessed person is not. In most possession cults described in literature, the relation between a medium and his or her usual attendant is regularly expressed in terms of marriage or sexuality (I.M. Lewis), but here, the matrimonial metaphor is displaced and characterizes the relation between the owner of the sacred objects and the divine power. By marrying *Nya*, a polymorph but rather female super-power, men try to domesticate her in order to serve their interests and to overcome witchcraft. But they also say that they try in vain because *Nya* can never be totally controlled and submitted. However, as healer, magician and adviser, the chief of *Nya* has a 'clientele' and is a powerful rival for diviners and marabouts. The distinction between chiefs and possessed men is of great significance. As in the vodun cultural area on the coast of the Gulf of Guinea, most of the adepts of possession cults are never possessed. Chiefs of *Nya* societies themselves are not possessed, except when they have inherited the status of chief while they were already officially '*Nya*'s horse'. In this case, they generally ceased to be 'taken by *Nya*'. After their death, *Nya* chiefs are reputed to remain powerful ancestors, keeping close contact with *Nya*. Every prayer begins by the enunciation of their names. A parcel of their bodies is incorporated in the altars and these incantations are supposed to 'wake up', to 'excite', or to 'warm *Nya* up'. During the ceremony, when the possessed men go through the first gate of the village, they walk backwards, because they are in the world of the dead where all is reversed and where they are in contact with the ancestors. Up to a certain point the power attributed to *Nya* subsumes with that of the ancestors who have created *Nya* and brought it to the village. If *Nya* arises at midnight – that is to say, possesses someone – he or she will go to the cemetery in order 'to listen to the ancestors and to know which offerings are to be made'. The relations between the mediums and the living chief of *Nya* are those of political allies, with eventual tensions, quarrels and reconciliations. Every public manifestation of *Nya* is preceded by secret meetings between the chief, the medium and if required, the singers and the sacrificer.

Powerful objects

Among the Hausa and the Songhay, the cults where altars (fetishes) are important, are separated from possession cults. In south-eastern Mali, altars are of great importance in possession cults. All the deities who take possession of men are honoured through sacrifices on sacred objects themselves named after the deity. Possession cults as well as mask cults (like *Komo*, *Kono*, *Namakoro* and *Tyi-wara*) always require taking care of sacred *boliw*. These objects, fabricated in the utmost secrecy by bringing together parts of mineral, animal and vegetal worlds are said to be charged with formidable specialized powers that they keep only if they are 'nourished' by sacrificial blood. While seldom stressed in the literature on possession, this feature is not really exceptional: it is also the case of many possession cults of the West African coast among the Yoruba, the Ewe, the Aja-Tado and the Fon.

The status of the possessed people

Nya possession is not a means by which underdogs (women and men of low status) bid for attention. Spirit possession cannot be seen as an oblique strategy or weapon against humiliation. Mediumship is restricted to men of powerful lineages and seldom used to insinuate grievances. Mediums do not belong to the categories of persons who are most readily prone to possession in the epidemicological trends deployed by I.M. Lewis in his comparative study (Lewis 1996). Women are reputed not to be strong enough to resist *Nya*'s strength. In principle, *Nya* 'takes' anybody for messenger, but practically the mediums are always chosen from the same lineages. This recruitment, generally prescribed by heritage or announced 'by *Nya*' through its possessed man, is never expressed in terms of solution of a suffering subject. Of course, idiosyncratic psychological factors may play their part, but the 'calling' of the possessed person is never revealed by sickness and the ritual does not transform mental disorder into religious office. The institutional factors seem to be more relevant to explain how mediums become the chosen and respected agents of the deity. Consequently, *Nya* societies (Nya-*ton*) are in no way formed, as is so often the case in African possession cults, of cured sick people who became priests through a healing initiation (Lewis 1971, 1996; Zempléni 1966, 1967, 1973, 1984, 1985, 1987; Monfouga-Nicolas 1972; Stoller 1989; Boddy 1989). The pattern is also quite different from North African examples as the Gnawa, Hamadsha or Hasawa sects, where the finality of trance is to cure people (Crapanzano 1973; Achouba 1982). The only cases reported are those of young boys who have inherited the role of possessed and have refused it. In this case, their misfortunes, eventually including nervous breakdown or madness, are attributed to a punishment inflicted by *Nya*. But it is unthinkable that, as among the Songhay, spirits send a sickness to their future mediums (who belong most of the time to the lineages of actual mediums) that can only be cured through initiation and possession (Stoller 1989).

It is important to stress that most of the time, the fate of a possessed boy is revealed by *Nya* during a ceremony, soon after the birth of a boy or even before. If *Nya* (that is to say the medium) sees a boy, he may say : 'That boy will be my horse when he grows up.' When he is 'blessing' a pregnant woman of his own lineage, he may say : 'Her child, if it is a boy, will be my mount.' Thus possession can be decided long before a state of trance has occurred. *Nya* is said to choose boys who are strong: 'If you cannot stand its force, then *Nya* let you go.' Possession is not desired by young boys or adults but it is no case interpreted as a response to affliction. In general, we find peaceful acceptance of this destiny. Well considered, healthy in mind and body, the 'messenger of *Nya*' (Nya-*tutumo*) leads the normal existence of a family father. His role is beneficial for the community and he enjoys a certain prestige. He is even feared, as are all those who keep company with sanctuaries and manipulate *boliw*. It is also said that women are attracted by him. Endowed with occult knowledge, trained as diviner, protected by *Nya*, he is very much appreciated as a husband.

A spirit possession crisis lasts for about two hours, seldom more. It can be induced by a wide range of stimuli but no particular one seems to be necessary. Generally, the possessed goes into a trance when hearing the music, the songs, or the praises of *Nya*. To refer to *Nya* in front of an entitled possessed man is otherwise considered improper. As release mechanism, music is not always necessary, although some informants insist on it. A band is composed of two harp-lutes (*ngoni*), one big gong (*kenke*), one pressure drum (*tanga*) and one iron scraper (*kara*). Three singers shake rattles. The *ngoni* contain a secret object, belonging to the category of *boliw*, which is reputed to induce possession. A relation is thus established between music and possession. A ritual song says: 'Strike briskly the drums, *Nya* (it means the possessed man) will dance!'

However, *Nya* often 'takes' somebody before the musicians start playing. Some operations, partly symbolical, partly related to the pharmacopeial, command the 'fall of the possessed'. Sometimes a powder composed of animal and vegetal substances – among others an hallucinogenic plant (*datura*) – contributes to induce the trance. But this powder is seldom used, and then mainly as a trigger mechanism for young possessed men. Anyway, the drug does not explain stereotypical ritual behaviour: possessed men behave in an accepted and expected fashion; observe a precise choreography, make codified gestures, follow a fixed itinerary, carry the bags containing the altars and pronounce consecrated wordings.

The relationship of the possessed and *Nya* oscillates between violent seizure and ecstatic illumination, and varies in the course of his life. A possessed man can never pretend to control the deity: he is captured and dominated. Following a widespread symbolism, *Nya*, when incarnated in its human host, is said 'to ride its horse'. A horse which has to be broken in: to become a 'saddle horse' which has a wild mount to learn. Particularly for young possessed men, trance is often an ordeal: *Nya* is said to torture its horse. But with experienced possessed men, trance manifests itself in a more restrained manner and is sometimes hardly visible.

One distinguishes three states of possession by *Nya*. The first is called *comato* (taken and fallen). It is a violent uncontrolled crisis, brief and occasional, seen as a simple manifestation of *Nya*'s strength. It can happen to anybody, even to women, though 'true' possession is a man's matter. Occasional *comato* crises are suspected to be faked. On the contrary, when crises are repeated in certain men, they may bring about a state of ritual trance. Those men then take up a career which leads to mediumism. They first become *bortala* (bag carriers). At the time of ceremonial, they carry the three bags containing the altars (*boliw*) to the sacrificial area. After several years, they may become mediums.

The cults as power associations

The notation of Patrick McNaughton concerning the *Komo* societies is relevant for all the cults quoted here: 'They are essentially fraternities that manipulate power, and to reflect that fact, it is useful to label them power associations' (1979: 10). By manipulating social crisis, *Nya* officiants exercize an important political as well as ritual power. As elsewhere in Africa, animosities between individuals as well as among groups are the believed sources of sickness and death (Augé & Herzlich 1984). Mainly concerned by social disorder, the deity shows disapproval by afflicting those involved with misfortune. The imagery is rather fierce: '*Nya* is nastier and better in witchcraft than any human being.' Whole villages that disappeared after diseases, famines, disputes and defections are reputed to have been destroyed by *Nya*. As a witch-hunter, *Nya* is actually a supreme witch, in charge of the repression of attacks against the initiates. Misfortune is seen as the consequence of breaches of the ritual rules or of mistakes in mystical actions. Through its medium, *Nya* acts as a public censor. Possession exposes social tension, synthesizes and neutralizes it. This is why the possessed have to remain above all parties. Because he has the authority of *Nya*, the medium can reprove a person who has broken the moral code which no one else would dare to do. These whispered messages are passed on to the guilty side by the witness (*sere*) of the messenger. If the transgression is very serious, the messenger reprimands the guilty person publicly. An informant who has served in the French army says that '*Nya* operates as a police force for the adepts of the cult and the villagers, while behaving as an army towards the exterior.' But the speech of the medium only carries weight if expressing a certain consensus or common opinion. Arbitrary and ambiguous, he is nevertheless supposed to give expression to the feelings of the local people when he is asked to decide about quarrels. *Nya* (the medium) has to negotiate and may reach a solution with some difficulties. The ethical position of *Nya* is by no means absolute: judgement in terms of good or bad depends upon the position from which it is viewed in terms of kinship, village, or initiating group solidarity, or individual status based on well-known knowledge. This point is crucial because *Nya* can be influenced by those who know its attributes; but when neglected, the deity is also prone to withdraw its benevolent patronage and to become actively hostile. Until the independence of Mali, possessed men promulgated the names of people 'who had been killed by *Nya*' for their misbehaviour, and the singers transformed these sentences into *Nya* praises, but today this 'death penalty' – even as interpretation a posteriori – is only evoked in general statements, formulated in a metaphoric way. The situation is exactly the same for other 'power associations' like the *Komo*, the *Kono*, the *Namakoro* and the *Tyi-wara* who fear the complaints of villagers to the tribunals. This loss of power, conjugated with factors cited above, has contributed to the relative decline of all these cults.

A shamanistic dimension

Let us agree upon a non-dogmatic opposition between possession and shamanism as two polarities rather than as two separate domains. In the possession cults, gods and deities pay visit to people; in shamanism, men travel in the world of the gods (Eliade 1951; de Heusch 1971; Bastide 1972; Rouget 1980). In that sense, even if shamans are in some cases possessed, possession is not the main characteristic of shamanism. The shaman travels symbolically to reach the spirits and tries to control them, while in possession cults, the possessed person is taken by the spirit or the deity and becomes his instrument, very often against his proclaimed will. The shaman goes into trance in order to allow his soul to travel in the sky, under the ground or in the deepness of the ocean. The idea of magic travel is essential. The soul of certain shamans goes to the moon or turns in the space around the earth. A staged ritual often illustrates the trip.

Without belonging to shamanism, a few African ceremonies which are based on the idea of magic travel admit a shamanistic dimension. A healer in trance goes and matches a spirit that cannot be seen by normal human beings. It is the case among the Lovedu of South Africa, the Ethiopians of Gondar, the Kuba of Zaïre and the Thonga of Mozambique. At Gondar, healers possessed by the *Zar* spirits are organized in societies composed of chronic patients. If a new sick person arrives, the healer enters voluntarily into a state of trance and invites his own *Zar* to come into himself in order to defy the unknown *Zar* of the patient and to force him to introduce himself. Here too, trance and possession play a therapeutic role. (S.D. Messing 1958: 285; Boddy 1989)

Without any healing function, the *myanka* of possession has nevertheless something to do with shamanistic travel: the malevolent actions of the witches are considered by *Nya* as provocations that motivate a hunting expedition against them. The world of the witches is supposed to double the visible world: witches part with their charnel shell to go and eat in the bush the souls stolen from the villagers. Thanks to the magic knowledge concentrated in its altars, *Nya* leads a shamanistic war against them.

During large public ceremonies, the 'walk out' of *Nya* stages dramatically this cathartic hunting party. The possessed moves in a symbolic world. 'As the turtledove on a wall of the courtyard that looks inside and outside', *Nya* sees at the same time the world of the living creatures and that of the dead and of the witches. When the possessed carries the three bags containing the altars, he sees the witches and hunts for them. His dance celebrates the invisible hunting expedition led by *Nya* in the bush. Suddenly, he runs quickly after a malevolent altar 'sent by witches'. Sometimes, he even finds one in a tree or under leaves on the ground. The crowd of villagers, dancing and singing in an amazing cloud of dust moves on to an area transformed into a sort of ritual stage (Colleyn and Péché 1983). The singers praise the exploits of the supreme hunter who dances carrying his weapons: the altars and the magic stick to finish off the witch. This epic episode culminates with a sacrificial meal taken by *Nya* in the bush in the enclosure set up near the village.

These religious practices unite the techniques of possession and shamanism. The possession crisis permits this symbolic witch-hunting journey to be staged. The fact that the possessed encounter witches instead of spirits, souls, or deities does not change anything, it is the idea of travel in a special space that is essential. In classic forms of shamanism, the shaman often goes after malevolent spirits which can be compared with African witches.

Conclusion

In this chapter, possession has been studied in relation to social institutions and religious systems, social tensions, sorcery and witchcraft. The bi-annual possession ceremonial reveals the quarrels and the rivalries simmering during the previous period and permits their expression in a more or less public debate. Anxieties, resentment, revenge and even hatred are released, but in a controlled manner. They are instutionalized and instantaneously taken up into a code of attitudes and wordings. This social control is always local and inconstant, as the Myanka distrust any concentration of authority. Power is always divided. The scattered sanctuaries, the differences between religious fraternities, their specific esoteric knowledge, and even their antagonism are so many different ways of organizing social complementarity and ensuring exchanges between social groups. Possession is thus not monopolized by a clergy operating within the context of a higly centralized religious system. Hundreds of little sanctuaries, each of them with its 'know-how', its priests and its mediums (possessed or wearing a mask), may claim to divine truth.

Note

1 In Mali, the term *bamana* is very often understood in the sense of 'animist' rather than as an ethnic group.

References

Augé, M. & Herzlich, C. (1984) *Le sens du mal: anthropologie, histoire, sociologie de la maladie*, Montreux: Éditions des Archives Contemporaines.

Bastide, R. (1972) *Le rêve, la transe et la folie*, Paris: Flammarion, Coll. Nouv. bibl. Scient.
Boddy, J. (1989) *Wombs and Alien Spirits.:Women, Men, and the Zar Cult in Nothern Sudan*, Madison: University of Wisconsin Press.
Crapanzano, V. (1973) *The Hamadsha: a Study in Moroccan Ethnopsychiatry*, Berkeley: University of California Press.
Echard, N. (1989) *Bori. Aspects d'un Culte de Possession Hausa dans l'Ader et le Kurfey (Niger)*, CEA EHESS, Documents de travail, 10.
Eliade, M. (1951) *Le Chamanisme (et les techniques archaïques de l'extase)*, Paris: Payot.
Heusch, L. de (1971) *Pourquoi l'épouser et autres essais*, Paris: Gallimard.
Gomm, R. (1975) 'Bargaining from weakness: spirit possession on the south Kenya coast', *Man*, 10: 4, 530–43.
Lewis, I.M. (1971) *Ecstatic Religions. An Anthropological Study of Possession and Shamanism*, London: Penguin Books.
—— 1996 *Religion in Context*, Cambridge: Cambridge University Press. (First published in 1986).
McNaughton, P. (1979) *Secret Sculptures of Komo: Art and Power in Bamana (Bambara) Initiation Associations*, Philadelpia: Institute for the Study of Human Issues.
Messing, S. D. (1958) 'Group therapy and social status in the Zar cult of Ethiopia', Middleton, 1967.
Middleton, J. (1967) *Magic, Witchcraft and Curing*, Austin & London: Texas Press.
Monfouga-Nicolas, J. (1972) *Ambivalence et Culte de Possession*. Paris: Anthropos.
Rouget, G. (1980) *La Musique et la Transe*, Paris: Gallimard.
Stoller, P. (1989) *Fusion of the Worlds: An Ethnography of Possession among the Songhay of Niger*, Chicago & London: University of Chicago Press.
Zempléni, A. (1966) 'La dimension thérapeutique du culte des rab. Ndöp, tuuru et samp, rites de possession chez les Wolof et les Lebou, *Psychopathologie africaine*, II, 3, 295–439.
—— 1967 'Sur l'alliance de la personne et du rab dans le Ndöp, *Psychopathologie africaine*, III, 441–50.
—— 1973 'Pouvoir dans la cure et pouvoir social', *Nouvelle Revue de Psychanalyse*, 8, Pouvoirs, 141–79.
—— 1984 'Possession et sacrifice', *Le Temps de la Réflexion* V, 325–52.
—— 1985 'L'enfant Nit Ku Bon: un tableau psychpathologique traditionnel chez les Wolofs et les Lebou du Sénégal', *Nouvelle Revue d'Ethnopsychiatrie*, 4, 9–42.
—— 1985 'Du dedans au dehors : transformation de la possession-maladie en possession rituelle', *International Journal of Psychology* 20 (4–5) 663–79
—— 1987 'Des étres sacrificiels', Cartry (éd.) *Sous le Masque de l'animal*, Paris, P.U.F 1987, 267–317.

Film

Achouba, A. (1982) *Assawa. Confessions des possédés*, Morocco: Achouba Films, 75 min.
Colleyn, J-P. et Péché, J-J. (1983) *Les Chemins de Nya*, Mali: Acmé-RTBF-CBA, 54 min.
Rouch, J. (1948) Initiation à la danse des possédés. Niger: CNRS Audiovisuel.
—— (1954) *Les Maîtres fous*, Ghana: Les Films de la Péiade. 30 min.
—— (1972) *Tanda Singui*, Niger: CNRS-Audiovisuel, 29: 20 min.

III

Spirit Possession & Gender

6

Defunct Women

Possession among the Bijagós Islanders

Alexandra O. de Sousa

Bijagós spirit possession is one of the most original forms of possession described in the ethnological literature. It is a non-pathological possession (Canguilhem 1943; Boddy 1988). Whereas elsewhere in Africa, spirit possession usually calms or heals suffering individuals (Lewis 1971: 223; Rouget 1980: 494), here possession is unrelated to any previous life accident, it is not considered as a sickness, and trance has no therapeutic dimension. Furthermore, if a function is ascribed to possession, the 'problem' to be resolved is not on the human side but on that of the spirits, the wandering souls lost in the forest. Another originality is that while possession crises are usually individualized (Colleyn 1988: 221), among the Bijagó possession is collective and prescribed to the whole group. It is performed by all women – at the same time. To reach adulthood, women must be invested by the spirit of a dead man. Through this male reincarnation they allow accomplishment of the man's initiation, and most importantly, at the end of the women's lives, they will have converted their possessor into an ancestor. Thus, the Bijagós women are being possessed by a virtual ancestor. Indeed, the question most commonly asked, when a visitor first arrives in the Bijagós archipelago, concerns those noisy groups of women-warriors that are frequently dancing and wandering in between the villages and the forest. They are called *orebok* (in bijagó) or *defunto* (in creole). These women, each possessed by the spirit of a young man who died before accomplishing initiation, periodically lose their identity to be invested by that of defunct males.

The Bijagós live in an archipelago composed of eighty-eight small islands and islets, situated some twenty nautical miles off the Atlantic coast of Africa and just north of the eleventh parallel. Only twenty islands are inhabited. The others are reserved either for seasonal rice cultivation, or are kept unoccupied for religious purposes, such as the celebration of initiation ceremonies. Some islets remain deserted because they have no fresh water. These small flat islands are covered with an opulent vegetation in between the tropical forest and the wooded savannah. Its water's richness in fish and exotic sea animals, such as manatees, salt-water hippopotami, and turtles, makes the archipelago an important marine life reserve. Spread out over dozens of miles, the Bijagós islanders manage to maintain close social and economic relations. Contacts with the continent, however, are sporadic and communication difficult. Nevertheless, their history has been tied for the last five centuries to that of Guinea Bissau, to which today the archipelago belongs.

In 1457, Alvise Ca'Da Mosto, a young Venetian serving under the infante Don Henrique, anchored off the Bijagós islands (Schefer 1895). The archipelago became a possession of the Portuguese crown. But, we have to wait until the next century to learn about their inhabitants. The Cape-Verdian Alvares d'Almada, a trader and expert on the area, wrote in 1594 about the islanders: '... great capriciousness ... men do only three things: make war, build boats and collect palm wine' (Almada 1964). It is the war against their neighbours from the continent, the Beafadas and the Pepels, but also between the islands of the archipelago, and later against the Europeans, for which the Bijagós have been renowned throughout their history. The archipelago has been for centuries the staging ground of bloody battles. Originally, the people who later became the Bijagós islanders were pushed from the continent on to the islands by the Beafadas, themselves threatened by the expansion of the Malinké empire in the seventeenth century. Later, the Beafada's attempt to gain the islands, by then the Bijagós' new domain, made them mortal enemies. With the beginning of slavery, what started as a defensive war became predatory (Henry 1991). The Bijagós began to raid the continent. They sacked the villages and captured the Beafadas, whom they contemptuously called their 'chickens'. These quarrels carried on for centuries and involved progressively more and more actors. From the seventeenth to the nineteenth century the archipelago participated in the slave trade for which this region of the African coast was a stopover. Yet, the Bijagós were rarely enslaved. This was partly because they were involved in trading their Beafadas prisoners for cows and other goods, which made them precious partners for the slave traders, and also because the Bijagós slaves did not survive very long. As Lemos Coelho, a slave driver from the seventeenth century, warned: 'The blacks from these islands are good to sell but not to buy because they think that if they die far away from their land they will return to it after death, and this is why they kill themselves with their own hands, like two of them have done to me, so quickly that one would say that the Devil had helped them' (Peres 1953: xxxi). The ease with which the Bijagós committed suicide was noticed later in the writings of Marques de Barros. 'Death for a Bijagó is no more than a short sleep. Because he is certain that he will be instantaneously reincarnated in his country, a Bijagó puts a rope around his neck with the same facility that we put on a tie' (Barros 1882).

In the nineteenth century war broke out between the imperial powers in the region, and later between them and the Bijagós. British, French and Portuguese fought over the control of the territory and meddled with local affairs. In 1810, Portugal signed an agreement with Great Britain in Berlin, banning the slave trade in Guinea. Yet, because of their inaccessibility, the islands soon became a comfortable place to hide an illicit traffic, and the Portuguese administration, weak and impoverished, turned a deaf ear to British indignation. Finally, the few but tragic punitive expeditions that the French organized against the islands in order to intimidate the Portuguese and repress the native's piracy against their ships, killed off the maritime inclinations of the Bijagós warriors (Pelissier 1989). 'Zealous friends of the Portuguese, they carried a matchless hate towards the other European nations ...' (Mollien 1822). The British and French, especially, became the worst enemies of the islanders. This situation allowed the Portuguese administration, worried at the other colonizers' incursions in the area, to establish new alliances with the Bijagós and recover their predominance over the archipelago. The governor of Guinea signed a peace treaty with the Bijagós kings and imposed the payment of a land tax.

But what the native kings signed with the Portuguese leaders had very little influ-ence over the population and did not last long. The pacts were successively violated and subsequently restored by the following administrators. New military expedi-tions were sent to repress the rebellion in the islands and finally in 1937 the Bijagós warriors laid down their arms.

However, the Bijagós submission was veiled. They kept cordial relationships with the Portuguese governors who occasionally served them as mediators against the merciless despotism of the Cape-Verdians post chiefs, their new enemies. In 1963 the independence war of Guinea Bissau began. The archipelago, geographically apart, participated only through the action of the young men who escaped from the islands to join the liberation army on the continent. After ten years of war, the young agronomist, Amilcar Cabral, theoretician and founder of the liberation party, PAIGC, was killed. Still, a few months later Guinea Bissau declared herself inde-pendent, which was only recognized by post-revolution Portugal a year later, in 1975. In each village a committee was elected to represent the party and the gov-ernment from Bissau. But in order to deal with village affairs, these new enterprises collaborated with the council of elders.

These daring islanders, accused of piracy, rebellion and insolence at various times and by different enemies, have since become the focus of worry for some and curiosity for others. Their geographic situation and their urge for independence have preserved them from the Manding and Fula Islamic influence that spread throughout the continent, and from that of the Europeans coming from the sea. From maritime warriors the Bijagós evolved into peaceful farmers. Their social orga-nization was certainly altered but its main principles were largely preserved.

The Bijagós descend by maternal path from four sisters : *Oraga, Ogubane, Orakuma* and *Ominka*. (Duquette 1983: 261) These four primogenitor clans are settled on all of the inhabited islands. Although each island belongs to only one clan, the owner clan gives permission for the other clans to use its land. Each village is founded by a clan and forms an independent social entity, with its kingship (*oronho*), its priestess (*okinka*) and its god fetish (*orebok*). However, Bijagó society is not organized accord-ing to clans, which do not form organic groups, but mainly in conformity with age classes. Strongly hierarchical and without central power, since kings have essen-tially a religious role, the society is ruled by a council of elders that reserves for itself juridical functions, governs the social activities and economic interests, and holds religious power. As we will see the age-set system is very much related to their ancient military organization. In fact, age groups, initiation, and possession are pieces of the same pattern – war.

A young man is not considered an adult before he has completed his initiation. During the initiation period which can take five to ten years depending on the island, he is not allowed to take a wife or have a house in the village. He is a resi-dent of the forest. He loses his name and must earn a new initiate name. All links with the past have to be broken, and previous wives and children must be aban-doned. Once initiation is completed, a man acquires full civil rights, such as the ownership of a rice field, the freedom to build a house where he can live with his wives, the right to keep the children born out of his new alliances, and the privilege of sculpting fetishes and addressing demands to them. According to the rules, unions formed before the initiation must not be carried over. The newly initiated man must disown women and sons from his 'former life'. He will establish a new

family after the initiation. Traditionally, a woman engaged with a non-initiated man
will remain at her father's house, and their children will belong in their maternal
grandfather's home. But times have changed and the suppleness of the system
together with the customs of the neighbouring societies are beginning little by little
to influence the islanders' social organization. Nowadays, unions formed prior to
the initiation are sometimes maintained at the price of heavy material compensa-
tions, and the initiatic seclusion period in the forest is no longer continuous. Initially
because of colonial imposition and later following a ruling of the Guinea administration, long forest life is forbidden and the initiation period of seclusion is reduced
to a few months per year. Nevertheless, the initiation cycles altogether still last several long years. In each island the cycles alternate between male and female periods.
While women are 'in defunct' on one island, the young men from that island wait
until their defunct colleagues finish their initiation. And vice-versa, only when the
masculine initiation has ended can the feminine cycle start.

A Bijagó reaches a higher age group every time an initiation cycle ends and a new
generation of initiates is integrated into the adult world. It is a progressive and not
a cyclical system. The initiation rites are organized between two or three neighbouring villages that do not necessarily belong to the same clan, suggesting a link
between an ancient warrior's solidarity and the modern initiation cycle. The male
age classes are divided into five groups: the *kanhokan* (7–17 years); the *kabarros*
(18–25 years); the *kamabi* (26–40 years); the *kassuka* (40–50 years), and from then on
everyone is considered an *okoto* (elder). The *kabarros* already receive some preparation for the initiation, but they will only name themselves *kamabi* when the initiation has formally started, and they submit to its rules. Women have only two age
classes that are defined according to maternity: *kampuni*, before, and *okanto* (literally
woman) after the first pregnancy. However, they can place themselves by proxy in
the male age group. Female initiation is in fact a posthumous male initiation. When
a man dies before finishing his initiation he is sheltered by a woman who, invested
by him, completes his initiation. It is thus possible to hear a woman say that she is
a *kamabi* when she has accomplished the first steps of initiation. She is referring to
the social age of the man that possesses her. It is this peculiar female-male initiation
that makes the Bijagós the focus of great anthropological interest.

The native explanation for spirit possession is that men cannot reach their ancestor's land, *an-orebok* (bijagó) or *glória* (creole), before they have completed their initiation. Thus, male initiation has to be performed regardless, if not by the young
man himself, as in case of premature death, then by a young woman who will carry
his spirit in her. All girls have, before maternity, the duty to incorporate one of those
dead beings that otherwise would wander in the forest, scaring the living (de Sousa
1995: 109). As they initiate the young deceased men, the defunct-women convert
those inauspicious wild powers into favourable domestic powers controlled by the
village, and re-integrate them into the continuous circuit between life and death.
There is no loss of substance. The *orebok* will be carried either by initiated men or by
possessed women, and at their death it will lead to 'glory' (de Sousa 1991: 109).

When possessed, girls adopt a warrior's behaviour appropriate to the age group
of the young men they incarnate. They spend their days walking around the villages and in the forest singing, dancing and drinking palm wine and the very strong
local spirits. The women no longer exist as female but as male on initiation. House-
work and nursing are totally abandoned. They exchange their baby for a spear,

nursery rhymes for war songs, and their coloured short skirts for a long undyed one. Wives and mothers are now warriors. As night falls the defuncts arrive in the village, dressed in their long fibre skirts and manifesting the fiery warriors that possess them.[1] The whole village celebrates the defuncts' visit by chorusing their songs and drums, but it is mainly the dead men's parents who escort their sons and push them to dance. Under the influence of alcohol, music and the crowd, some possessed women show a trance-like behaviour, although no dramatic convulsions, screams and fainting are seen. They shake prudishly and gaze at the crowd while dancing. In one island the defunct women are called canoes, suggesting their role as *orebok*'s conveyors. Here, when the beat of drums warms up, the possessed women dance like rowers and sing '... come and help me ... come and help me, because the canoe is heavy', to which the public enthusiastically answers in chorus 'the canoe is heavy' (de Sousa *et al.,* 1991a). The mothers of the deceased scream with joy and the party continues through the night, while the canoes carry the souls of those that are no longer there.

The term *orebok* poses a problem for the anthropologist and forces one to explore that vast domain that is the notion of person. To simplify the question it can be reduced to the ethnographic descriptions. *Orebok* covers three main categories: the women undergoing initiation, possessed by a dead uninitiated man; the anthropomorphic statues of the village's main god, 'the founder and owner of the land' (de Sousa, Colleyn and de Clippel 1991b); the spirit that inhabits the body and that escapes at death to join the '*orebok*'s land' (*anorebok*, bijagó) or 'glory' (*glória*, creole). The temptation to translate *orebok* to soul is great because it allows a quick and comfortable interpretation on the notion of person. But it would be an error to take for granted that a 'person' in this case is the reunion of a body with an *orebok* and in that way make a correlation with the Christian notion of soul. The first objection comes from the presumption that since women, as well as non-initiated young men, do not have *orebok* (as explained above, they carry *orebok* but do not own it) we could deduce that they do not have souls. What would then spirit their bodies? When I asked the villagers whether women had souls or not, my informants looked stupefied and went into deep reflection, finally to conclude that they did not know. The question just does not make sense. *Orebok* is not a male substance denied to women, thereby rejecting them into a future with no 'glory'. The division of individuals into those who have *orebok* and those who do not have it, is certainly not related to their gender but to their initiation status. Not only non-possessed women but also uninitiated men are deprived of *orebok*. *Orebok* is a substance acquired at the initiation when the symbolic death takes place and another individual is born as 'a complete being' with an *orebok*. On the other hand, *orebok* is not an essence proper to human beings. It is also present in the anthropomorphic statues protecting the village and representing the founding ancestor, the 'god owner of the land'. Some big trees, like the kapok trees (*Cebia guineensis*), also have *orebok*. They receive offerings and requests for favours during therapeutic rites. *Orebok* would then exist in adult men, in protectors' god-objects and in sacred trees. However, if we listen to the vernacular language, Portuguese Creole, we will see that what, in the local language, is a matter of *orebok*, in creole is a matter of soul (*alma*), fetish (*iran*) or defunct (*defunto*). These distinctions are related to the context, and the translations were probably made under Christian influence during the colonial era. Because of semantic needs when describing the possession phenomena, I choose to keep the creole terms. That is why words such as 'souls', meaning human spirit and defunct, when referring to a possessed woman, are used here. This choice is not different from that of Lévi-Strauss when, talking about the Bororo from Brazil, he uses the term 'souls visit' (Lévi-Strauss 1984).

Bijagós possession is a posthumous male initiation. The steps of the initiation cycle, no matter whether they are carried out by a living man, or a dead one invested in a woman, conform to the same general rules. Once an initiation cycle begins, the man dies symbolically to be re-born with a new name. Similarly, the defunct initiation occurs when the death of the young man is not just symbolic but real. In such case, he is re-born in a woman. In both cases, the initiates are kept for a few months in sacred and secret places of the forest. For each village, or group of villages, there is a place set aside for the initiation of men, and another for women. Usually situated by the sea or on unoccupied islets, the initiation sites are surrounded by prohibitions. The most important of these is the site's inaccessibility to non-initiated individuals. It is here that the solemn and secret ceremonies are performed, at the end of which the initiate takes another identity. Men come out with a new social status, they are now *kamabis*, with a new name; women come out possessed by a defunct and known by their possessor's new name.[2] Once back at the village, they do not share any community life. The women sleep at the defunct's temple, and the men at the granaries. In both cases they must respect sexual abstinence and are forbidden to talk with non-initiated people of the opposite sex. The initiation does not last more than a few months per year, but the complete cycle lasts several years. The initiates go through periods of reclusion, during which they perform sacrifices and give important allowances to the elders. In return, the elders give advice, narrate important historical features and reveal some 'secrets' and rules of social behaviour. Men finally come out as adults and with an *orebok* capable of rejoining the ancestor's land at death. Women retrieve the system's losses. They bring back the wild spirits of dead 'children' and redress them through a posthumous initiation. The Bijagó possession allows a complete recovery of *orebok*. It is a mechanism of restoration.

To consider women as simple carriers of souls would mean sentencing them to an empty and apathetic destiny. On the contrary, during their initiation women acquire an *orebok* that will go to the ancestors' land at their death. A woman who fully completes the initiation of her defunct will receive the same funeral homage as any male *kassuka*. From a social point of view, defunct initiation gives women an enormous power in the organization of matrimonial alliances. Because initiation cycles alternate, men have to wait until the end of a feminine cycle before they can start theirs. Legal marriages are delayed, since they cannot take place until the males are initiated, and this has economic and political implications. Indeed, women never lose an opportunity to exercise their power. The arguments older women use to delay the term of a feminine initiation are as unpredictable as they are indisputable. Any event in the village might be considered disturbing and can be used as an excuse. However, in order to keep a certain balance between the interests of both groups, men are invited to supervise these manipulations. Thus, male priests, called *orase* (bijagó), take part in the women's councils. In general, *orases* are chosen among the most wise and powerful men in the village. They are said to have been kidnapped by the defuncts and taken to their secret initiation site. Once there, they cannot refuse the role of a defunct's priest. In fact, it is an extremely prestigious function that, besides them, only kings may have. They attend all women's initiation rites and are consulted for important decisions concerning possession. As members of men's groups and defunct's advisers, the *orase* priests serve as ambassadors at women's councils. Possession is clearly not exclusively a women's affair. It involves men's society, both directly as far as its religious meaning and its manipulation are concerned, and indirectly through its social consequences.

But the initiation duties and the consequences resulting from the lengthy cycles also raise conflicts between elders and juniors. The elders' fear of losing their young people to urban modernity, together with the desire for reverence and the economic benefits obtained during the initiation, contribute to extend the duration of their time. This is commonly observed in both female and male initiations. Because there are few possible strategies to avoid these delays, some adolescents and young adults run away to escape the system. They generally abandon their island to be initiated on another island, amongst strangers, and where, although there is no family to protect them, their position as foreigners somehow keeps them from being overtaxed. In men's society, the conflict often breaks out when the desire of young males to live with their wives and children overcomes their fear and respect for social rules and the elders' threats. The women's case is no less obvious. The impossibility of carrying a foetus and a defunct being at the same time, a mother and a warrior, makes it easy to understand that maternity and possession cannot be simultaneous. A choice is necessary, and here religion and social functions take precedence over biology and individual priorities. The initiation of a defunct – women's possession – have to be performed before maternity. This is why women are generally initiated at an earlier age than men. This is also probably one of the reasons why the incidence of abortion is four times higher in the archipelago than in the neighbouring groups from the continent (de Sousa 1995). Whereas in the past uninitiated pregnant girls were banished from their villages, today they either bring on a miscarriage or accept their disgrace. Once more, the pressure generated by possession determines individual behaviour as much as social events. Although the features of Bijagós possession place it as an example of a non-afflicting cult, the intolerance of the system towards its youth replaces it as an age-conflicting rite.

In conclusion, Bijagós spirit possession remains a unique example of a non-pathological and collective possession creating future ancestors. It is performed by women as a posthumous male initiation, with the objective of restoring the harmony between gods and men, the forest and the village, broken by death. It ultimately places women in a position of exceptional control over the religious system and as a consequence assigns them an unequivocal partnership for social life.

Notes

1   There are some behavioural differences between elder and younger possessed women. The former bear more mature and powerful warriors' souls, while the latter carry those of naive and very impulsive young men. At her first public appearance as *defunto*, the young girl wears goat leather shorts and dances frenetically miming a crazy goat that makes everybody laugh. Later on, the *defuntos* carry over their heads a miniature of the masculine cow mask (*vaca-bruta*, c; *esene*, b). They mimic wild cows and try to impress the audience with their bravery and dancing skills. Finally, as they become 'adults', they put on a colonial hat or a wooden-carved imitation.

They don't have to dance any more for an audience, but they will accompany a young *defunto* when that pleases them, often driven by the influence of alcohol.

2   Each woman has her own dead man to be initiated. The choice of her *defunto* is made by the priestess (*Okinka*) and the *defunto*-priest (*Orase*). It happens in the forest, when the girl is possessed for the first time. The defunct man that possesses her will talk or dance in such a way that he'll be recognized and individually identified by the priests. At this point he will receive his initiatic name. In the following days, when presented to the village, there will be no longer any question of a girl being called Isabel, nor of a dead boy called Tempo, but of a defunct warrior named Ompané. The spirit of a dead man possesses only one woman, but if she dies before accomplishing his initiation, his spirit will stay in the forest to be taken by another girl. This maintains the system, since at times there aren't enough souls for every woman to initiate. The male death rate is not high enough to allow each woman to have one dead man's soul. At the initiation moment, priest and priestess may be in the embarrassing situation of not having enough dead males from which to choose, and one way to circumvent this deficiency is to recuperate the souls released upon an adult woman's death. The opposite situation, where there would be too many dead men to be initiated and not enough women to be possessed, would not be demographically possible and certainly does not occur in times of peace.

References

Almada, Alvares (1964) [1594] *Tratado breve dos Rios de Guiné e do Cabo Verde, desde o Rio de Sanaga até aos baixos de Santa Ana*, Brasio, A. 2° série, III. Agência geral do Ultramar, Academia Portuguesa de Historia.

Barros, Marques (1882) *Guiné Portuguesa ou breve noticia sobre alguns dos seus usos, costumes, linguas e origens dos seus povos*, Boletim da Sociedade de Geografia de Lisboa, 3° série, 12.

Boddy, Janice (1988) *Horses, Musicians and Gods: the Hausa Cult of Possession-trance*, Massachussetts: Bergin & Garvey Publishers.

Canguilhem, Georges (1943) *Le normal et le pathologique*, 2 éd. augmentée.

Colleyn, Jean-Paul (1988) *Les Chemins de Nya*, Ed. EHESS.

De Sousa, Alexandra O. (1995) *Motherhood among the Bijago of Guinea-Bissau: an interdisciplinary approach*, CEPED Studies N°9, University of Paris VI.

—— (1991) *Une Approche de la Notion de Personne chez les Bijagos de Guinée-Bissau*, Masters thesis in Social Anthropology: Ecole des Hautes Etudes en Sciences Sociales.

De Sousa, Alexandra, Colleyn, Jean-Paul, De Clippel, Catherine (1991a) *Le Voyage des Âmes* (documentary film), Acmé films: Paris, 23min.

—— (1991b) *Naître Bijago* (documentary film), Acmé films, Paris: 30min.

Duquette, Danielle (1983) *Dynamique de l'art Bidjogo (Guinée-Bissau)*, Instituto de Investigação Científica Tropical, Lisboa.

Henry, Christine (1991) *Rapports d'âge et de sexe chez les Bijago (Guinée Bissau)*, PhD thesis in Social Anthropology, University of Paris X.

Lévi-Strauss, Claude (1984) *Paroles données*, Paris: Plon.

Lewis, Ioan M (1971) *Ecstatic Religion: An Anthropological Study of Spirit Possession and Shamanism*, Harmondsworth: Penguin Books.

Mollien, Gaspar Théodore (1822) *Voyage dans l'intérieur de l'Afrique, aux sources du Sénégal et de la Gambie*, 2° ediação, Arthur Bertrand, Paris.

Pélissier, René (1989) *Naissance de la Guinée. Portugais et Africains en Sénégambie (1841–1936)*, Orgeval: Pélissier.

Peres, Damião (1953) *Duas descrições seiscentistas da Guiné. Academia Portuguesa de Historia*, Lisboa.

Rouget, Gilbert (1980) *La Musique et la Transe: Esquisse d'une théorie générale des relations de la musique et de la possession*, Paris: Gallimard.

Schefer, Charles (1895) *Relation des Voyages à la Côte Occidentale d'Afrique d'Alvise de Ca'Da mosto 1455–1457*, Paris: Ernest Leroux.

7

The Case
of the Butcher's Wife
Illness, Possession &
Power in Central Sudan

Susan M. Kenyon

what possessed women portray is not the power of the powerful or the men's dominion, but rather the whole spectacle of life with all its contradictions and problems (Kramer 1993: 114–15)

The following case study describes the course of action adopted by a Sudanese woman to deal with ongoing health problems, drawing on her own narrative to show how she became involved with the spirit possession activities known as *zar*. The account is based on taped interviews I made in 1981–2 and my field-notes from a *zar-burei* ceremony held in the town of Sennar, Central Sudan, in August 1981.[1] This was never a large affair; at its most lavish, there were perhaps forty guests while for the most part, around twenty people were present. In many ways it was typical of such ceremonies held regularly in the Sudan as a way of staving off misfortune and ensuring well-being for the participants. At the same time, it was a unique occurrence, focusing on the needs and problems of one particular woman – Amna, the butcher's wife.[2]

Zar is a widespread phenomenon in northern Africa and the Middle East and has been particularly well-documented in the Sudan (Boddy 1988, 1989; Constantinides 1977, 1991; Kenyon 1991a, 1991b, 1995; Makris and al-Safi 1991; El-Nagar 1975, 1987; Zenkovsky 1950). The term *zar* refers to both a type of spirit and to various practices and rituals associated with those spirits; it also encompasses several different 'ways' or organized sets of practices. In Sennar, for example, two distinct types are recognized today: *zar-burei* and *zar-tumbura*. While they differ in ritual and organization, the belief in *zar* (albeit in contrasting types of spirits) is at the core of both groups. *Zar* spirits, often referred to as 'the red wind', are basically benign although they can bring disorder to the lives of people they actively possess and have been known to cause fatalities. They are also represented as foreigners rather than familiars, with distinctive dress, food, perfume and musical preferences. We are increasingly aware that they are part of a highly complex and elaborate system of knowledge which is both widespread and probably very old in Africa (Ranger 1993).

Not all people are involved with *zar* in the same way. Gender, age and residence are important variables in determining a person's association with the spirits. Children learn about such things from an early age as they observe local rituals or hear adults analyse life's crises in spiritual terms. While a certain knowledge about *zar* is thus shared by men and women, young and old, urban and rural, elaboration of that knowledge into an organized system of activities is almost entirely in the hands of middle-aged women in the larger towns. These activities are further controlled by formally-trained female leaders who are past child-bearing age, known in Sennar as *al-umiyat* (sing. *umiya*).[3] The fact that *zar* organization is predominantly female has been interpreted as evidence that it is a deprivation cult (after Lewis 1971, 1986) in the sense that 'women and other depressed categories exert mystical pressures on their superiors in circumstances of deprivation and frustration when few other sanctions are available to them' (Lewis 1986: 39). Such cults are further described as 'peripheral' because not only do they 'not embody the main moral code of the societies in which they occur', but also in such societies 'women are in fact *treated* as peripheral creatures' (Lewis 1986: 42). More recent studies have tried to avoid this androcentric bias and have seen *zar* rather as a different perspective or 'way of knowing' (after Lambek 1993), as well as an alternative formulation of social and spiritual relations than that commonly described for Central Sudanese Islamic society. It is certainly the latter approach that is suggested in the butcher's wife's own narrative, as she describes the different choices available to her in dealing with her affliction, the wide-ranging help and support she receives from family and friends in the long healing process, and the complexities of the therapeutic ritual of *zar* possession in which this culminates.

Those who participate in *zar* are drawn from the full spectrum of socio-economic backgrounds, including the poor and illiterate as well as people of substance. Initial involvement often comes through misfortune or illness though it may later be diagnosed as an inherited condition.[4] When a problem occurs, Sudanese feel they have a range of options to resort to, of which *zar* is but one. Biomedicine, Islamic healing, and different traditional healers and home remedies often overlap in the pluralist medical system of the Sudan, and the choice of one strategy over another, or the concurrent use of several strategies, is not readily apparent. Individuals' choices are usually determined less by their own preferences and resources than by those of people close to them: their family, neighbours and friends. As will be clear below, this resource group (what Janzen 1978 refers to as the 'therapy-managing group'[5]) is a major factor in making decisions during the therapeutic process, both in the early stages of the disorder and as the course of treatment proceeds. Furthermore this process is largely managed by women. It is striking that while men may attempt to solve their own difficulties, women generally assume responsibility for their close kin as well as themselves (Kenyon 1991a: 163ff). Assisted by their various support networks, they are adept at exploring the available possibilities. When accepting treatment through a male-dominated system (such as biomedicine or Islamic healing), they may temporarily surrender control of the process to a husband or brother, but their mothers and sisters are still likely to be checking out other options, ready to step in if necessary. They may also be adopting parallel courses of action as a safeguard, since they view all systems of curing as relatively equal but different. If knowledge is power, then women in this part of the world possess distinct advantages; they have access to multiple domains of knowledge, being less bound by the constraints of hegemonic ideology than many men.

Therapeutic choices are ongoing. Even when dealing with the same problem, an individual and her support group continue to look for the best alternative as they implement a course of action. For most participants, *zar* possession provides only one set of answers to a particular circumstance; and even for the most committed, beliefs and practice in *zar* do not provide an exclusive dependence. There are always other explanations, other courses of action, which may be taken if the specific situation warrants it.[6] Thus the only way that we can properly understand decisions about possession and affliction, and thus ultimately about the praxis of power and possession, is in the broader cultural context through which such decisions are made (Boddy 1988, Giles 1987, Lambek 1993, Sharp 1993, Stoller 1989).

In the wider Islamic society of Central Sudan, ecstatic experiences generally are accorded respect. Men, for example, who become entranced through their participation in *zikr*[7] are thought to be touched by God, and the *baraka* [holiness] this brings is shared by others in the group. Holy men [*al-fuqara, al-faki* sing.] with special knowledge of God's word [*al-Quran*] and often with particular powers of divination and healing, may communicate with spirits or non-human helpers in the course of their work. In the town of Sennar, there is even a woman of great repute who practises curing and divination through possession by a spirit named Bashir, whom she describes as '*Fath al-Rahman*', opening from God. Each of these experiences is based on possession trance and is individually empowering, bestowing considerable spiritual and social prestige on those affected. It is also socially sanctioned by popular Islam and fully acceptable within the dominant discourse of the region: a patriarchal discourse, the parameters of which are defined and maintained by men but respected by all.

From an emic point of view, however, it is important to note that in the Sudan, qualitatively different states of trance are recognized, just as the beliefs associated with those states and types of possession experiences vary, depending on the cultural context of the experience and the status of the individual affected (as Lambek 1993 also points out for Mayotte). The first altered state of the novitiate in any activity involving trance, for example, varies a great deal from that of the seasoned practitioner who inherited his powers at a young age from a close relative. Even on a single occasion in which trance plays a part, several factors may be at work and should caution us against generalizing about either possession beliefs and practices, or about those people affected by such beliefs, without taking into account the range of experiences encountered. It is particularly important to recognize this diversity without endorsing the dominant 'prestige structure' of the culture (after Ortner and Whitehead 1981), which leads us, with Lewis and others, to regard some experiences as 'better' or 'more sacred' or at least less 'peripheral' than others.

To the Sudanese, *zar* possession is readily distinguishable from those experiences described above, even though in practical terms trance may be achieved in similar ways. A major difference is that the above examples are associated with *baraka* or holiness in some way; trance possession by *zar* spirits may also endow a certain 'potency' (after Errington 1990: 42) but is very definitely not regarded as respectable within the Islamic tradition which dominates this part of the world. Possession by *zar* carries neither the sense of blessing nor the socially sanctioned empowerment of other types of experience. In the wider Islamic society of Central Sudan, attitudes to *zar* range from total rejection, as sent from Satan (*al-Shaitan*), to reluctant acceptance because it is mentioned in *al-Quran*. Whatever their preconceptions about the nature of *zar*, however, people invariably accept active possession by *zar* in themselves unwillingly, not least because it implies a long-term surrender to an uncertain destiny. Controlling these spirits can take an enormous amount of effort and energy which includes accepting the intermediary of the *umiya*. Nobody admits to seeking out a *zar*.

On the other hand, as is evident below, *zar* possession is also clearly empowering. In the case of the butcher's wife it enables her to deal with a range of health and social issues in a highly structured and elaborated way. Furthermore it provides alternative approaches to understanding those issues which are largely independent of the dominant patriarchal discourse of this part of the world, and which continue to be articulated by practices outside the control of formally vested authorities. Finally *zar* continues to meet many peoples' needs in strikingly dynamic fashion, despite the upheavals of the twentieth century. In fact it appears to be spreading, into areas where it was not previously known[8] and among a broader cross-section of the Sudanese population (Kenyon 1995).

In the case of the butcher's wife, as the main participants (the resource group referred to above) carefully and repeatedly weighed up all their options, *zar* seemed to be the best, indeed at times the only course of action. Once committed to it, they went ahead to the best of their ability, to appease the spirits and to meet their demands as interpreted by the leader of the local *zar* group. They always described their choices in the same breath, with the same hesitation, as they talked of various hospital diagnoses (biomedicine) or religious interpretations (represented in a town like Sennar by the holy men, *al-fuqara*). While they accepted the *zar* diagnosis as probable, people retained a certain scepticism until the efficacy of the treatment became apparent. This uncertainty contributes to the fact that *zar* occasions are filled with a great deal of anxiety and friction among human guests themselves as well as in relation to the spirits. *Zar* ceremonies are real-life dramas, partly because the spiritual enactment develops in often unpredictable ways, but also because of the tensions engendered among the various participants. As dramatic texts the ceremonies portray highly significant historical themes encoded in a variety of mediums (music, scent/incense, dress, food as well as behaviour), an approach which has received significant, long overdue attention in recent years.[9] In this chapter, however, it is the second sense of drama, that of tensions between the human and non-human domains, and within each of those domains themselves, that is being underscored. Such tensions create significant currents of 'creative energy'[10] within the ritual events, which variously transform both participants and ritual into empowered and empowering vehicles.

Finally, while the case of the butcher's wife supports Lambek's (1993) view that possession is a form of knowledge, it also reinforces the point that in practice (if not always in ideology) it is perfectly congruent with other forms (such as Islam), and the reasons for choosing one form over another cannot readily be anticipated. And while I agree with Boddy (1989) that the discourse of *zar* can be read as a metalanguage, a counter-hegemony which is vividly illustrated in the enactment of the more extended formal ceremonies, it is important to stress that such counter-hegemony is grounded in its own discourse, rather than a reaction to the hegemonic ideologies of the larger society. Furthermore the narrative and description below remind us that on a daily basis it is not always clear what that counter-hegemony (or more accurately counter-hegemonies) reveals and in what way it is empowering. Tensions, inequalities and biases among participants themselves fragment our notions of what such metalanguages say or do for ordinary people and return us to 'the whole spectacle of life with all its contradictions and problems' (after Kramer 1993).

Amna, the butcher's wife: affliction and possession

I first met Amna, the butcher's wife, through her teenage daughters, Asha and Selma; the latter was a student in the local secondary school and they were both friends of my neighbour's daughter. They talked lovingly of their mother, who was obviously the focus of their home, and proudly took me there to meet her. She beamed with pride at them too, and told me she had seven children altogether, although the house seemed to be bursting with more. Later I learned that she had ten surviving children but was afraid that if she had told me the exact number she would have upset either the 'evil eye' or the government. The 'evil eye' would fall on her or one of the children because of their abundant good fortune, while the government was believed to be enforcing a policy of sterilization for women with more than seven surviving children. Amna lived in dread of being found out by either secular or supernatural authorities simply because she thought that she was more fortunate, more blessed, than any one individual ought to be.

As I got to know her better I realized that Amna lived in dread of many things and was in a constant state of nervous excitement. She was a small, gaunt woman in her early forties, with a high pitched voice and a way of wringing her hands as she talked. When I first met her, she already looked frail. Her face was shrunken and her cheek bones stood out below large, protruding eyes. Her family was concerned about her health and had taken her to several western-trained doctors, one of whom had suggested that she had a toxic goitre. She rejected that diagnosis and went into a fit of depression, muttering that she knew she was going to die and that her family should just leave her to do so. When she continued to deteriorate, her children persuaded her to go back to the doctor; but she claimed that on the second visit, he changed his diagnosis. He told her she did not have a goitre at all, that her problems were all caused by 'nerves' and she should pull herself together.

Amna had not always been ill or thin. When she was young, she said, she had been plump and beautiful. Indeed Asha and Selma were both very attractive young women and it was easy to see what their mother must once have been like. She had been born in the north of Sudan to the Shygiya people and many of her family still lived around Atbara. She was just thirteen years old when she was married to Ahmad, who was about ten years older, a close maternal relative though through his father he belonged to the Danagla people. They had been happily married for over thirty years, and he was most concerned about her poor health.

Amna had a conservative upbringing. Her paternal grandfather was a 'hard' man, who believed that girls should not leave the house and would not let any of them go to school, even Quranic school. She never learned to read or write, not unusual for a woman of her age but it leaves her feeling sad, especially since her own daughters did well at school. Her brothers, meanwhile, were all educated and were successful businessmen. One was working in Saudi Arabia when we met.

Her husband trained as a butcher like his father and soon after their marriage came to Sennar to seek his fortune in the main market. He was moderately successful though Amna commented that their income never seemed enough. Their oldest son also trained as a butcher and worked with his father. Their oldest daughter, Asha, left school after the intermediate level to care for her mother, who was already beginning to suffer health problems. Asha had started a nursery school in the vacant site next to their home and cherished ambitions of a teaching career. Except for the youngest, all the other children were in school at the time of these events.

In moving to Sennar, Amna and Ahmad left all their relatives in the north, something Amna still found difficult. They settled on the outskirts of town where for a modest sum they purchased a house site. Twenty-five years later they were the proud owners of a large home, with two brick living rooms, a detached bathroom area, a grass hut which served as the kitchen and an adjacent lean-to [rakuba] where the women spent most of their time. Their courtyard, in which they grew fruit and vegetables and kept a few livestock, was one of the more spacious in the area; chickens ran freely round the house and yard, and goats and sheep grazed under the trees.

Amna's neighbours were concerned about her declining health. She was a warm-hearted individual, always ready to help others despite her very real health problems. If guests arrived in the neighbourhood, she was the first to send over a dish of food. She was also modest and self-effacing, listening with sympathy and encouragement to the difficulties of others. Her own troubles started just before she became pregnant with her last child. She described her condition as '... a beating in my stomach, headaches, pains, cramps and vomiting ... vomiting until I fainted,' so severe that she consulted a *faki*. Her oldest daughter went to him on her mother's behalf and he declared that someone had put the 'evil eye' on her. Amna recalled:

> He sent a *mihaya*[11] and I drank it and vomited. After that I slept till the morning. He told them to bring me to him. I said I could only go if they carried me. I couldn't even go to the toilet alone; they had to bring the chamber pot to me. I said to him, I can't come ... and so I was ill for a year, unable to go out or visit him. Then he died ...

Amna was still not well but soon after, her mother was taken ill and sent for her. Amna did not hesitate to go north, though the travelling was difficult. Happily, her mother recovered, and while she was resting in her home village, Amna tried again to find treatment for her own problem: I used to be very strong, like a horse, but had become very thin. We have a *shaikh*[12] in our village.

> I went to see him and he gave me medicine and said it would strengthen my nerves. It did not do me any good. I kept drinking the medicine and vomiting. Then they said they wanted to do the *zar*. When my mother saw me she had said 'You have to beat and open the Box.[13] You have *zar*.' So they opened the Box for me there and beat me a *yumiya* [one-day ceremony]. Then I became better. We beat the *zar* for one day and the next day I became well. I was able to come from my mother's home. Our journey was very difficult ... but after the *zar* I was very fit.

By the time she returned to Sennar, Amna was also heavily pregnant. She had believed she was too old at 39 to conceive again; her youngest child was already five years old and Amna had assumed her child-rearing days were over. Both pregnancy and delivery were difficult:

> I had to go to the doctor at the hospital, Dr. H. When I first went to him, my stomach was very small. I thought I had a fibroid but he said, 'No, no, no, you have a child but you are very anemic. It is a child, but it is not moving because of your blood. It is just hiding. You are thin and weak, you have no blood. It does not move about in your stomach. You will have to deliver it in the hospital.' When I was ready, I went and they gave me drips and injections and after that the doctors came and I gave birth to her. Before that I used to deliver my babies very quickly ... The baby was very, very small. Her head was tiny. I thought she would die, but look at her now! She

is very fat. I never had any milk for her, though; she only had it from the bottle. I was fine in childbirth. It was when I got up from the lying-in that I became ill. Forty days after the birth I got up, really fat and well. My health had come back to me, I was beautiful. Then within three months, illness came to me once more. I had a terrible shock because my oldest son was admitted to hospital. He suddenly was taken ill with a fever and they took him straight to hospital and gave him stomach surgery. He was there for eight or nine days. He recovered, but I became sick instead.

Her earlier symptoms returned. She consulted all sorts of experts but was only confused by their conflicting advice:

> I had been to different doctors and to a gynaecologist for my pregnancy. I had been to holy men. I even went to a very famous holy man in Khartoum, in Umm Beda. He just told me, 'No, I can't help you, your illness is one of the *zar*. You just have to beat [the drums] for it.' He was a famous man, he knew everything, both a *faki* and a doctor. If the illness was not of *zar*, he told you which doctor to see. He knows all about every type of sickness and he could take you anywhere for treatment. He said to me 'You have got *al-Jamaa*.[14] You need to make a ceremony (*karama*) for them.' Straight-away we said we will make a *karama* and we will beat for them.

Sara, one of Amna's neighbours, was particularly concerned about her friend. It was she who had persuaded Amna to visit the famous *faki* in Umm Beda, a man from her home village, who she felt could convince Amna what her problem really was. She described the visit:

> Amna hesitated. She did not want to waste money and said that it might not be *zar* and she might not be all right. Then we went to this man. He told us everything that was happening to her, everything that she felt in her body, the heartbeat, the disturbances in her body, vomiting, diarrhoea, leg aches, feeling scared, everything that hurt in her body he told her about. Maybe he spent an hour talking with her. After he finished he said, 'Listen. You do not have any doctor's illness. You don't have a rash or a debilitating sickness or high blood pressure or diabetes. You don't have anything in your body except the Red Wind. This is the *dastur*.[15] These people have taken over your nerves and your heart.' He told her that the shaking and disturbances were from them and said 'Maybe you have not held a *karama* for them? They only want a *karama* from you. After you do this, after the seven days, they will leave you alone and you will become well.' So she agreed ... But she had two doubts in her heart. She thought maybe this is not the *dastur* and she would waste all this money and then find that it is not the *dastur*; and maybe she would not recover. But this man had told her, 'You do not have anything but the *dastur* so go straight away and beat for them.'

On her return from Umm Beda, Amna started to see the leader, *al-umiya*, of the local *zar* group on a regular basis.

> I had already been to the *umiya*; when I was very ill they had taken me there. Really they had to lead me there. They had opened the tin Box[16] for me and I had paid LS3. They told me to bring pigeons and a box of cigarettes and they wanted a bottle of liquor (*araqi*), so I gave them money to buy it. Then they opened the Box again and said 'Bring the pigeons.' I brought the pigeons and they cleansed me. I had a silver ring on my finger and they cleansed that too. They said 'That's it!' I came home that night and slept and then they told me it was *zar*. I said 'no, no, no, it is not *zar*'.[17]

Amna believes she caught, rather than inherited, *zar*:

> My mother herself does not have *zar*. In the north we do not know the *zar* like they have here. We do not have cigarettes or *araqi*; we only beat the *daluka* [tambourine drum], that's all. Here they smoke and drink and have no shame ...

She thinks she knows the occasion when she was affected:

> This was the cause. I got it from a woman over there [the other side of town] who had the *zar*

of the Chinese. I went to visit her and when they took me to her, they [the spirits] caught me as she went down.[18] She had on her jacket and was carrying her *zar* stick. They had a table and on it they had put all her things, everything, sweets, the supper and the drinks … She was the hostess of it. They had their sticks and their *tarbosh*[19] and they were walking round the table. I called to them, 'Hey!' and since that day I was ill. I had a pain and I came back shivering and since that day three years ago I have been ill. I don't know who they were, the cause of my misfortune. Other people said to me this is *zar*.

That was the beginning, when I went to that *maidan*, that place of *zar*. That was where I got ill and then I didn't know what I had. I came home and this neighbour of mine, Wakil, who is dead now, said 'Let me take you, Amna, let us make the *bakhur* [incense] for you and open the Box.' Still I did not know anything about the Chinese… It was then that we first went to *Umiya* Rabha, to have the *bakhur* and smoke my clothes with it. The drums were beating for the Sudanese [Black] *zar*. I went down with them and they called me to open the Box and asked for LS5 …

After the *umiya* had opened the Box and saw me and told me it was *zar*, I still did not believe her. I told her they were liars and went up to Omdurman … to the man at Umm Beda. He confirmed it was true: I had the *zar*.

Besides the *zar* of the Chinese, I have Hakinbasha, I have Luliya and again I have Bashir. This is what the *umiya* said.

The holy man in Umm Beda had convinced her that she should try to seek a cure through *zar*. Amna and her family began to save for a *karama* as the *umiya* advised, although they knew that their resources would not stretch to a full seven day ceremony, a Chair.[20] Instead they agreed to sponsor a half Chair, which would last three to four days. Her husband was particularly supportive and showed no sign of disbelief or irritation.

The father of my children accepts the *zar*. He tells us to do anything which will make me strong again. He said beat the *zar* even though it takes a lot of money.

Her daughters agreed. 'He gives her the money,' they replied, 'he wants her to be well.' They added that their father does not like *zar* and would not be around during the ceremony; but he was prepared to do whatever was necessary for her recovery.

It was not until August 1981 that they were able to hold the *karama*[21] to honour or at least propitiate the spirits who they now believed possessed her: the individual spirits known as Hakinbasha, Luliya and Bashir. The family was ready to hold the *zar* ceremony at the end of Ramadan, in June, when Amna's close friend, Wakil, died suddenly. They supported the bereaved family through the funerary *bika*, but the effort left Amna weak. She seemed to be fading rapidly and her family worried that unless they held the *karama* soon, it would be too late. Amna herself was convinced that she was dying. She never left the house, rarely leaving her bed; she looked drawn and haggard and was very weak indeed. Her youngest child was also not doing well, becoming even more nervous and withdrawn.

A second attempt made to hold the ceremony in July also fell through when the *umiya* had to leave for the town of Gedaref to help her own family with an unexpected *zar* ceremony. Finally, in the middle of August, Amna's daughters came to announce their *karama* at the end of the week. The family was already busy preparing all the food and inviting relatives, friends and neighbours as well as those known to be involved with the *zar*. The expense was horrifying; well over a LS100[22] was already spent. Amna's husband had provided most of the costs but her oldest son, the butcher, had given what he could; her second son, still at school, had been going back and forth to negotiate with the *umiya*; her daughters were all helping with the cooking and sewing. 'Really,' grumbled Selma, 'it's worse than a wedding!'

The wedding imagery lasted for much of the next few days. Amna was referred to as the bride, and many of the preparations and symbolic acts of the ceremony reflected the wedding ritual, as she was prepared for the big event by her relatives and neighbours in cultural ways very like those employed to create a bride. The day before the ceremony was to start, for example, Howa the hairdresser (cf. Kenyon 1991a) was braiding Amna's hair in the traditional bridal style, taking the whole day to plait it as finely as possible and entwining black thread to make it look longer and thicker. For them it was a restful day, punctuated by many cups of tea shared with neighbours who dropped in to see how things were coming along, and meals served by Amna's daughters, as if the party had already begun.

Friday, the anticipated opening of the ceremony, came and went. The *umiya* and her family simply failed to show up.[23] At some expense, Amna's son hired a public car to fetch them in mid-afternoon, only to be told that they would come after sunset and start promptly the following day. When they did not come or send any excuse the assembled friends became very upset. Sara, Amna's neighbour mentioned above, went to remonstrate with the *umiya* over her rudeness. The *umiya* said she could not start the ceremony for a few more days, but promised that she would then give Amna the full half-Chair for which she had already paid.

Despite this very unpromising start, the ceremony finally got under way a couple of days later and was to last for three full days and four nights as promised, followed by Amna's seclusion with the *umiya* for the same length of time. This whole period continued to be fraught with tension: among the spirits, between the *zar* leader and her assistants and friends, and among the participants. The frail figure of Amna herself was almost lost in the mêlée on several occasions, but she steadfastly tried to concentrate on following the *umiya*'s instructions as closely as she could, on making a success of the *karama* in both a spiritual and a secular sense, and on coming to terms with her newly acquired spirits.

It was just before sunset on Sunday when the *umiya*, her mother and sister struggled into the courtyard, carrying three hide drums, two baskets of equipment, the large blue tin Box (*al-ilba*) containing all the ritual paraphernalia, and a bunch of walking sticks: the so-called *idda*[24] of *zar* which they carried through to the room on the vacant site next door. Clean mats had already been laid on the dirt floor and it was here that Amna was to spend most of the following week, secluded from contact with most people, but especially male company. Provisions supplied by Amna's family – sweets, cigarettes, drinks and clothes – were already displayed, as the *umiya* rubbed down her equipment with a special perfume. The incense of *zar* began to waft around the courtyard and one by one women went to greet her, paying a small sum to be perfumed with the *zar* incense. The *umiya*, her mother and sister soon took their places against a wall, picked up their drums and began to beat a welcome song, the 'thread' to the opening ceremony known as 'The Laying of the Mats.' Two women immediately started to gyrate on their knees.[25] No one seemed to know who they were though earlier I had heard one explaining abruptly that she was very sick with *zar*, and had been told of the ceremony by the *umiya* so that she could come to obtain some relief. Amna sat between the *umiya* and one of her neighbours, Munira, who periodically nudged her to touch her head to the ground. Gradually she acquired confidence to do so spontaneously, and Munira moved away, later becoming possessed herself.

During the evening, the whole assembly of spirits [al-Jamaa] descended in turn, each being summoned by a specific drumbeat. Amna was one of those who got up to dance on her feet for the first time, cautious and apprehensive, as the spirits began to make themselves known to her. Most of the women present were possessed at least once, including fourteen year old Amira, who danced on her knees. It had been her mother, Wakil, who had died earlier in the summer. 'Amira is still full of grief,' murmured the women as they mopped her brow and offered her support in words and caresses once the spirit had left her.

The following day, 'the Day of Henna', the weather was dreadful and heavy rains made the roads impassable. We were late reaching Amna's house but everywhere seemed strangely quiet: the drummers had yet to arrive. We learned later that mud-soaked roads prevented anyone getting through from the centre of the town, but when Zachara the midwife (Kenyon 1991a) arrived, she was plainly annoyed that the drummers had failed to come. Sitting behind one of the drums, she said that rather than leave Amna to suffer she would play herself. The others, almost all neighbours and friends of the sick woman, giggled but were evidently dissatisfied with the state of affairs. The umiya busied herself with warming the drums over the incense and said nothing. Finally Sara joined Zachara on the drums, slowly at first but warming to her task, and the whole evening turned out to be highly successful as first the Ethiopian spirit Josay,[26] then the Pashawat Hakinbasha, spirit of a medical doctor, and finally the Ethiopian Bashir responded to the beats. Amna was possessed by each in turn, being helped by her friends to dress in the appropriate costume as she struggled to her feet. The clothes were far too big for her diminutive frame, but she danced on, oblivious to the unkind giggles and whispered comments from some of the onlookers.

The afternoon of the third day, 'the day of sacrifice', the umiya held a coffee party [jabana] for the Ethiopian spirit Bashir. Sometimes described as the servant of the other zar, he takes messages back and forth and this was an opportunity for people to consult with him privately. The event, however, grew tense as Bashir, always capricious and difficult, began to make rude comments through the umiya on the generosity of Amna and her family. More people than expected were attending the ceremony and had to be fed; this was putting enormous strain on the family's limited resources. Those of us who were Amna's friends squirmed uncomfortably and tried to ignore the criticisms, while we encouraged her daughters and friends in the kitchen and quietly joined in a series of counter-criticisms.

Later in the afternoon, rugs and a mattress were brought outside and Amna, now dressed in a plain white dress and scarf, was led out to the renewed beat of the drum. The umiya, no longer possessed, knelt before her, showered her with perfumes and decked her with necklaces, charms [hijab] and finally the red silk bracelets [jirtiq] of the bride. The red jalabiya of Bashir was pulled over her head, for this was to be a night especially in his honour. As sunset approached, a sheep was dragged into the courtyard and ritually sacrificed. A bowl of its blood was brought back to the courtyard and daubed across foreheads, while the remains of the sheep were taken to the kitchen to be prepared by Amna's family.

Drumming and dancing again continued until two in the morning. Generous quantities of refreshments were served – special beans with honey in the early part of the evening, bowls of mutton stew later. Many women became possessed by Bashir, the only spirit to descend and in whose honour the sacrifice had been made. When the *umiya* was possessed she danced alone in the centre of the courtyard with the other women encircling her, clapping with awe, especially when she pulled Amna into the circle with her. However, there was also a lot more quarrelling, especially between the *umiya* and some of her assistants, and it was not always clear who was possessed. The assistants kept demanding more refreshments and cigarettes, blaming the *umiya* when they were not available. There were obviously dramas within dramas.

On the final day of the ceremony, drumming began early, well before dark. Fewer women attended and the subdued atmosphere was in sharp contrast to the near frenzy of the previous evening. Amna, looking very demure, was wrapped in a *firka garmasis*, the women's brightly-coloured ceremonial cloth which indicated that part of this evening's events was in honour of the female spirit Luliya, sister of Bashir. Activities began with the highlight of the whole *karama* when the *umiya* carried out a large metal bowl holding the head of the sacrificed sheep, and performed the ritual of 'the Opening of the Head'. With drums pounding, Amna knelt before her. The sheep's head was held aloft and the *umiya* poured a glass of water into its mouth, as if to welcome the guest. Later the cooked meat was stripped off the head and passed around for those brave enough to eat, which they did with great reverence. Refreshments for Luliya – Pepsi, candies, sweet beans and cookies – were shared and then, rather suddenly, Luliya left. A different beat, another style of dancing, signalled the reappearance of the spirit Josay, as women he possessed strode round with exaggerated gestures, toying with spears. Josay 'played' for a while, left and finally Bashir returned for the rest of the evening. By this time Amna was completely exhausted. She had to be helped to stand and to dance; but she again was possessed by each of the spirits in turn.

The ceremony thus ended. Life began to get back to normal for most of us, though Amna was confined to her room for four more days, tended only by the *umiya*. The final scene of the *karama* was played out a week later in a procession, *al-saira*,[27] to the banks of the Blue Nile. The family rented a public car to take ten women, drums, coffee cups and pots, cooking stoves [*kanun*], and clothes to the river. There at the water's edge the *umiya* beat the drums to summon the spirits to Amna for the last time.

Amna recounted the events:

> Ahh! That day at the river! Here at home, we had made *lugma* [sorghum porridge], *mulah rob* [sour milk stew], *sharmut* [meat sauce], we had bought sweets and had twelve cups and twelve *finjan*. Then before we went to the river we made coffee, just like the first day of the *zar*. They poured out the tea and coffee into the twelve cups and twelve *finjan* and served the people inside and outside the house. Rabha the umiya had come and bathed me herself. She brought the water, washed my hair for me and told me to wash myself. Then she took me to the river. All the way to the river, the women were singing. Rabha herself was singing …

> They had dressed me up with beads … plaited cowrie shells into my hair and then covered me up. I couldn't see till we got to the river, I was so covered up. There I asked them which way I should go. They said you have to go into the water. When I saw the spray and foam from that dam, well … I covered my face and Zachara held me. I said 'Never! No, no, no, leave me alone.' Water from the dam was coming from on high. I washed my face with it. They kept pushing me to go in and I said to Rabha she should. She just said 'Do you think I don't have any children?' I felt dizzy, all the women were dizzy … After that, they brought the pigeons. They threw them

at the water, but the pigeons returned to us, they came back from the water. Rabha took them and picked them up and killed them. Then she filled a plate with blood and sweets and beans and dropped it all into the river. She washed the plate.

They sang for Hakinbasha. They sang and dressed for all of them [the spirits], but for Hakinbasha they walked around the garden. There he came to us. The girls had brought the plates and fed us stews and sweets and cream caramelle and a box of cigarettes. We ate and smoked and then we were ready to go.

After that I felt fine. Thanks be to God, I felt calm and relaxed.

I did not see Amna for several weeks, but heard that she had recovered quickly after the trip to the river. When I finally met her I expected a more dramatic improvement. At first glance, she looked as frail as ever, but she was cheerful and confident that she would fully recover.

Thanks be to God, I am much better. Before that *zar*, I could not sleep at night. My eyes used to swell and hurt me. Now I sleep. Since I beat that *zar*, I take my bed outside to the courtyard and sleep till morning. Thanks be to God.

Of the *zar* practitioners in Sennar, on the other hand, she felt more than a little disillusioned:

That *zar* of theirs is just money. Money! Altogether that *zar* cost me too much money. Probably LS250 in all. … That *zar* really needs a lot of money. And now, every time there is a *maidan* they send for us. … Are these women playing? We just run away from them. Really, this *zar*, it is bring this and bring that and drink this, things which I know nothing about.

Discussion

Several themes emerge from this detailed description of one woman's encounter with *zar*. It reminds us of the 'world of ethnographic things', the sights, sounds, smells and tastes (after Stoller 1989: 5), symbols which are fundamental to understanding the many dimensions of such ritual events. Besides detailing the decline of Amna's health and the course of a single *zar* ritual, it illustrates indigenous attitudes to health and sickness; the processes of different curing systems and the decisions associated with choosing one over the other; and the richness of belief and practice associated with the system known as *zar*. In addition it offers insight into the contradictions and complexities of ideas about a woman's individual identity, autonomy and power in relation to possession by spirits. What is lacking in this account, however, is any indication that the butcher's wife and her friends are, or regard themselves to be, a 'depressed category', 'deprived' or 'frustrated'; that they are trying to exert any type of 'mystical pressure' on either spirits or humans; that they regard anyone, either male or female, spirit or human, as their 'superiors', or that they feel they have limited resources at their disposal (after Lewis 1986). On the contrary, Amna's own narrative makes clear that while she saw herself as a sick woman she attributed this mainly to her own abundant good fortune, and had a range of options to deal with her problems, which she and her supporting kin and friends carefully weighed up in an ongoing fashion. Furthermore the description of the culminating ceremony shows that, while fraught with tensions, it is a complex and empowering event for many women, and one which is redolent with symbolism reinforcing female power and control in the wider social world.

Power, like possession, comes in diverse forms. It is not simply coercion or dominance, and is certainly far more than a reflection of political ideology or hegemony (as Errington 1990, after Anderson 1972, showed so effectively for Southeast Asia). In order to appreciate the nature of this form of empowerment we need to understand how power is conceived of in context (cf Giles 1987); otherwise we fail to understand why possession offers such a 'powerful' alternative in a wide range of situations. In this case study we are dealing with at least two understandings of power. First, there are the social and cultural inequalities which to some extent reflect the wider society. These are based on age as well as gender, but also include more specialized levels of knowledge and ability. Within *zar* society, there are distinct hierarchies based on experience within the organization as well as in relation to the spirits themselves and these are largely independent of secular society. Secondly, and from an emic perspective more significantly, *zar* possession, like that of Islamic trance such as in *zikr*, carries an electrifying potency. Once a spirit 'comes down' and actively possesses a person, she is felt to be surrounded by an aura of spiritual energy which should not be breached. No one should touch a possessed individual, for physical contact with the spirit domain is highly dangerous.[28] This potent 'charge' is most highly developed by the *umiya*, who is in more or less constant contact with this spirit domain; but even a relative sceptic like Amna is infused with an energy or strength to make a valiant if not total recovery, and to regain some control over her physical well-being.

All the participants in this ceremony were touched by this energy and the range of voices they express through their participation is one of the strongest indications of the empowerment such activities bring. Voice in itself is a confirmation of power: it is the silenced who lack the means to assert their autonomy and are more properly deprived.[29] On this occasion a multitude of voices is clamouring to be heard, reflecting differences and inequalities within the possession state but none are helpless. Indeed the boundaries between 'hegemonic' and 'counter-hegemonic' discourses are often blurred in individuals' own words. In Sennar no less than elsewhere, social relationships do not fall into neatly drawn categories; and in relation to the spirits as well as in relations mediated through the spirits, significant and often unpredictable dynamics are evident.

This becomes clearer as we look at the loudest voices being expressed: those of the butcher's wife and the *umiya*. What is striking, as we follow Amna through the course of her illness and her evolving relations with the spirit world, is how her relationship with the spirits was largely mediated by or through her social relationships. She herself retained a certain scepticism throughout the process as well as a strong awareness of self. For example, she always tried to be a 'good Muslim' in the traditional/orthodox sense and was concerned that involvement in *zar* was contrary to Islamic tenets. All those she consulted, friends, relatives and even religious figures, reassured her on this point but throughout the ceremony we see her and her support group finding their own accommodations so that their perceptions of what it means to be a 'good Muslim' remain intact. It was important that prayer mats be laid out at the proper times during the ceremony and that her submission to Islam should be visible. *Zar* activities invariably cease briefly when the Islamic call to prayer is heard in Sennar, in this way reinforcing a spatial and temporal separation of the two domains of knowledge. The extent to which they can overlap on any one occasion varies enormously; in this case, Amna and her family took the lead in infusing her experiences in *zar* with public Islamic submission. Furthermore, they also drew boundaries between their family life and the domain of *zar*, as they made sure that most of the formal activities were held in the empty site next door, space that they already used but which did not 'belong' to them. The ceremony inevitably spilled over into Amna's own courtyard and kitchen, where much of the preparation occurred, but Amna's efforts to contain the boundaries of the spirits in both religious and domestic terms are significant commentaries on her own sense of self and autonomy.

Amna did indeed have real problems and did not enter her relationship with the spirits from a position of strength. She became involved with *zar* for several reasons, most notable of which were serious physical symptoms. She lived in dread of all sorts of things; she was constantly told she was suffering 'from her nerves', and seemed to be physically fading away. Pregnancy was a contributing factor although not the precipitating cause and it is worth noting that Amna's problem was excessive fecundity rather than infertility.[30] Furthermore she, like her neighbours, was upset by rumours that women were being routinely sterilized in hospital if they give birth to more than seven children.[31] She was less afraid of the fact that she could have no more children – she really did feel God had been more than generous to her – than she was of surgery. This type of medical procedure is far too drastic a measure for a condition which she knew would be taken care of naturally in a short time. 'Cutting out her stomach' (which is how she always described it) seemed a totally alien and intrusive response to what she saw as a purely natural state.[32]

Physical problems were compounded by social and family difficulties. The ill-health of her mother and the fact that her relatives lived so far away were ongoing sources of stress. Her youngest child was difficult: small and thin, incredibly highly strung. The illness of her son (for which he actually had stomach surgery, an interesting recurrence of this theme) caused a very real setback from which she was not able to recover although he appears to have made a quick return to health. Money was an ongoing problem; there was never enough to meet the costs of schooling, taxes and other necessities. The strenuous demands of her social networks, in both Sennar and the north, added to Amna's general fatigue. The death of her close friend, the widow Wakil, and concern for her orphaned children were final straws in what can be seen as a steady process of decline.

However Amna was not allowed to decline alone. What is striking about her case is the strength of her support group, and the various roles each person played in facilitating the therapeutic process: her mother, friends such as the widow Sara, midwife Zachara, teacher Munira and the neighbours who attended daily to help out as needed. Sara especially was torn between her sense of social propriety and anxieties concerning potential menace from the spirits, as she urged Amna's daughters to cook more food for the unexpected guests, and at the same time tried to make sure that the family was properly prepared for this encounter with the spiritual domain. When she took the drum on the night of the storm to ensure the ceremony continued, she was fearful the spirits would be disturbed by one of two things: on the one hand they might be offended by contact from someone not ritually qualified, on the other they would be angry at an abrupt halt to the proceedings. Her actions (like those of Zachara) showed courage and presence of mind; they also highlighted the dangers felt to surround any contact with the spiritual world.

These were expressed even more dramatically in the mercurial behaviour of the *umiya*. Often unreliable in her relationships in the human domain, she was held to be unfailing in her control of the spirits and the sometimes extravagant demands they made, even through her. The difficulties she encountered in trying to hold a curing ceremony for Amna suggested to many guests that she was callous and irresponsible. Her clients however were aware that she was constantly wrestling with volatile spirits and the unpredictable ways they assert themselves against any form of human control or manipulation. For long periods she sat taciturnly by, oblivious to rising tensions around her, as when bad weather held up the *karama*. Rubbing down her equipment with the special oils of *zar*, warming the silent drums, she was already engaged in holding back the spirits. Nobody looked to her for guidance on this occasion; indeed she herself rarely spoke. She responded to the spirits and to the demands that they laid on her and those who were reached through her. The fact that these demands were often unreasonable in terms of human social conventions only heightened the powers she was felt to command.

The *umiya*'s main assistants, equally demanding, also added significant voice to the occasion through both their presence and their absence. Both women shared the *umiya*'s potency but lacked her total commitment to the spirits. Each had her own separate relationships with the *zar*, which are touched on only lightly here. The *umiya*'s mother was the main drummer and held great stature within the circle of *zar* devotees, even though she herself was rarely possessed.[33] Usually a sweet old lady, in the company of spirits she could be highly unpleasant to human guests. Her second daughter, the *umiya*'s younger sister, was the other main assistant. Like her mother, she also claimed to have no personal relations with *zar*, but because of her proximity to the house of *zar* she was felt to have special powers in relation to the spirits. She expressed this by repeatedly taunting the spirits (in or through the possessed), adopting behaviour regarded as suitable only for spirits (aggressive 'manly', 'rude' behaviour) and addressing the spirits directly in this way. Her own life style was also unconventional: she was unmarried and had a child, she worked in the market, she was loud and unrestrained. In all this she was regarded as running a narrow line between danger from the spirits on the one hand and social ostracism on the other.

Each of these voices is engaged in communicating not only with each other but also with the spirits. In addition to human interactions, the *karama* is a forum for the spirits themselves, their various sounds and presence. Although in the opening ritual the 'whole assembly of spirits' was summoned by drum-beats and was thus regarded as attending briefly, Amna's ceremony was dominated by the few individual spirits who were believed to be troubling her and in whose honour the *karama* was held as a major step towards conciliation. The aloof, professional silence of Hakinbasha contrasts with the rough and demanding (but more popular) tones of Bashir and (to a lesser extent) of Josay, or with the gentler and less noisy demands of Luliya. Each of these spirits has a history, a ritualized interpretation which articulates public and individual, national and local events in discourses which are simultaneously widely shared and yet unique. All four spirits are well-known throughout the Sudan today, and the contours of their individuality or 'spirituality' are sharply drawn. However, there is always a hint of unpredictability. The way in which they might interact with Amna, in Amna, left an element of suspense which heightened the emotions throughout the ceremony. No two manifestations of a spirit are ever the same; and particularly those *zar* described as new spirits, the

Ethiopian spirits Bashir and his sister Luliya, are likely to defy conventional expectations of how a possessed individual might behave.[34] Other categories of *zar*, such as the Pashawat Hakinbasha, are rarely individualized in this way and their collective behaviour is much more predictable and controlled.

The total effect of a ceremony such as this is one of richness and complexity. This form of ritual embodies an enormous wealth of knowledge, unevenly shared and constantly recreated in new and unique situations. And more than anything else, it symbolizes the domain of women. As I have noted elsewhere (Kenyon 1991) birth, circumcision and marriage, the major rites of passage in the Sudan, are all part of the same ritual complex and are all largely controlled by women. Not surprisingly, *zar* ritual shares much of the same patterning. The wedding is the cultural event which best epitomizes women's knowledge, the occasion on which it is most fully expressed and acknowledged, and as noted above in *zar* ritual wedding imagery occurs frequently. However, there is no suggestion that in the *zar* ceremony, a woman is married to (becomes the bride of) the spirits, as is found elsewhere in eastern Africa (Giles 1987). Rather the connection is firmly between *zar* and the other major rituals controlled by women. On each of these occasions, women are in charge of events: it is their knowledge which shapes the occasions and which reinforces the pivotal importance of women not only in the female domain but in the larger social and spiritual worlds to which they belong. Symbols of that knowledge, of women's creative power as well as of their sexuality, are embodied in the special materials, perfumes and jewellery; in the language reserved for the participants; in the music and dance performed on such occasions. All these are heady reminders, not simply of an immediate event but rather of the significant cultural roles of women and the knowledge that these are built on.

In terms of *zar*, women's experiences find further validation in the creative energy unleashed on these ritual occasions, when through their own spiritual connections participants are transformed from the local and particular into the global and supernatural. This process is one over which they not only have control but one which is infused by women's own understanding of local and national-international events. As Kramer (1993: 116) again so aptly noted:

> When the women represent figures from society, they are not bowing to the power of the society; on the contrary they are acting in contradiction to this power when they present themselves as changed or as others, or, putting it another way, when they represent the social world as it appears to them and not as it pretends or wishes to be.

As such, one can call the viewpoint of the spirit hosts 'dehierarchizing.' It does not give any preference to the important, the significant – the 'sublime' – over that which society views as trivial.

Postscript

I returned to Sennar in 1988 for a brief visit and spent an afternoon with Amna. She was looking much better and proudly updated me on her children's progress. As far as her own health was concerned she felt she had largely recovered, not simply because of her *karama* though this was part of the total process. She continued to support the *umiya* who opened the box for her, but had not hosted another ceremony and did not attend those of others with any frequency. However she had been to see another medical doctor about a different complaint. He had again diagnosed a goitre and prescribed a course of medication. She was making remarkable progress and was even putting on weight.

Acknowledgements.

I wish to thank the many women in the Sudan who shared their experiences in *zar* with me. This chapter is indebted to the late Rabha Muhammad, the late Soad al-Khoda, Nafisa Muhammad, Halima Ahmad, Zachara Ahmad Seif al-Dien, Miriam Idris and Najat Abbas. I also want to express my gratitude to Jeanette Dickerson-Putman, Baqie Mohammad and Lesley A. Sharp for their insightful and helpful comments on an earlier version of this chapter. Responsibility for the final version is of course my own.

Notes

1 Fieldwork in the Sudan was carried out between 1979 and 1985, with a short return visit in 1988. During this time I lived mainly in Sennar and Khartoum, though I was able to travel widely throughout most of the country.

2 Most names are pseudonyms.

3 Elsewhere in the Sudan, the term *Shaikha* (masc. *Shaikh*) is preferred. While female leaders are more common in *zar-burei* throughout the Sudan, male leaders are also found occasionally (e.g., El-Nagar 1980). In *zar-tumbura*, on the other hand, the symbolic head of each group, known as al-*sanjak*, is always male.

4 The most common way of acquiring *zar* is through inheritance from a close, usually female, relative.

5 As Janzen (1978) noted for Zaïre, the composition of this group is flexible, changing throughout the course of a single illness episode and including both kin and non-kin.

6 Soreya, the *umiya* described in Kenyon 1991a: 184ff, underwent surgery not long after we made the interviews on which that chapter was based.

7 Literally 'remembrance' it refers here to Sufi rituals of prayer in which the name of God is frequently invoked and trance is a common outcome. Such forms are associated with the Muslim Brotherhoods (*al-tariqa*, pl. *turuq*), certain of which are very popular in the Sudan.

8 Such as the far West. My own research with a leader of *zar* in Nyala, Darfur province, in 1982 suggests that *zar* had been spreading into this area within the previous twenty years.

9 For *zar* specifically in Boddy 1989 and Constantinides 1972; for other regions, Sharp 1993 and Stoller 1995.

10 Described by Masquelier (1993: 3) as 'the creative energy focused through ritual and the imagined community of spirits'.

11 *Mihaya* refers to one of the major cures used by Islamic healers. Specifically it is the water used for washing off Quranic verses written on a wooden board by the *faki*, and believed to have vital medicinal properties.

12 A tribal leader or important or learned man in the village. It could also be used, in a more specific sense, to refer to a male leader of the *zar* cult. Here it is not clear in what sense she is using the term.

13 i.e., the tin box, in which is stored all the ritual paraphernalia of the cult leaders. See Kenyon (1991b).

14 i.e., the whole assembly of *zar* spirits. This means that she is possessed by several *zar* though they would only 'come down' or be active one at a time.

15 Literally 'hinge' or 'constitution', this word is also used to refer to the *zar* spirits in a euphemistic way. Devout Muslims often refuse to utter the word *zar* itself.

16 This signifies the leader is inviting *zar* spirits to come down and actively possess the human guests. She herself may or may not be in a trance state (Kenyon 1991b).

17 Her initial reluctance to accept this diagnosis is typical. *Zar* is widely regarded as un-Islamic, and indeed since the Islamization policy of the present government was imposed, *zar* activities have been officially banned.

18 i.e., was possessed by a *zar* spirit.

19 The hats worn by colonial officials. In fact they are Egyptian (and thus Pashawat) rather than Khawajat dress, but this sort of distinction is not always important in *zar* performance.

20 In the Sudan, the term Chair [*Kursi*] refers to the formal seven-day ceremony, and the derivation of the term has provoked some interesting hypotheses (in Kenyon 1991a). The term recurs in other types of spirit possessions, though with differing usages. For example, in Swahili possession the human hosting the ceremony becomes the Chair of the spirit (Giles 1987: 241); and in Madagascar there are colonial *tromba* spirits that sit in armchairs and are called 'Armchair Spirits' (Sharp, personal communication).

21 The same term is used for any type of thanksgiving event.

22 At the time, this was worth approximately $100, more than double what the butcher earned in a month.

23 We learned later they had to put on an unexpected *karama* for a nephew who had died recently in the east.

24 This term, which is used in other contexts to describe women's household equipment (Kenyon 1991a: 186, 249), refers to all the equipment used in *zar*.

25 Until a woman has offered an animal sacrifice to *zar* spirits in a formal ceremony, she is not able to stand during actual possession, an example of the very tangible boundaries that are drawn between different types of possession.

26 Or Jozay, as Boddy (1989) refers to him. He, like each of the spirits possessing Amna, is found in *zar* throughout Northern and Central Sudan.

27 This is the same term used for the procession in a wedding or naming ceremony when a trip may also be made to the river.

28 The exception to this statement is the fact that some spirits (notably the Ethiopians) like to be welcomed in informal contexts with a special handshake. However, any further physical contact with them is also avoided.

29 I wish to acknowledge the insight of Lesley A. Sharp in articulating this point.

30 When Amna felt that she was too old to have another child, she was reckoning her age in sociological rather than biological terms. Thirty-nine is not an uncommon age to have a child in Sudan. However several of Amna's children are already old enough to be parents themselves, although in fact none of them are yet married; it is this fact which makes her embarrassed by her continuing fecundity.

31 I was never able to authenticate this rumour, which was widely believed throughout Sennar. I also never met a woman who was actually deterred from having more children; they simply concealed the number of children they had in any official documents.

32 Comaroff (1985: 182) talks of a 'rejection of the categories of the cultural scheme in which healing was purely a matter of rational technical intervention, the repair of the body physical alone.' This rejection is explicit in Amna's double experience of stomach surgery.

33 She claimed to have little personal experience with the spirits. However, she had been married to a great leader (*sanjak*) in *tumbura zar*, had spent most of her life in the household of her mother-in-law, the 'Grandmother of Sennar *zar*' (Kenyon 1991b), and was locally regarded as one of the most knowledgeable individuals within *zar*.

34 For example, when the spirit Bashir arrived towards the end of the second evening and several women stood up to dance immediately, one had hard, wide, unblinking staring eyes which caused great amusement. The onlookers laughed, mocking the spirit. 'What is this?', they asked. 'Does Bashir look like this now?' as they copied the staring eyes and the vacant expression of the possessed woman and tried to provoke the spirit. The possessed woman danced on, apparently unaware of the comments, and Bashir also failed to respond, though on other occasions this could easily precipitate some sort of dramatic outburst from him.

References

Anderson, B. (1972) 'The idea of power in Javanese culture', In Holt, pp. 1–69.

Atkinson, J.M. & S. Errington (eds) (1990) *Power and Difference: Gender in Island Southeast Asia*, Stanford CA: Stanford University Press.

Barclay, H.B. (1964) *Buurri al Lamaab: A Suburban Village in the Sudan*, New York: Cornell University Press.

Boddy, J. (1988) 'Spirits and selves in Northern Sudan: the cultural therapeutics of possession and trance', *American Ethnologist* 15(1): 4–27.

—— (1989) *Wombs and Alien Spirits. Women, Men, and the Zar Cult in Northern Sudan*, Madison: University of Wisconsin Press.

Comaroff, Jean (1985) *Body of Power, Spirit of Resistance*, Chicago: University of Chicago Press.

Comaroff, Jean & John (eds) (1993) *Modernity and its Malcontents*, Chicago: University of Chicago Press.

Constantinides, P. (1972) 'Sickness and the spirits: a study of the Zaar spirit possession cult in northern Sudan', PhD dissertation: University of London.

—— (1977) 'Ill at ease and sick at heart: symbolic behavior in a Sudanese healing cult', Lewis (ed.) *Symbols and Sentiments*, 61–81.

—— (1991) 'The history of zar in the Sudan: theories of origin, recorded observation and oral tradition', in Lewis *et al* (eds) 83–99.

Errington, S. (1990) 'Recasting sex, gender and power', Atkinson & Errington (eds) 1–58.

Giles, L. (1987) 'Possession cults on the Swahili coast: a re-examination of theories of marginality', *Africa* 57, 2: 234–58.

Holt, Claire (ed.)(1972) *Culture and Politics in Indonesia*, Ithaca: Cornell University Press.

Janzen, J. (1978) *The Quest for Therapy in Lower Zaïre*, Berkeley: University of California Press.

Kenyon, S.M. (1987) *The Sudanese Woman*, London: Ithaca Press.

—— (1991a) *Five Women of Sennar: Culture and Change in Central Sudan*, Oxford: Clarendon Press.

—— (1991b) 'The story of a tin box', Lewis *et al.* (eds) 100–17.

—— (1994) 'Urban spirits in central Sudan: male voices in female bodies', paper presented at the Central States Anthropology meeting: Kansas City.

—— (1995) 'Zar as modernization in central Sudan', *Anthropological Quarterly*.

Kramer, F. (1993) *The Red Fez: Art and Spirit Possession in Africa*, trans. Malcolm Green. London: Verso.

Lambek, M. (1980) 'Spirits and spouses: possession as a system of communication among the Malagasy speakers of Mayotte', *American Ethnologist* 7 (2): 318–31.

—— (1981) *Human Spirits: A Cultural Account of Trance in Mayotte*, Cambridge: Cambridge University Press.

—— (1993) *Knowledge and Practice in Mayotte: Local Discourses of Islam, Sorcery and Spirit Possession*, Toronto: University of Toronto Press.

Lewis, I.M. (1971) *Ecstatic Religion*, Penguin, Harmondsworth.

—— (1977) *Symbols & Sentiments: Cross-cultural Studies in Symbolism*, London: Academic Press.

—— (1986) *Religion in Context*. Cambridge: Cambridge University Press.

Lewis, I.M., A. Al-Safi & S. Hurreiz (eds) (1991) *Women's Medicine. The Zar-Bori Cult in Africa and Beyond*, Edinburgh: Edinburgh University Press.

Makris G.P. & A. al-Safi (1991) 'The *tumbura* spirit possession cult of the Sudan', Lewis *et al.* (eds) 118–36.

Masquelier, A. (1993) *Narratives of Power, Images of Wealth: the Ritual Economy of Bori in the Market*, J. & J. Comoroff (eds), 3–33.

El-Nagar, S. (1975) 'Spirit possession and social change in Omdurman', MSc thesis, University of Khartoum.

—— (1980) 'Zaar practitioners and their assistants and followers in Omdurman', Pons (ed.), 672–88.

—— (1987) Women and spirit possession in Omdurman', Kenyon (ed.), 92–115.

Ortner, S. and H. Whitehead (eds) (1981) *Sexual Meanings: The Cultural Construction of Gender and Sexuality*, New York: Cambridge University Press.

Pons, V. (ed.) (1980) *Urbanization and Urban Life in the Sudan*, Khartoum: Development Studies and Research Centre, University of Khartoum.

Ranger, T. (1993) 'The local and the global in Southern African religious history', *Conversion to Chris-tianity*, R. W. Hefner (ed.) Berkeley: University of California Press.

Seligman, B. (1914) 'On the origin of the Egyptian *Zar*', *Folklore* 25: 300–23.

Sharp, L.A. (1993) *The Possessed and the Dispossessed. Spirits, Identity and Power in a Madagascar Migrant Town*, Berkeley: University of California Press.

Stoller, P. (1989) *The Taste of Ethnographic Things*, Philadelphia: University of Pennsylvania Press.

—— (1995) *Embodying Colonial Memories*, New York: Routledge.

Stoller, P. & C. Olkes (1987) *In Sorcery's Shadow*, Chicago: University of Chicago Press.

Trimingham, J.S. (1949) *Islam in the Sudan*, London: Frank Cass & Co.

Zenkovsky, S. (1950) '*Zar* and *Tambura* as practised by the women of Omdurman', *Sudan Notes and Records* 31: 65–81.

IV

Spirit Possession as Performative Ethnography & History 'from below'

8

Slavery, Spirit Possession & Ritual Consciousness
The Tchamba Cult among the Mina of Togo

Tobias Wendl

The relationship between slavery and spirit possession has hardly been studied in anthropology. Whenever the discussion has turned to this point, it has been within the framework of Ioan M. Lewis's (1971) deprivation theory. This theory holds that possession cults recruit their members from marginal and socially deprived sections of society, with women in the majority, followed by low-status men, such as day labourers, slaves, descendants of slaves and migrant workers. The cults are said to provide such people with therapeutic outlets for frustrations and a means of protesting social exclusion. What this approach has not considered, however, is that many possession cults include a special category of slave spirits, i.e., spirits that either represent slaves or descend directly from dead slaves. Illuminating examples are the *Abid* spirits within the *zar* cult of northern Sudan (Boddy 1989) or the *Gandyibi* spirits within the *holey* cult of the Nigerois Fulbe (Vidal 1990) and Songhay (Rouch 1989). In this chapter I shall try to examine the phenomenon of these slave spirits in more detail. My point of departure will be the *Tchamba* cult among the Mina in Togo: a *vodu* possession cult, in which, however, it is the descendants of the former masters who are afflicted by the spirits of their former slaves. My case study of the *Tchamba* cult may thus be considered, in some respects, to be even an antithesis to Lewisian deprivation theory.

I will first try to describe the character and extent of slavery among the Mina and then examine the transformation of slaves into slave-spirits. In the third part, I will focus on the image of slaves within the context of ritual symbolism and performance. Finally, I will discuss if and how slave spirits might represent a certain part of Mina history which was split from their 'historical consciousness' but which cannot be definitively repressed and therefore periodically re-enters 'ritual consciousness'.[1]

The Mina and the age of slavery

Mina society emerged as a political entity at the end of the seventeenth century when the transatlantic slave trade was already well underway. From the very beginning it was characterized by a relatively high degree of ethnic-cultural heterogeneity. In addition to the autochthonous Peda nucleus were large groups of refugees from the Fante, Ga, Anlo and Adangbe peoples as well as descendants of Portuguese and Brazilian traders. During the eighteenth century the town of Anèho-Glidji, the political and religious centre, experienced an economic upturn due to the expanding ivory- and slave-trades. This enabled the Mina to impose their rule over a large number of villages in what would later become southeastern Togo. However, the degree of political centralization remained relatively modest, especially when compared with the neighbouring empires of Asante and Dahomey; the latter of which was even briefly able to exact tribute from the Mina.

Mina society was composed of two main categories of persons: free men (*ablodeto*) who enjoyed full civil rights, and slaves (*adonko*), legal minors of foreign ethnicity. Between them was a third category of 'dependants' who were either of foreign origin or ethnic Mina. The foreign dependants were principally refugees who had placed themselves under the protection of one of the Mina clans. The indigenous dependants, on the other hand, were usually people who had failed to pay their debts and were forced into pawnship. The descendants of dependent people were able to attain full clan membership relatively quickly, or even to found their own descent groups. The descendants of slaves, however, remained legal minors. They were given plots of land on which they worked two days a week for themselves, while the rest of the time they tilled their masters' fields. Labelled as 'Born betweens' (*dzidzidome*), they were permitted to have a mate but not to marry; they were allowed to procreate but were prevented from founding their own descent group; they could worship their forebears but not practice a real ancestors' cult. Children of a Mina woman and a male slave remained slaves. Children of a Mina man and a female slave, however, were regarded as free, but were not entitled to hold political positions, because lacking complementary maternal kin they were considered to be too weak.

It is difficult to estimate the actual extent of slavery in Mina society. Claude Meillassoux (1986: 66), who based his comparative studies of African slavery on the extensive data of the French colonial administration, concludes that by the end of the nineteenth century about 25 per cent of the inhabitants of former French West Africa were enslaved; and in more than half of the 65 administrative districts the slave ratio was even greater than 50 per cent.

There was certainly less slavery in Mina society than in neighbouring Dahomey and Asante where one third and one half respectively of the total population had been enslaved.[2] In any case, the slave proportion of Mina society would have reached its peak in the second half of the nineteenth century when the transatlantic slave trade had collapsed. Meanwhile the demand for palm oil had significantly increased so that the slaves were also put to work on the new domestic oil plantations. To use Paul Lovejoy's (1983) terminology: slavery was more than a marginal feature of Mina society, it was an institution and by the nineteenth century at the latest, had turned into a slave mode of production, a system of exploitation of a captive population unable to sustain itself by natural reproduction.

In general, it is held that male slaves predominated in the transatlantic trade, whereas in the domestic African trade there were more female slaves. However, as Claude Meillassoux (1986: 79–85) has argued, this high esteem for women slaves within Africa cannot be attributed to the women's biological capacity to reproduce the enslaved population. All available statistics clearly indicate that the fecundity of slave women was reduced much below that of the simple rate of reproduction.

Meillassoux, who therefore prefers the term 'sterility' to fecundity, sees the main reason for the higher demand for female slaves as resulting from the fact that women generally contributed more to the production of African societies and were also more obedient than men (1986: 110ff). Because the slaves didn't reproduce themselves, it became necessary to resupply periodically with new slaves. From an economic perspective in most cases this was obviously cheaper than having to bear the costs of raising the next slave generation.

The Mina acquired their slaves either by purchase or by capturing them in wars that often may have been pretexts for slave raids. The killing of enemies seems never to have been an important aspect of Mina warmaking; rather, what mattered, as Westermann (1935: 248) put it, was getting hold of exploitable valuables. However, since most of the war captives were members of neighbouring peoples who would have seized any chance to escape, it wasn't very wise to keep them. Instead, the captors tried to sell them as quickly as possible to European merchants or their local intermediaries. A slight change occurred after 1806, when Francisco Felix de Souza, commander of the Portuguese fort in Ouiddah (later known as the 'Vice King of Ouiddah') set up a trading post in Anèho and – along with Late Lawson – gained the monopoly in dealing with European and overseas slave traders.[3]

The slaves used in domestic production were purchased from more distant regions to the north. Such geographic distance not only reduced the risk of flight, but also established, as Meillassoux (1986: 70) puts it, a maximal social distance, segregating the slave from his master and reinforcing his unalterable status as a foreigner. The acquisition of slaves sometimes was also considered as a kind of capital investment. Bonifatius Foli, Westermann's main Mina informant, expressed it in the following way: 'When our forefathers bought a slave, this was just as if they put money into a bank account. If you buy yourself a slave and he produces children, they will belong to you; they will till your fields and build houses for you.' (Westermann 1935: 127)

Both women and men were allowed to acquire and hold slaves. Sometimes they were resettled in larger groups outside the villages on special farm hamlets, where they continued to work four days a week for their masters and the rest of the time for themselves. They planted palm groves and processed the palmnuts and kernels into oil. Traders used slaves as porters and guardians, while chiefs used them as servants and soldiers. Clever and skilful slaves were also required to participate in trading. They were provided with money or merchandise and were expected to turn a profit. Among the trading slaves those of Yoruba origin had the best reputation. Slaves and their descendants could be bequeathed or sold; they were sometimes pawned, for example in cases of unsettled debts, or given as security for additional loans.[4] In cases of manslaughter, the guilty person was sentenced to provide one or more slaves as compensation to the lineage of the victim. However, the slaves were not completely at the mercy of their masters. When ill-treated, they could seek asylum with one of the cult groups.

A slave could buy his freedom by paying his master the selling price of two slaves. In such cases, a small ceremony was performed announcing that the slave had settled his debts and was then free. He became associated with his master's clan and thus acquired civil rights. There are numerous examples of former slaves who acquired great wealth after becoming free. However, the memory of their slave origins continued to stigmatize them. And only if a slave's origins were definitively erased from the collective memory, was the former slave truly emancipated.

The Mina slaves originally came from the northern hinterland. There, they were captured and brought to the towns of Togogdo and Sagada on the Mono River, where coastal traders acquired them in exchange for salt, guns, powder, textiles or cash. They were then brought to the coast – with eight to ten people tied to one iron chain. From these groups the Mina first filled their own needs; the rest of the slaves were sold to the Europeans.

Although the northern hinterland was ethnically a very heterogeneous area, the Mina referred to it globally as *adonko*, 'the slave country'. Whether they were Kabye, Tem, Bassar, Moba, Tchamba or Tamberma, the Mina considered them all as being barbarians and thus suitable for enslavement. They were regarded as being rude, ignorant, amoral, and stupid, in short, their capture and exploitation seemed to be justified. The majority of slaves, however, were of Kabye and Tchamba origin, and thus the terms *kableto* and *tchambato* sometimes were used as synonyms for *adonko*.[5] Next to these terms others existed that did less to indicate the slaves' presumed ethnicity than their status as unfree persons: *ame peple*, 'the bought person'; *ame kluvi*, 'the chained person'; *ame gato*, 'the iron person'; or *nekekevi*, 'child of the day' and *ngdogbevi*, 'child of the noonday heat' – which allude to them as having been purchased during the day as opposed to normal people who were fathered at night. The fact that slaves were usually tied with iron chains during transport but sometimes also at home in order to prevent them from fleeing, later became one of the major symbolic attributes of slave status for the Mina.

The exclusion of the slaves and their return as spirits

Dead slaves were buried without any particular funeral rites outside the villages, in the wilderness. This was considered to be the proper place for all kinds of 'bad dead'. In Mina funeral rites, the dichotomy of 'village' and 'wilderness' is used as a metaphor for the social centre, on the one hand, and for the social periphery on the other hand. Anyone who died in old age or after a long sickness was classified as a 'good dead' and was buried within the village. Criminals and strangers, however, as well as those who died in an accident or from a contagious disease, were referred to as the 'bad dead', and their place of burial was outside, in the wilderness. The 'good dead' were transformed by expensive funeral rituals into ancestors and could then return through reincarnation. People classified as the 'bad dead', however, were excluded from this possibility. Anyone buried outside, in the wilderness, was not able to transform himself into an ancestor. The only way he could return was as a malicious dead spirit, as *amekukuvodu*. And this is what happened to the slaves.

The Mina pantheon is a most flexible and dynamic structure. Old spirits are sometimes forgotten and eventually disappear, while new spirits arrive and make themselves known in a permanent cycle which shapes and reshapes the pantheon. Nobody (except perhaps a very strange, highly meticulous ethnographer) would ever venture to establish a definitive list of them. Although the Mina themselves are convinced that they have never encountered all the spirits, they use two different taxonomies to classify them.

First, a distinction is made between personal spirits (*dzodzome-vodu*) and clan spirits (*kota-vodu*). The latter are considered to be the property of a certain clan, and only its members have a ritual tie with them which includes the right to practise the cult. Just as the clan spirits define, sociologically speaking, the corporate identity of the individual clans within the society, the personal spirits define the personal identity of the individuals within their clan. The personal spirits are free. They are considered to be the property of certain individuals, and there are no precise rules regarding their succession in priesthood. Each person is supposed to have ties to spirits but will not necessarily encounter them in a crisis situation. Some may be lucky throughout their lives because of ongoing harmonious relationships with the spirits. Others, however, are seized and may become possessed later on, or fall sick, and the only way to regain their health and vigour is to honour the spirits with special altars and shrines.

In another classification, the Mina associate their spirits more closely with certain phenomena of the outside world. They may speak of 'heaven spirits' (*dzime-vodu*), of 'water spirits' (*tome vodu*), of 'savanna spirits' (*gbeme-vodu*), of 'animal spirits' (such as those of the serpent, crocodile, monkey and hyena), or of spirits representing the forces of nature as they manifest themselves in thunder, rainbows or in dangerous epidemics such as that of smallpox. Yet another category refers to spirits of certain professions such as those of the hunter and the blacksmith. And a final category refers to spirits of foreign people, strangers and slaves, as well as to the 'bad dead' in general, who have been buried in the wilderness. Actually, this last category is the only one in which the spirits' potential to act is genetically traced back to the dead and thus displays a 'manistic' component, as it would have been labelled by the earlier German-Austrian cultural-historical school. All other spirits, however, are forces that act out of their own, representing rather the animated or 'animistic' aspects of nature and the outside world.

Another distinguishing feature of the slave spirits, as well as of the 'bad-dead spirits' in general, is their distinctive lust for revenge. However, a parallel may be drawn to the spirits of certain animals killed in the hunt. Herrmann Baumann (1950) emphasized the transafrican dimension of this religious pattern of ideas and practices, and to describe it, coined the expression 'Nyama – the power of revenge'. Mina hunters too, build up special shrines, called *adee*, to protect themselves from the vengeful spirits of certain animals they have killed. In these shrines they keep and venerate the animals' bones, in particular their lower jaws. Both the hunting of animals and the seizing of slaves represent intrusions into the outside world's resources. In the former case it concerns the fauna, in the latter it concerns the demography of other peoples. For the intruders, both cases are associated and experienced with distinctive lusts for revenge from each of the aggressed species; and both intrusions require protective counter-measures, such as building shrines. One might argue that these intrusions are, if not atoned, at least symbolically represented.

The slave spirits were called *Tchamba* because of the slaves' presumed ethnicity and origin.[6] Later, this name was also used for those spirits to whom the slaves themselves were tied: the spirits of the north. Similarly, the *Mami Wata* spirits comprise both 'white spirits' and 'spirits of the whites', which are Christian saints and angels as well as Hindu deities. The Mina were convinced that the slaves (and this held for Europeans and East Indians, too) had similar prenatal ties to the spirits of their own homes, just as the Mina had to theirs. If a slave then reincarnated himself – a possibility for those who had bought their freedom and were then buried in the village inside – his ties to the spirits of the north could indeed pass on to a Mina.

These notions about 'bad death', reincarnation, and ties to alien spirits in connection with the historical background of slavery have resulted in the fact that the Mina pantheon today includes a considerable number of *Tchamba* spirits. Of course, these don't really exist in the north. Rather, we might conceive them as projective transfigurations, by which the Mina have articulated their own experience with the otherness of the people from the north in symbolic and ritual terms. Within this discourse, the Mina's observations about the life of the slaves obviously provided the model for *Tchamba*'s fictive culture of reference to which the priests for their part tried to adapt their rituals.

Slave image and ritual performance

If today someone learns – when consulting a diviner for example – that a *Tchamba* spirit may be with him, he will try to start honouring this spirit by erecting a shrine. First, he will get two iron bracelets, made of twirled red- and yellow-painted iron wire, flattened at the ends. These bracelets serve as a metonymy for the slaves' iron chains; they refer to the condition of being enchained. The next item to be added to the shrine is a wooden stool, which condenses two complementary significations. On the one hand, it is supposed to serve the *Tchamba* spirits literally as a seat; by placing the stool, the seized person begs the spirits to come and take their seats. This is the first aspect. The second refers to the fact that the slaves formerly used to carry the stools for their masters; in this context the stool as a symbol refers to the slave's role as a stool carrier. Third, cowrie shells are added, either on strings in rows or set in piles. Cowrie shells were the currency of the slave trade. Symbolically, they emphasize the nature of the slave as a person who has been bought. In the early colonial period, the purchase price for a slave varied between (400,000 and 1,200,000 cowries, which corresponded at that time roughly to a sum of between 100 and 300 German Reichsmark.

Iron bracelets, wooden stools and cowrie shells are the focus of every *Tchamba* shrine, representing the slave as a chained person, a stool carrier, and a person who has been bought. Further items and objects referring to the slaves' world and their home in the northern savanna include: cola nuts, jewellery, musical instruments, teapots, textiles, iron chains, long clothes, fez-like and turban-like headgear, food stuffs and much more. Gradually a shrine is erected that closely resembles a collection of 'northern ethnographica'. All the objects displayed refer to the strange culture of the *Tchamba* spirits that the Mina, by means of their knowledge and observations of the slaves, have constructed in a process illustrating what Roy Wagner (1981) calls the 'invention of culture'. The arrangement of the whole shrine resembles a synecdochical representation. First, the alien culture as a whole is reduced to a certain number of spheres or synecdochical (pars pro toto) fields, such as 'feeding', 'clothing', 'body care' and 'religious practice'; then these particular fields are illustrated by suitable artefacts (Wendl 1991a).

Within ritual practice which I conceive, following Fritz Kramer (1987), as a steady interplay of fixation and incorporation, the shrines represent the quiet resting pole. It is the place where the tiresome spirits are confined. By offering the spirits their favourite dishes and other imagined comforts related to their northern culture, the afflicted person liberates himself temporarily from their grip. At the same time, the spirits find a home and peace. Incorporation, the kinetic counterpart of banishment, occurs during the possession ritual. It is then that the dancers let surface their inner anxieties, passions and past experiences, condensing them into dance images which express and portray all those forces that normally are confined to the shrines. In the case of the slave spirits, these images also emphasize the slaves' otherness and alterity.

One index of this alterity was the slaves' facial marks. The Mina disapprove of such marks, as do the neighbouring Ewe and Asante, whereas the peoples in the northern savanna decorate their faces with numerous small vertical and horizontal scars. The Mina consider these facial marks to be barbarian, even as evidence of savagery. A very laconic proverb says: 'When eating *fetri* the slave doesn't draw strings',[7] which means that the slave will avoid everything that might remind himself or others of his scarifications. *Tchamba* murals, which sometimes decorate the shrine's exterior, often depict these marks in a very realistic style. And if somebody is seized by *Tchamba* during the possession ritual, his face is usually painted by the cult assistants with similar chalk marks.

The costumes that the dancers subsequently put on also refer to their origins in the north. They wear long flowing robes, fez-like headgear, Mossi and Fulbe hats, sometimes even a turban (Figure 8.1, page 118). And they chatter a language that is supposed to be a language of the north. Some *Tchamba* dancers walk as if their feet were chained. Others balance a teapot filled with water on their heads; they take a mouthful, rinse their mouths and spit out the water. Then they start washing their faces, hands and feet, and finally pour the remaining water on the ground. Thus they imitate Muslim ablutions.

In the nineteenth century, however, only a very small number of the slaves actually were Muslims; and I doubt that the Mina would have had many occasions to observe such ablutions among their slaves. It is more likely that these observations came from the Islamized Hausa traders who started to found trading colonies in all major towns and villages at the turn of the century. These settlements, often referred to as *zongo*, evolved at about the same time that the institution of slavery became increasingly suppressed and thus obsolete. So it might well be that the Mina slowly started to integrate their new experiences with the foreign Hausa traders into the old image of the slave spirits. In the *zar*-possession rituals in northern Sudan, the slave spirits usually wear black clothes that are very old, too small or too short, and sometimes animal skins. The main attributes of male slave spirits are spears, sticks or clay pipes; and their favourite drink is cow's milk. One of the outstanding figures is *Maryjan*, an old male spirit, who walks heavily bowed down, marked by hard physical labour. Female slave spirits often request grinding stones for crushing millet and other plants (Boddy 1989: 297f). In the *holey*-possession rituals among the Nigerois Fulbe on the right bank of the Niger River, the slave spirits beg the noble spirits for alms. They, too, sometimes start to crush millet, but then are allowed to keep only the bran for themselves (Vidal 1990: 270).

If the performances and gestures of the slave spirits seem to be quite similar in the various cults, there are nevertheless some significant differences as far as the

Figure 8.1 Tchamba Dancer dressed in a fictive northern costume, Togo, 1986.
(Tobias Wendl)

composition of the cult groups is concerned. According to Laurent Vidal's statistics,
collected in the Fulbe villages of Tuluare and Kareygoru, respectively 74 per cent
and 90 per cent of the possessed people (which, of course, refers not only to those
possessed by slave spirits but by all kinds of spirits) belong to the social category of
unfree people, which means that they are descendants of former slaves (1990: 156,
162). Among the Mina however, the situation is reversed: there it is the social category of the free ones – and particularly those whose ancestors had been well known
for holding slaves – that become possessed. Among them one finds more women
than men, most of whom are tied to other *vodu*-spirits as well.

Elsewhere, I have examined the biographies of Mina priests and devotees in some
detail. I discovered that these people do not belong, either socially or economically,
to any marginal or deprived section of society, but rather are distributed over various different descent and professional groups. Most of them entered the cult groups
at major turning points in their lives or during periods in which they faced strong
psychological strains and distresses (Wendl 1991a). While interpreting their biographies, I tried to use Vincent Crapanzano's (1980) distinction between the 'autobiographical truth' and the 'reality of life history', and then to read the first one as a
metaphor for the second. In the texts I collected, 'autobiographical truth' provided,

on the one hand, a framework for representing, as well as for interpreting, individual life experiences. On the other hand, it obviously also served as a kind of exemplary biographical post-hoc verification of some fundamental religious axioms.

In some biographies the narrators explained their ritual ties with *Tchamba* in more detail by evoking a motive that I would like to label as the 'reversal of protective magic'. The slave-holding ancestors of the affected narrators once had got hold of some protective magic to counteract the dead spirits of their slaves, which were almost always seeking revenge. After the abolition of slavery, this protective magic – consisting of various medicinal items sewn into cloth and attached to the masters' ceremonial stools – gradually fell into oblivion. Suddenly, however, these protective medicines became the main target of attacks by the vengeful slave spirits. They entered into the medicines and thus strengthened their magic powers. But what previously had been harmless protective medicines then turned into powerful aggressive spirits, who claimed their own shrines and priests by taking possession of the narrators.

Heike Behrend (1993: 161) writes that spirit possession reveals a striking fundamental paradox which is that a person *is* and at the same time *is not* what she or he *seems to be*. A somewhat similar paradoxical performance may be seen in the *Tchamba* cult, in which Mina society reveals itself on the one hand as a slave-holding society, thus extending a part of its history into the present. At the same time, the society dissociates itself from this part of its history by the very ritual character of the performances, which are simultaneously funny and frightening. In this respect, the *Tchamba* cult certainly resembles other performative strategies and bodily practices of remembering as they are used by social memory (Connerton 1989: 22ff); and it is not surprising that the cult was expanding at the same time that slavery was disappearing.

Legally, Mina slaves were free after the colonial intervention; however, in fact they remained dependent on their former masters as far as their access to cultivable land was concerned. It seems that slavery in Southern Togo disappeared gradually rather than abruptly without causing social eruptions on a larger scale (cf. Miers and Roberts 1988). Many of the liberated slaves then started purchasing or leasing land. Some found homes at the missionary stations, and later on became integrated into the churches. Others tried to return to their homes in the north, and still others started to work as migrant labourers on the oil plantations, or for the colonial railway and roadworks.

Spirit possession and ritual consciousness

Anthropological theory has assumed and formulated various different positions and paradigms at the different periods of its history in order to interpret African cults of spirit possession. According to early German cultural-historians such as Leo Frobenius (1933), these cults expressed a strong antithesis to the 'manistic' awareness of life as he associated it with ancient African civilizations. He even saw them as a kind of rebellion against the natural order of reality. More recent approaches, inspired by text and discourse theory, as they have been proposed and applied with some different emphasis on details by Lambek (1981), Kramer (1987), Giles (1987),

Boddy (1989), Behrend (1993), and myself (Wendl 1991a), studied possession rituals as cultural texts and tried to analyse their inherent structures. The focus was on isolating constitutive elements with their connotative and denotative meanings, on determining the rules according to which these elements could be combined; and finally, on the problem of how the established rules generate and evoke complex messages within the frame of individual experience and more general social discourses. Recently, Paul Stoller (1994) has tried to challenge this approach by pointing to the very bodily and sensuous experience of spirit possession, triggering a whole range of cultural memories scholars previously have tended to overlook or to 'oversense'. However, I would argue that this is more an empirical problem for field work than for theorizing, because text and discourse theory can easily respond to these additional qualities of spirit possession simply by acknowledging the multisensory channelling (tastes, smells, sounds, textures, sights) of the possession-texts under examination.

Writers inspired by psychoanalysis, such as Crapanzano (1973), have focused more on the therapeutic aspects of spirit possession and examined its significance in coming to terms with individual life crises. Sociological approaches as they have been put forth by Lewis (1971) and others were above all interested in studying the machinery of social exclusion and ritual compensation; and feminist theory finally saw possession cults as an expression of women's culture: as a gender-specific form of interacting and communicating in order to overcome women's sickness and suffering (cf. Luig 1991).

These last three approaches have in common that they rather tend to ignore the problem of meaning in terms of a proper syntactic and semantic exegesis of ritual performance, and prefer to focus on their functional-pragmatic dimension: how do people use possession cults to manipulate everyday life? These functional-pragmatic approaches have proven themselves to be quite prolific. The problem, however, is as Fritz Kramer (1987: 233) has clearly pointed out, that possession cults very often fulfil a whole range of different functions at the same time. These may become so numerous as to almost contradict and start to cancel each other out. They serve as therapy, as entertainment, as social criticism, as art, as a means to differentiate oneself from one's society, and sometimes even as a form of performative ethnography. I think the most reasonable way of doing justice to this phenomenon is to conceive of it in terms of variable multifunctionality. In this respect, the Mina *Tchamba* cult, too, seems to have all the features of such a multifunctional institution. However, aside from the above-cited aspects, one more may be added, which had not yet been considered in the discussion about spirit possession: the aspect of ritual consciousness.

Not only did the Mina withhold basic civil rights from their slaves, they also excluded them from the stream of historical tradition and social memory by burying them in the wilderness outside of the villages. There, however, the slaves transformed themselves into dead spirits and returned. They demanded that shrines be erected to them in the village inside and thus insisted on a re-inscription in the social memory. In this respect, I view the *Tchamba* spirits in fact as referring to a repressed part of Mina history and existence, a part which has been expelled to the silent outside world of the unconscious. There, however, it seems that it cannot permanently be repressed and so returns periodically – by means of a possession cult – into the society's ritual consciousness. A similar interpretation may be given to the

Mina's *Toxosu* cult as well. The *Toxosu*, which represent the spirits of deformed children that used to be drowned in swamps and rivers outside the villages, are similarly excluded from the historical consciousness. They, too, sue for the right to be remembered by taking possession of people until they are honoured with shrines, and thus get access to the ritual consciousness.

Finally, in order to stress the transcultural dimension, a third example, this time from the Bijagós islands. Among the Bijagós it is the spirits of young men who died before finishing their initiation and who therefore are not entitled to be included in traditions and chronicles. These spirits usually seize women and force them to terminate the initiation rituals on the men's behalf. Only when this has occurred and the men posthumously have become full social persons who can begin their journey into the ancestors' world, will the possession of the women come to an end (Colleyn, de Clippel, and de Souza 1992). In this case, the ritual consciousness has shifted into a historical consciousness, allowing spirit possession to disappear completely.

Possession cults may, under certain circumstances, serve to challenge and correct a people's mainstream historical tradition, thus constituting and articulating a kind of ritual consciousness that tries to fill in the lacks of the historical consciousness. Of course, I do not claim that this is a general, transculturally-valid functional aspect of all possession cults. Rather it seems to be an aspect that may attach itself in certain historical and social contexts of ambivalence to a particular cult. However, future research is needed to study such contexts and discourses of ambivalence in greater detail and in comparative perspective.

Slavery is not an ambivalent subject only for the Mina. This becomes evident if one looks at the relevant debates in African history and anthropology (Wright 1993, Clarence-Smith 1994). There was, for example, the attempt to conceive of African slavery as an antithesis to American slavery, and thus to humanize it. Miers and Kopytoff (1977) referred to the strong assimilation potential of African societies and emphasized the common features of slavery and other forms of dependency such as clientelism, pawnship or even relations between father and children. Viewed in this light, African slavery appeared somewhat embellished as an extension of traditional forms of dependency on strangers. This view was, however, heavily criticized by scholars such as Paul Lovejoy (1983) and Claude Meillassoux (1986). The former emphasized the historical transformations of African slavery; the latter stressed the great structural similarity of any slave mode of production and referred to enslavement as a process of radical and systematic de-socialization and de-personalization, of de-sexualization and even de-civilization.

For Mina society the institution of slavery is both a present and sensitive memory. On the one hand, slavery appears to have been an economically rational action, justified by the enslaved populations' evident lack of civilization. On the other hand, its evocation arouses great uneasiness with regard to the official national discourse. This discourse postulates equality; it posthumously depicts masters and slaves, exploiters and exploited as brothers, beautifying painful and ugly historical experience. Ethnic sensibilities and differences are minimalized in an attempt to build a nation; and such an effort cannot admit memories of slavery. By reactivating these very memories in its ritual performances, the *Tchamba* cult creates a kind of counter public. It re-shapes an image that has not only been expelled from the Mina's own historical consciousness but also from the official discourse of national history. Obviously, this re-shaping and ritual re-staging does not lack a certain political explosiveness in the present situation where the country is largely dominated by the Kabye, one of the peoples that the Mina used to enslave.

In this chapter I have attempted to focus on some of the relations between slavery and spirit possession that previously have been neglected in anthropology. Using the case of the *Tchamba* cult among the Mina, I have tried to demonstrate that the memory of slavery is still a very vivid and sensitive one. I have arrived at the concept of a 'ritual consciousness' that sometimes seems to challenge and correct the 'historical consciousness'. And in my opinion this concept may fit very well into a more general theory of spirit possession that conceives it, not as a static and monolithic phenomenon, but rather as a flexible one characterized by variable multifunctionality embedded in multiple and multisensory discourses and performances.

Notes

1   This chapter is an extended version of a paper originally presented at the biannual meeting of the Deutsche Gesellschaft für Völkerkunde (DGV) in 1993 in Leipzig. It is mainly based on material collected during twelve months' field research among the Mina and Ewe in Togo and Ghana in 1985 and 1986. I was then primarily studying the Mami Wata cult (Wendl 1991a, 1991b, Wendl and Weise 1988), but also had numerous opportunities to interview *Tchamba* priests and devotees as well as to participate in their cult performances. I would like to thank the German Academic Exchange Service (DAAD) for financial support, and Laté Lawson Molevi, Elise Jibidar, Daniela Weise and Nancy du Plessis for their suggestions.
2   Cf. Hebenbrock 1991: 59; Kaese 1991: 77; Lovejoy 1983: 171; Law 1991.
3   Akle-Agbomina 1983: 64ff; cf. Westermann 1935: 126 as well as Cornevin 1987: 147.
4   Westermann 1935: 284ff.
5   Whereas Kabye culture has recently been studied by a number of scholars, the 30,000 Tchamba living in the prefecture of the same name east of Sokode, have yet to meet their first ethnographer. They seem to assimilate themselves more and more to the neighbouring Tem and are today among the most Islamized ethnic groups of Togo. Frobenius (1911: 359) considered the Tchamba to be a splinter group of the Bassar, who took refuge during the Dagomba war and eventually settled with the Tem. See also Cornevin 1987: 55ff, 103, 389 table.
6   The spelling varies: *tchamba, tsamba, tsaba, tsemba,* and *tseba.*
7   *Adonko mekploa fetridetsi o* (Westermann 1905: 122).

References

Akle-Agbomina, Yvette (1983) 'Histoire d'une ville et d'un royaume: Anèho-Glidji'. Unpublished Mémoire de Diplôme, EHESS Paris.
Baumann, Herrmann (1950) 'Nyama, die Rachemacht', *Paideuma* 4.
Behrend, Heike (1993) *Alice und die Geister: Krieg im Norden Ugandas,* München: Trickster.
Besmer, Fremont E. (1983) *Horses, Musicians, and Gods: The Hausa Cult of Possession-Trance,* South Hadley: Bergin & Garvey.
Boddy, Janice (1989) *Wombs and Alien Spirits: Women, Men, and the Zar Cult in Northern Sudan,* Madison: University of Wisconsin Press.
Clarence-Smith, Wiliam G. (1994) 'The Dynamics of the African Slave Trade', *Africa* 64/2: 275–86.
Colleyn, Jean-Paul, Cathérine de Clippel and Alexandra de Souza (1992) *Le voyage des âmes,* 30-minute documentary film distributed by ACME-Films (Bruxelles) and ORSTOM (Bondy).
Connerton, Paul (1989) *How Societies Remember,* Cambridge: Cambridge University Press.
Cornevin, Robert (1987) *Le Togo: des origines à nos jours,* Paris: Académie des Sciences d'Outre-Mer.

Crapanzano, Vincent (1973) *The Hamadsha. A Study in Moroccan Ethnopsychiatry,* Berkeley: University of California Press.
—— (1980) *Tuhami: Portrait of a Moroccan,* Chicago: Chicago University Press.
Frobenius, Leo (1911) *Auf dem Wege nach Atlantis,* Berlin.
—— (1933) *Kulturgeschichte Afrikas: Prolegomena zu einer historischen Gestaltlehre,* Zürich: Phaidon.
Giles, Linda L. (1987) 'Possession cults on the Swahili coast: a re-examination of theories of marginality', *Africa* 57/2.
Hebenbrock (1991) 'Sklaven aus dem "Bauch des Dan": Sklaverei und Sklavenhandel in Dahomey', Bley, Helmut *et al.* (eds) *Sklaverei in Afrika. Afrikanische Gesellschaften im Zusammenhang von europäischer und interner Sklaverei und Sklavenhandel,* Pfaffenweiler: Centaurus.
Kaese (1991) 'Sklaverei und Staat in Afrika: Das Beispiel Asante', Bley, Helmut *et al.* (eds) *Sklaverei in Afrika. Afrikanische Gesellschaften im Zusammenhang von europäischer und interner Sklaverei und Sklavenhandel,* Pfaffenweiler: Centaurus.
Kramer, Fritz W. (1987) *Der rote Fes. Über Besessenheit und Kunst in Afrika,* Frankfurt am Main: Athenäum.
Lambek, Michel (1981) *Human Spirits: A Cultural Account of Trance in Mayotte,* Cambridge: Cambridge University Press.
Law, Robin (1991) *The Slave Coast of West Africa 1550–1750: The Impact of the Atlantic Slave Trade on an African Society,* Cambridge: Cambrige University Press.
Lewis, Ioan M. (1971) *Ecstatic Religion. An Anthropological Study of Spirit Possession and Shamanism.* Harmondsworth: Penguin Books.
Lovejoy, Paul E. (1983) *Transformations in Slavery: A History of Slavery in Africa,* Cambridge: Cambridge University Press.
Luig, Ute (1991) 'Besessenheit als Ausdruck von Frauenkultur in Zambia', *Peripherie* 47/48.
Meillassoux, Claude (1986) *Anthropologie de l'esclavage. Le ventre de fer et d'argent.* Paris: Presses Universitaires de France.
Miers, Suzanne & Igor Kopytoff (eds) (1977) *Slavery in Africa: Historical and Anthropological Perspectives,* Madison: University of Wisconsin Press.
Miers, Suzanne & Richard Roberts (eds) (1988) *The End of Slavery in Africa,* Madison: University of Wisconsin Press.
Rouch, Jean (1989) *La religion et la magie Songhay.* Brüssel: Editions de l'Université de Bruxelles. (Expanded version of the French original edition from 1960.)
Stoller, Paul (1994) 'Embodying colonial memories' In *American Anthropologist* 96/3.
Vidal, Laurent (1990) *Rituels de possession dans le Sahel,* Paris: L'Harmattan.
Wagner, Roy (1981) *The Invention of Culture,* Chicago: Chicago University Press.
Wendl, Tobias (1991a) *Mami Wata – oder ein Kult zwischen den Kulturen,* Münster and Hamburg: Lit.
—— (1991b) 'Kamm und Spiegel. Notizen zum Europäerbild in einem westafrikanischen Besessenheitskult', *Kea – Zeitschrift für Kulturwissenschaften* 2.
Wendl, Tobias and Daniela Weise (1988) *Mami Wata: The Spirit of the White Woman,* 45-minute documentary film. Distributed by IWF Göttingen.
Westermann, Dietrich (1905) *Wörterbuch der Ewe-Sprache,* Berlin: Reimer.
—— (1935) *Die Glidji-Ewe in Togo. Auszüge aus ihrem Gesellschaftsleben,* Berlin: de Gruyter.
Wright, Marcia (1993) *Strategies of Slaves and Women. Life Stories from East/Central Africa,* London: James Currey.

9

Constructing Local Worlds

Spirit Possession in the Gwembe Valley, Zambia

Ute Luig

During the cholera epidemics of 1993[1] Minalungu, a locally famous spirit medium in her fifties sent out messengers to the surrounding homesteads. They were instructed to ask an equal amount of beads from each family as it had members. Minalungu then dipped the beads in medicated water in an old wooden Tonga bowl and prayed to the basangu[2] spirits of the wild, to save her people like she had done for many decades. But only a few villagers in Mweemba sent her beads in 1993. Many laughed at her messengers and ridiculed them for believing in these superstitious practices as being relics of the past. But while the mourning from near and afar was heard day and night when the cholera epidemic reached its peak, those who had followed Minalungu's advice did not fall ill, as I was told by a young, well educated woman who was one of her devout followers.[3]

This incident gives a vivid impression of the ambiguity spirit mediums are exposed to at present in the Gwembe Valley, situated in southern Zambia. It seems that many people (from all social strata) have lost faith in the *basangu* who may be laughed at or even compared with Satan (Colson, unpublished fieldnotes 1982). Yet, during the nineteenth and the first half of the twentieth centuries *basangu* mediums were influential ritual leaders (see O'Brien 1983). Some, like the prophet Monze who deeply impressed Livingstone in 1865, or Gokwe who lived at the Zambezi near Binga (in present-day Zimbabwe) even commanded respect from people living far away who came to consult them in times of severe drought.

Although the decline of *basangu* mediumship might be attributed to processes of secularization as a consequence of the fundamental changes people in the Gwembe Valley underwent in this century, the answer seems not so easy. The most important argument against this assumption of disenchantment is the proliferation of Christian churches and the continued success of *masabe* spirit possession, which attract people in great numbers. It seems therefore not to be a problem of secularization as such, but a question of how meaningful the interpretations of specific cults still are for local people to come to terms with their increasingly complex worlds in times of radical social change.

In order to better understand these connections, I will look into the contributions spirit possession cults and cults of spirit mediumship[4] offer to the construction of locality in a world of globalized cultural flows. Since according to Gupta and Ferguson (1992: 9-10) 'actual places and localities become ever more blurred and indeterminate, ideas of culturally and ethnically distinct places become perhaps even more salient'. It is this kind of dialectic which intrigued me into writing this chapter.[5]

In the first section I shortly describe the transformations the Tonga as the dominant group in the Gwembe Valley had to cope with between 1950 and 1990. In the second part I analyse the success and failures of the *basangu* prophets in defending their idea of locality against the multiple challenges resulting from processes of fundamental change. And finally I discuss (very selectively) the achievement of *masabe* healers by describing how they appropriate and integrate outside forces in their vision of the local world they live in.

A vanished world: the Zambezi Valley before independence

In 1958 more than 2000 square miles of land along the Zambezi river were inundated as a result of the construction of the Kariba dam (Colson 1971: 26). In this process not only most of the Valley's fertile soils were destroyed, but the inhabitants' way of life was radically altered. Apart from a small group of Shona immigrants (see Lancaster 1981), the Valley was settled by Tonga speakers who differed culturally and politically in significant ways among themselves as well as in regard to the Plateau Tonga (Colson 1962) and the Ila-Tonga (Smith and Dale 1920). Yet, despite these local differences the Valley Tonga shared a common way of life consisting of a complex system of riverine and dryland farming, fishing and cattle keeping (Scudder 1962) which was complemented by labour migration to (then) Southern Rhodesia and South Africa (Luig 1996).

The enforced resettlement of 34,000 people from the north bank of the Zambezi by the colonial government as a consequence of the construction of the Kariba dam caused a great amount of uncertainty and eventually led to violent turmoil in one region (see Colson 1971). Enforced by the colonial state in the name of progress for the area, the resettlement represented a more radical break with the past than had the many years of colonial power before, during which the Gwembe Valley had acquired the reputation of being a backwater among European administrators and missionaries alike. This was due to the harshness of its climate, the few resources it offered (Matthews 1976) and the remoteness from the railway line which had rapidly become the economic artery of the country after its completion in the beginning of the twentieth century. The construction of the dam changed all this, since the Valley people experienced dramatic changes when in addition to their dislocation and homelessness, the struggle for independence came to a successful end in 1964. It is therefore not out of sheer nostalgia that the image of this lost culture is invoked, but in an effort to remember a period of singularity.

The period of the resettlement embodied the experience of a violent rupture with the past which was symbolized in the destruction of the ancestral and local shrines (*malende*), of which only a few were rescued. The abandonment of these shrines depicted the total defeat of a group of ritual leaders (*basikatongo, basangu*) who were convinced that their spirits had forsaken them (Colson 1977). They therefore decided against further performances of ritual because their spiritual force was lost. In order to understand the rational in that self-proclaimed abandonment of power

it seems necessary to know more about their role in the social organization of the
Tonga.

Bwami bwa invula: the lords of the rain

The Tonga[6] precolonial political system was based on widely dispersed matri-lin-
eages (*mukowa*). Political power[7] which was fluid and temporary was wielded by
'big men' who were able to control a following, but did not hold an office. They
lived in small polities, which most of the time consisted of a single neighbourhood.
Although the political structure was transformed due to the imposition of chiefs by
the colonial administration and the later changes of the postcolonial state, the core
religious institutions of the neighbourhoods continue more or less unchanged in
their organizational structure.[8]

Social life among the Tonga, therefore, still revolves around the neighbourhood.
It is marked by a local rain shrine (*malende*). Its custodian is the *sikatongo* (sg.) who
represents 'the matrilineal descent group of the founder of the shrine and the
founder himself' (Colson 1977: 121). *Katongo* means deserted dwelling, a synonym
for the ancestors. The *basikatongo* (pl.) are the 'guardians of the land'[9] (see also Maddox *et al.* 1996). They control the agricultural cycle, order, when and what to plant
and sometimes how to plant and when to harvest. They are responsible for all rituals connected with the land and the neighbourhood and have the power 'to heal or
harm the land' (Feierman 1990: 69ff). They bless the seeds before planting, receive
the first fruit of the harvest, placate the ancestors when they feel insulted and have
therefore withheld the rains. After the *basikatongo*'s death, their successors, always a
man and his ritual wife, are chosen matrilineally. The ritual wife is responsible for
the fertility rites when the ancestors at the *malende* are approached.

The duties of the *basangu* complement these tasks of the *basikatongo*, but quite
often overlap or even rival them. Ideally[10] the *basangu* are appealed to and called
upon in times of crisis after the efforts of the *basikatongo* have failed. This happens
especially during droughts, invasions of locusts, and epidemics, like cholera, smallpox or measles.[11] Since the welfare of the community, its fertility, wealth and reproduction lies in their hands, their most important duty is the 'control' of the rains,
that is to 'give' or to withhold rain as well as to stop the whirlwinds which quite frequently occur in the rainy seasons and devastate houses and crops. However, their
'power' over the rains is rather a form of mediation than actual control because ultimately God (*leza*) is thought to be responsible.

As diviners and prophets, the *basangu* are interested in the reasons why the rains
have failed, in order to know how to placate the spirits. Natural disasters and catastrophes are rarely explained in scientific terms[12] but are attributed to social dishar-
mony and conflicts, transgression of taboos or the neglect of *mizimu* (ancestral
spirits) or *basangu* spirits. It is this moral discourse which is debated and contested
among the people who even in times of crisis may refuse to follow the orders of the
basangu or only enact them half-heartedly. The role of the *basangu* is therefore quite
precarious. They are accepted as the spirits' voice when they are in trance but neither before nor after the seance are they given special respect or shown deference.
The *basangu*, then, have no power in the Weberian sense of enforcing their own will

upon others, but come close to what Hannah Arendt (1986) called 'communicative power' since the results of divinations and successive plans for action have to be communally approved. The communicative dimension of their power has two important consequences. First, their role as mediators legitimizes their intervention in social conflicts. By defining the causes of these conflicts and the resulting natural disasters they exercise what Feierman (1985: 75) has called the power of naming.[13] Secondly, this act of naming enables them to innovate and shape controversial developments in their communities by privileging certain ideas and values and rejecting others. It is this creative potential and in the view of Arens and Karp (1989: xx) their 'transformative capacity which is the key element in people's understanding of [the *basangu*'s] power'. Based on a certain kind of charisma their power is extremely fluid and has to be defended against resistance of the people as well as of the spirits.

The *basangu* as spirits are beings of the bush in contrast to the *mizimu* who represent the ancestors of the lineage. The *basangu* live in big trees or in rocks outside the villages. Although *basangu* spirits have names and their places of origin are known, they are neither personalized nor attached to lineages.[14] They are not linked to any particular community, but roam from one village to the next. In this sense, they are not localized. This independence of the spirits manifests itself in the fact that dead *basangu* mediums do not receive a shrine. And in addition no certainty exists that they will have a successor in their village; this often was and is not the case.

Locality then, for *basangu* spirits and mediums alike, is not a bounded space nor a 'timeless given', but a spatial arrangement for a certain time. Its boundaries are open and negotiable from generation to generation. Although *basangu* mediums are engaged in constructing local subjects and local knowledge, they do strive to enlarge their inter-regional influence, taking Monze or Gokwe as an example. How this leads to and what it contributes to the 'construction of locality' will be analysed in the next section.

Localities as context – context of localities[15]

The double relationship between the *basikatongo* and the *basangu* is inscribed in the construction of Tonga neighbourhoods which I refer to in a more abstract sense as locality. In Appadurai' s understanding (1995), locality is defined as the appropriation or colonization of space which is transformed through time and socialized through ritual activities. For him, as well as for Gupta and Ferguson, locality is a relational term since it has to be set against other localities. This implies that localities have to be differentiated from their surroundings by marking boundaries and in-between zones (see Luig 1995a). These are constructed according to cosmological and moral principles which are embedded in systems of economic production and social relation. A case in point is the drawing of boundaries between human settlements and the 'wild' with several zones of intermediacy (van Beek and Banga 1992) on the one hand and the differentiation of the 'wild' on the other hand. The *basangu* excelled in this spatio-temporal production of space by carving out fields, fallows, waste land, etc. as distinct markers of social and economic interaction. While these distinctions followed socially–determined rules and ecological knowledge, religious and aesthetic principles prompted the differentiation between places of power and land shrines. According to Colson (1997: 48) places of power are mountains, rocks, baobab trees, pools or waterfalls which are often situated in isolated or otherwise marginal areas. They are 'regarded as inherently sacred and as *loci* of spiritual power', (ibid.), transmitting through their colours, lights, whispers, heat or coldness a special atmosphere of awe and respect. Among the Tonga, the baobab trees especially are associated with the *basangu* spirits who dwell in them. When these trees are situated outside the community, in the borderland between fields and bush, they represent meeting places for diverse groups, like labour migrants, local seekers for help, or immigrant communities.

In contrast, land shrines (*malende*) stress their attachment to local people and their involvement in local history. Guarded by the *basikatongo* and embodied with the power of the deceased, also named after them, they are rather fragile structures, left to decay after one or two generations. Their material and their outlay reflect the fluidity of social relationships in Tonga neighbourhoods. They are restricted to local groups and deeply involved with local history. This attachment to specific localities, however, limits their range of influence in times of general crisis where places of power appear more attractive. Yet, both places, together with the *katongo* and the *cipito*[16] are important ritual markers in the Tonga landscape. These sites convey a feeling of belonging and knowing the land, of history as well as past and present conflicts. The construction of locality therefore transcends a pure spatial arrangement, and is also more than just a socialization of space and time as Appadurai (1995: 206) suggests. It creates part of a social and moral landscape imbued with emotional and aesthetic qualities, as Ikemefuna Okoye (1997) has argued, in which the 'poetics of space' (Bachelard 1957) are inscribed. *Basangu* mediums excelled in this spatio-temporal and cultural production of space by carving out places of power as distinct markers of interaction between humans and the spirit world.

This structuration of local space is embedded in a dialectical or hierarchical relationship with other localities which Appadurai (1995: 208) frames as a theory of context. In his reading, localities 'are contexts and at the same time require and produce contexts' (ibid.: 209). They are contexts insofar as their setting provides the frame for human action or the creation of new life worlds; they create new contexts by setting themselves apart from other contexts which exist in a larger frame of reference. This context-generative process links localities in an ever–widening chain with outside forces, like the nation state or the world market. 'In this way through the vagaries of social action by local subjects, locality as context produces the context of localities, which over time changes the conditions of the production of locality' (ibid.: 210). These interconnections pose the question of social power, since the nation state or the world market shapes, influences or even drastically limits the context-producing activity of local subjects. It is therefore mainly a question of power and not necessarily of preference whether locality production remains autonomous or if it becomes more and more subdued to outside forces. Departing from these considerations we can pose the question of the *basangu*'s decline again.

My contention is that together with the *basikatongo* they successfully manage to construct localities as contexts, but that they are less successful in handling the contexts of localities. The recent history of the Valley gives some clues in this direction. Although the Gwembe Valley has been part of the developing hegemony of South Africa since the beginning of this century, the influence of outside forces was and still is comparatively small. Outside influence became more intensive during and after the resettlement when the people of the Valley got more involved with the Zambian state. In addition, the education system and the Christian churches made their impact felt. Ministers and adherents of the churches attacked local beliefs in spirits as well as in witches as superstition, sometimes aggressively burning people's 'fetishes' as they called them, in order to demonstrate their own power. Due to the intensified interrelations with national politics and economics the Valley was exposed to a constant flow of immigrants, who looked for jobs and opportunities in cash crop agriculture and the fishing industry, bringing with them new ideas and images.

As a consequence of these globally and nationally induced transformations the former homogeneity of the neighbourhoods changed and increased the dependency of the Valley people. They became more and more involved with these hegemonic forces and the inequality of power widened. It was in this situation that the *basangu* lost their control over the construction of locality. They were not only materially unable to prevent the resettlement of the people, but were and are only partly able and willing to cope with this new situation. They tried to defend local specificity and local identity by guarding them against those foreign influences which they fear as destructive, like for instance the selling of grain (Luig, Ul. 1997: 39), the use of buses and taxis as well as certain commodities, like rectangular houses, shoes and money. This type of selective resistance to Western commodities reflects a deeper insight into the destructive aspects of commodification and commercialization (for similar processes see Masquelier this volume). However, their (selective) distancing from Western commodities and values does not imply that they opt for a closed society being parochially local. On the contrary, *basangu* mediums were and are in no way inimical to all innovations. They only try to adapt foreign ideas and translocal practices in such a way that local values become enriched, instead of being threatened or even lost. In this way they persist in their ideal of community which was and is ' local in its teleology and ethos' (Appadurai 1993: 11), contrary to *masabe* healers who stepped in and exploited this situation for their own benefit. In the following paragraph I shall analyse the differences in their approach to the confrontations of 'global modernity'.

Masabe spirit possession and the construction of locality

Masabe possession is organized as a cult of affliction which addresses itself to the individual instead of the community. *Masabe* spirits afflict a person with illness in order to make their wishes known and disclose their identity either in dreams or through divination by a *masabe* healer. The spirits want to be recognized as partners in a relationship which changes from subjugation to mutual reciprocity when it is successful.

It is without doubt this very personal relationship which accounts for the attractiveness of *masabe* spirit possession which differs fundamentally from the public accountability of *basangu* mediumship. While *basangu* mediums have to be publicly confirmed, *masabe* healers are judged informally by their success in healing which involves a complex therapy, including herbal treatment, counselling of patients and family and performances of rituals. This complex therapy is oriented towards the socialization of spirits into the world of humans and the gradual familiarization of humans with the spirit world.

Performing local worlds

To do *ngoma* (Janzen 1992), to play drums, is the symbol for the complex interaction of possessed and unpossessed, of dancers, drummers and singers with the spirits. As in Kauli seances which Schieffelin (1985) has so aptly described, Tonga possession dances are social constructions of spirit identities which emerge in a dialogic fashion between their mediums, the drummers and the public, while onlookers join in the singing and clapping of hands necessary to attract the spirits. Although *masabe* spirits, like all other Tonga spirits, are considered as formless and bodiless *muuya* (breath or wind) before they afflict a person, they change their identity in the course of the ritual process from an immaterial being into a spirit of 'something' which can take a great variety of embodiments (see below). The spirits' individuality is acted out in a complex dramaturgy which depends on sounds, colours, and material objects. The rhythm of the dance, the succession of particular tunes, the colours of the costumes and accompanying beads fuse with the emotions expressed by the dancers and the public. Especially in the *masabe* songs invaluable knowledge about the spirits' character, their history and expectations in the interaction with their hosts is revealed. *Masabe* songs can be interpreted as a cultural archive where events are evaluated and commented upon from an emic and gendered point of view (see Luig 1993a and 1993b) as a *history from within*.[17] However, at the same time these dances are forms of playful, sometimes even ribald, entertainment where the images of *passiones* (see Lienhardt 1961) are dramatically enacted, depending entirely on the medium and the public in which way they are negotiated.

In the following paragraph I analyse the world of the spirits as part of a performative ethnography which reveals and interrogates the spirits' significance or strategies in their construction of locality. According to the negotiations of the spirits' identity their characteristics are not fixed but change over time. In order to convey some insights in their historical depths and changing nature I haven chosen two periods for comparison. The first period refers to the 1950s when Elizabeth Colson (1969) was able to record an impressive list of spirits,[18] while the second period is related to my fieldwork between 1987 and 1993.

Constructing locality during the 1950s

Although *masabe* spirit possession was already introduced to the Central Zambian plateau in 1918[19] (see Jaspan 1953), *masabe* spirits only became influential shortly before and during the resettlement when they filled the vacuum other spirits, like the *basangu* and *mizimu* had left. Elizabeth Colson observed and noted a great variety of spirits over three decades, which represented nearly all domains of social life. The specificity of these spirits gives insight into the forms in which Tonga constructed their local world and the way they represented it to themselves and others during colonial times. Although we lack detailed information about the specific characteristics of the spirits since few songs exist (or have been recorded), *masabe* spirits clearly personified a wide spectre of the everyday experience of the Valley Tonga at that time. An important group of spirits represented animals which were classified as animals of the bush and animals of the house. And they were differentiated according to their local or exotic (European) origin. While local animals appeared as signifiers of the wild (lion), the untamed (vulture) or the unpredictable (baboon), little was known about the symbolic meaning of foreign animals, like ducks and pigs, which had only recently been introduced to the Valley (see Colson 1969). Even now people do not know much about their meaning or do not care any more. Yet, the sheer quantity of animal dances compared with other spirits (see Colson's list) reveals their importance for the construction of the *Lebenswelt* in the Valley. However, contrary to the *basangu* which occupied themselves primarily with the 'domestication' of nature – in the form of designing spaces for social or ritual use – animal *masabe* spirits were individually appropriated for their specific qualities like physical strength, force, power, cleverness and shrewdness. Comparable to the animal stories in Tonga oral traditions, the appearance of the possessed as baboon, snake, lion, vulture, etc., implied a discourse on moral values which was remembered, interpreted, ridiculed or even rejected in the ongoing negotiations of the evening performances.

The important role of animal spirits in the construction of locality as context was complemented by various stranger spirits who represented the contexts of locality, that is its relationship with outside forces. Of particular importance were the southern neighbours of the Tonga, like the Shona, Ndebele and Zezuru, but also a European spirit called *mazungu*. Colson dates his existence before the 1940s. He can be seen as a precursor of *mangelo*, meaning angel or just white person (see below). The common features of all stranger spirits were their strange languages (heteroglossia) and the even stranger eating habits which were enacted in the dances as celebrations of otherness and self-assertiveness. They conveyed a picture of the Tonga's main social relations which during the 1950s were predominantly oriented to the south of the Zambezi. It was in the mines around Bulawayo (see Luig 1996) and to a lesser extent in Johannesburg where male Tonga migrants encountered these neighbouring groups as fellow workers and where they had a profound experience of the superiority of the Europeans who controlled their life and working conditions. Thus male labour migrants played[20] (and still do) important roles in *masabe* spirit possession since their concrete experience is translated and reworked by possessed females as *passiones*.

Whereas these spirits from afar represented the various facets of alterity and its social implications, other spirits stood for agency and power. Among them were incarnations of *maregimenti* (soldiers), *mapolis* (messengers), *matingatinga* (carriers), *matobela injanji* (railroad followers), or *madyabantu* (cannibals) who embodied the colonial state with its many facets from repression to cultural diversity. Although the impact of the colonial state had been rather marginal in the Gwembe Valley up to the 1950s, compared with other regions in Africa (see Luig 1993b), the conception and realization of the resettlement programme had intensified the state's influence on people's lives. The symbolic and actual violence of the resettlement was visualized and objectified in the impressiveness of the machines used for preparing the land for the resettlement. Spirits with such powerful names as *siacilipwe* (bush clearer), *kanamenda* (motorboat), *citima* (train), *incinga* (bicycle), *indeki* (aeroplane), *kandimu* (boat engine) performed this drama again and again during the dances at night, articulating the construction of locality with the deeply resented colonization of space.

The intrusion or even invasion of the colonial state was also delightfully enacted in the following performance of *indeki* (aeroplane), observed by Elizabeth Colson in her 1955 unpublished fieldnotes (Scudder and Colson 1956). While at first the possessed women only waved their arms like the wings of aeroplanes, in later performances of *indeki*, they were more concerned with the behaviour of the district governor. He was shown in the dance leaving the plane and joyfully greeting the villagers in a 'new language', mixing Tonga with English and words of other languages as well. The spirit of the district governor wore a male hat, black cloth and leg rattles, called *musangusangu*. After he had greeted everybody, he sat on a stool and mumbled something about *pandamushaka*. *Pandamushaka* means cutting the bush (Scudder and Colson: unpublished fieldnotes 1956), but symbolically referred to removal from the land. The depiction of the district commissioner's part in the resettlement programme repeated and parodied the behaviour of 'government agents', but also drew attention to the different sources of his power since he combined European status symbols (hat) with African symbolic items from the wild (especially *musangusangu*). The representation of European power in the images of the wild interpreted this power as all-embracing, combining local and outside resources into one powerful image.

Constructing locality in the 1950s relied on European influences in other domains as well. Spirits, like *guitar, ma-dance* and *cilimba* (accordion) represented aspects of European urban culture which infiltrated the Valley with the help of migrant labourers and the commodities they brought with them. This interplay between rural and urban cultural ties and exchanges dramatized the context of a changing locality in a fundamental way. It was accentuated by the introduction of new commodities, like soap, perfume and dresses, which were heavily sought after and constituted part of a mimetical urban world in the villages (see Colson 1969, 1971; Kramer 1987).

To sum up – what did construction of locality mean during the 1950s and 1960s and how was it manifest in *masabe* spirit possession? From the beginning, *masabe* spirit healers played an active part in constructing the contexts of locality. Despite the scant information we have, it seems safe to say that the representation of locality was based on concrete relations (to animals or neighbouring tribes) which became part of the symbolic construction of the world. This context of locality however changed drastically through the impingement of powerful outside forces, which were represented by the colonial state, its technology and its culture. *Masabe* spirit mediums actively adjusted and adapted these forces by ritually converting them from menacing powers to protective ones. In contrast to *basangu* mediums who tried to come to terms with the enforced changes by condemning them, *masabe* mediums transferred their power through a process of symbolic appropriation which was enacted through ritual. In this way they symbolically tried to gain control over the processes of locality construction and its contexts.

Variations of difference: Masabe *spirits in the 1980s*

At the time of my research from 1988 to 1990 and again in 1993, the earlier peripheral situation of *masabe* spirit possession had given way to popular recognition; it had changed from a nearly exclusive domain of women to an arena for men as well. Though contested, especially from Christian church leaders, but also from some *basangu* mediums, *masabe* healers had become a force to reckon with. Even hospital personnel had discovered their merit for healing certain diseases and voluntarily transferred patients from Western type clinics to the therapy of *masabe* healers. What were the reasons for this success?

Apart from its individual form of healing and empowerment, the permeable nature of the spirits is one of the main reasons for this achievement. The representation of the spirits seems unlimited, their world boundless. This leads to the invention of new spirits[21] and to repeated incorporation of 'new' cults, such as *bulengelenge, bamuba, bampande*[22] or *basangu* into *masabe cults*. However, the not very successful attempt of *masabe* healers to pass themselves off as *basangu* mediums who are still regarded as being more powerful, refers to certain limits of this permeability. In order to differentiate the *masabe-basangu* from the *real basangu* new classifications were invented: *masabe* healers claiming to represent *basangu* spirits were either referred to as *white bampande*, being identified with white clouds which was a synonym for their lack of control over the rains, or as *black bampande* which affirmed their control of rain but may not have included control of epidemics. In both cases, however, people denied them recognition as *true bampande* reducing the power of their spirits either to healing or to some form of control over wind and cloud formation. That these were not insignificant struggles for names, but serious fights for positions of power was borne out by the case of a *masabe* healer who tried to pass off as a *basangu* medium. His claim led to an embittered conflict between two families for two generations. Even after the death of the culprit, the conflict which was framed in accusations of witchcraft flared up again when his brother's daughter-in-law died. The case had to be negotiated again and only after heavy compensation by the nephews of the accused did peace regain.

The above example proves that despite the constant drawing and redrawing of boundaries between cults, the expansion of the spirit world is in no way contingent, but depends on the power relation among the healers, on the overall ritual situation as well as on the spirits' continuing significance for the people. Spirits are either neglected in the dances or forgotten when their message is no longer meaningful. Others acquire new identities through associations with new events or through the process of Christianization. An interesting case is for instance *ma-soldier* (which is another name for *maregimenti*) who was described by Colson (1969: 85) as a symbol for the colonial army. In my interviews however, in the 1980s, he was mentioned either in connection with the Zimbabwean guerrilla forces or with the white Rhodesian army. Both armies operated in the southern part of the Gwembe Valley during the Zimbabwean civil war, destroying villages and terrorizing their inhabitants. For many of my informants then, *ma-soldier* symbolized colonial domination and the terror of war, but for others he had experienced a Christian permutation. These informants classified him as a benevolent spirit who 'had undergone Christianization'. He had changed into a soldier of the Messiah and in this capacity became a saviour from witchcraft.

Similar shifts are characteristic for *mangelo* as well. Recorded by Elizabeth Colson in 1962 as a synonym for 'Europeans', who were differentiated into several ethnic groups, like English, American and Japanese, *mangelo* also became Christianized, representing a wide spectrum of meanings, including white person, angel, representative of God and even God himself. In a more abstract sense, then, he symbolized the power of *Europeandom* and embodied a powerful allegory of 'European' superiority which has become an idiom of modernity in the process of time. Remarkable in this shift of identities is the implicit Africanization of *mangelo* by including members of the African elite, named as *madyabantu*. (For a similar process of Africanizing European spirits see the contribution of Matthias Krings in this volume.)

The construction of Tonga locality has thus changed considerably over time although its principle of representation has not become transformed. Compared with the 1950s, locality is still expressed in relation to the forces of nature, the encounter and exchanges with neighbouring tribes, agents of government and the state and the many symbols of modernity. Despite this structural continuity in the production of locality, the spirits have undergone many changes. Most of the spirits mentioned in Colson's 1969 text have disappeared. This is particularly true of animal spirits since only two of her original nine are still remembered, including *baciwubwe* and *basokwe*. Other spirits have appeared in their place or have become more prominent than before, like *bamooba*, *cisongo* and *mweendajangule*. In contrast to the animal spirits they no longer represent the visual world of the bush but more abstract principles like knowledge (*mweendajangule*) or pain and suffering as represented by *mooba* and *cisongo*.

> *Mooba yee, mooba ndalipengela kuli ba Mooba*
> *yandaanda mpeyo ndalipengela*
> Chorus: *yandaanda mpeyo ndalipengela kuli mooba ye*
> *Mooba*, oh, *mooba*, I am troubled by *mooba*
> I am frozen by the cold, I am troubled
> Chorus: I am frozen by the cold, I am troubled by *mooba*
>
> *Mooba mooba ndipe mayamba mooba*
> *yandaanda mpeyo ndalipengela mooba*
> Chorus: *yandaanda mpeyo ndalipengela kuli mooba ye*
> *Mooba*, *mooba*, walking around because of *mooba*
> I am frozen by the cold, I am troubled by *mooba*
> Chorus: I am frozen by the cold, I am troubled by *mooba*

And in one of the texts for *cisongo* the singer complains:

> *Chilachisa mwana abaama – yeeye*
> *chilachisa mwana baama*
> Chorus: *yee ye mwana – bama yeeye*
> It hurts, child of my mother, yeeye
> It hurts, child of my mother,
> Chorus: yeeyee child, mother, yeeyee

While this noticeable change in the spirit world may be linked with the ongoing domestication of the bush, which has extinguished most of the more dangerous animals, the image of the wild has not lost its possible menace and ambivalence. This is captured in the endless verses of pain and suffering addressing the invisible spirits of the bush embodied in *bamooba* and *cisongo*. But apart from these highly emotional encounters, other spirits, like *baciwubwe* and *mweendajangule* symbolize the unlimited resources of the wild, its richness and proliferation, abundance and fertility . *Baciwubwe* (the hippo), one of the most popular spirits at present, represents quite well the shift in the interaction with the forces of nature . A symbol of physical strength (*nguzu*) and fertility due to its many offspring and its intimate connection with deep water, *baciwubwe* embodies the promise as well as the continuing danger of the wild. Its powers are limitless since it transgresses all boundaries as animal of the water and the land. This exceptional character allows for it to become a symbol of empowerment and protection.

Baama tuli bamu meenda – yee, baama tuli bamu meenda – yee
tuli bamu meenda, tuli bamu mayoba
Mother, we are of the water, yeeye, Mother, we are of the water, yeeye
we are of the water, we are of the clouds.

Kuchipongwe tukanywe meenda,
kuchipongwe tukanywe meenda basaa,
kuchipongwe tukanywe malowa
We go to Cipongwe and drink water
We go to Cipongwe, friends, and drink water
We go to Cipongwe and drink blood.[23]

It is this mixture of water and blood which is given to *masabe* initiates on the first day of the final healing ceremony. Both substances play important ritual roles because they are considered to infer new strengths to the possessed and bless them with fertility.

Equally exceptional as *baciwubwe* is *mweendajangule* who has only one arm, one leg and one eye. He was already mentioned by Jacottet in 1899 as a mythical figure among the Subiya in a text from 1895. At present, *mweendajangule* is one of the most influential spirits, closely associated with the bush and with the mountains, where he lures people after sundown. He has become a synonym for medical knowledge of the bush and for the control of natural resources. His power makes him exceedingly dangerous which is acknowledged by assigning him the colour red which in contrast to white and black symbolizes ambiguity, unpredictability and imminent danger. Despite this negative side his medicinal knowledge of plants – symbolized in the hoe for planting – is eagerly sought after.

Aka kaamba kamba kangu me, aka kaamba
aka kaamba, aka kaamba nkamuchelo
This little hoe, this little hoe is mine, this little hoe
This little hoe, this little hoe is to dig medicine

Mweendajangule zuba lyaaya tukasye michelo
Mweendajangule zuba lyaaya kobweza kaamba
Mweendajangula, the sun is going down, let us go to dig medicine
Mweendajangula, the sun is going down, take your little hoe

Mweendajangule yeee, yee, mweendajangule yee yee
mweendajangule imusamu wachoolunengu chaachaacha
Mweendajangule, yeeyee, yeeyee,
mweendajangule the medicine which brings luck, is *chachacha*.

The role of *mweendajangule* as purveyor of medicine, tapping the resources of the bush, puts him in a central position to control the health of the people. It gives him power by extension over the reproduction of the community. He is thus an ideal mediator between the wild on the one hand and the people on the other. And as with *baciwubwe* his power transgresses all boundaries, since his half-sidedness puts him above ordinary categories (see Beidelmann 1986). Beidelman endows him tentatively with Promethean strength which as Prins (1980: 157) remarks 'makes men mighty but can also easily break them'.

These interesting shifts in the representation of the forces of nature are paralleled in the symbolic representation of society. Those spirits which represented the colonial state and the period of resettlement with its technological challenges are completely forgotten. Neither *indeki* nor *kanamenda* or *matingatinga* are danced any more or have been replaced by other spirits of the same genre which has happened e.g., among the category of stranger spirits. Instead of the *Makolekole, Mazulu* or *Mangoni* who played prominent roles in the earlier performances, spirits from the north and from the north-east (*Bakasai, Baluvale*) have taken over. They respond to the changed social relations in the Valley where northern groups have considerably engaged themselves economically.

The changes in the symbolic representation of locality are an impressive document of the processes of transformation which were characteristic of the social history of the Valley in the last thirty years. However, spirit pantheons are not simple reproductions of social relationships but are cultural and historical constructions which only to a certain extent are embedded in social relations. They also have the capability to transcend social reality, to open new frontiers and create worlds of their own. These may be ideal constructions where new values are created and new visions probed. A case in point is a 'new' spirit with an old name: *mangelo.* The *mangelo* who was described to me by a healer in Mweemba in 1990 lived in a closed symbiosis with *mweendajangule* who has become incorporated as equal partner. The new *mangelo* is visually differentiated from the older *mangelo* through the construction of a hut with two openings – one being covered with red cloth for *mweendajangule*, the other with white cloth for *mangelo*. Yet, despite their continuing 'autonomy' (*Eigenständigkeit*) which is visualized in the colour symbolism, they cooperate closely in fighting the witches which very often harm *masabe* healers and their believers during dances.

This form of synthesizing is even more elaborate in another new spirit called *mizimu* (ancestors) which up till recently did not exist in the *masabe* pantheon as well, but had a cult of its own. But that it is not a simple incorporation, like in the case of the *basangu*-takeover, is evident from its characteristics. The new *mizimu* has nothing in common with the *mizimu* of the ancestral cults which represent the continuity of the lineage. Instead the new *mizimu* links the past with the present. He was described to me as a composite group of spirits working together for the well-being of the people. First among them are *Monze* and *Lewanika* representing the powerful leaders of the past. Although *Monze* was judged and sentenced to prison, for challenging the colonial government by declaring himself paramount chief of all Tonga, he is still remembered as *Monze mupati,* or *Monze mukulu: Monze* the great. In his role as *mizimu,* he is credited with the allocation of a *masabe* spirit to *Malia* and *Askia,* two women who are helpers for *masabe* healers. *Lewanika,* the influential Lozi king, is ranked second to *Monze,* although considered to be a powerful counterpart. His duty is to protect the fields from witchcraft through his countermedicine, which suggests that he is considered to be a witch himself. Part of *mizimu* are also *Johnny* and *Micheleki,* two European doctors, who always wear spectacles when treating patients. They are assisted by *mweendajangule* whose outstanding herbal knowledge is once more confirmed, since it is he who searches out medicine for the doctors in the bush. While *Micheleki* and *Johnny* are responsible for male patients, *Betty* and *Rita* treat female patients, especially for infertility. They are two sisters from Zambia, who visit the healer at night and explain to him what to do with his patients the following morning.

The complexity of *mizimu* has reached a new stage in the *masabe* healers' endeavour to construct their local world. All important strands of the social and historical experience of the Tonga for more than a century are woven into an intriguing parable of ancestry. In this respect *mizimu* becomes a symbol of Tonga identity which is anchored in time and in space. Of particular importance is the subtle manipulation of values which is independent of empirical reality. The claim of Tonga superiority over *Lewanika* is upheld, his portrayal as a witch expresses the fear and admiration the Tonga must have felt towards him as well as their conviction that all (unlimited) power depends on witchcraft. The globalization of the local is expressed through the introduction of the two European doctors who cooperate with Zambian women, *Betty* and *Rita*, in the struggle to preserve the fertility of women. The doctors techno-medical capacity is complemented through the knowledge of African medicine which is represented through *mweendajangule*. We find here another repetition of the structural complementarity of *mangelo* and *mweendajangule*. *Mizimu* is thus a metaphor for the embeddedness of the Gwembe local world in global contexts. The experience of these different relations is interpreted as enriching and supportive for the benefit of the people. Local identity is neither portrayed as inferior nor as parochially local but as sovereign, tapping all available sources and resources and pulling them together for the good of the community.

Conclusion

One conclusion of my chapter is that cults of spirit mediumship and of affliction contribute equally in the construction and reproduction of locality but with very different accentuation. While *basangu* mediumship produces and reproduces locality through local subjects with local knowledge, *masabe* cults of affliction reflect primarily the 'locality-producing capabilities of larger scale social formation' (Appadurai 1993: 7), but subjects them to local knowledge and local identity. In a way both cults have the same intention and objective, namely to uphold and strengthen local identity, but articulate them from opposite perspectives and with different methods. While *basangu* cult leaders defend their local world by limiting outside influences, *masabe* cult leaders absorb and accumulate new ideas, objects and methods to empower themselves. While both are engaged in locality production, they differ in the way they cope with the situation when the conditions of the production of locality have changed (ibid: 9). It is here where *basangu* prophets have their greatest weakness, considering the different interest groups in the Valley and their identification or non-identification with modernity. Unlike the *basangu*, *masabe* healers support constant processes of incorporation and differentiation. These expansionist strategies and competitiveness guarantee them a considerable amount of success; their main competitors being at the moment a multitude of Christian churches, sects and cults who have entered the Valley since the 1960s. Their variety led to a bewildering complexity of groups with competing messages of 'salvation' and methods of eradicating evil. In contrast to the *masabe* cults quite a few churches exorcise demons and eradicate witchcraft through special witchfinders, but for competitive reasons they simultaneously provide healing rites for personal misfortune and illness. While this versatility explains their temporary success, their reference and dependence on Christian eschatological discourses limits their ability to explain the changing world around them in terms of Tonga cultural identity. It is this particular limitation which explains in my view the superiority of the possession cults to offer meaningful explanations for the social problems of the time. Through the transformation of alterity into identity which lies at the heart of the healing ritual, they order the disorder or the menacing bricolage of cultural flows into a known system of meaning which constantly renews and differentiates itself. One aspect of the fascination of spirit possession lies in this particular strength to wield opposite and sometimes chaotic experiences into metaphors of local power.

Acknowledgements

I would like to thank various friends and colleagues for their discussion and critique of this chapter. A first version was given in Satterthwaite during the tenth colloquium on African Religion and Ritual in 1994. Apart from these helpful discussions Birgit Meyer, Jean LaFontaine, Peter Probst, Matthew Schoffeleers and Roy Willis shared their time to suggest improvements. Enoch Syabbalo was a most competent and patient partner in the Gwembe Valley who fundamentally influenced my understanding of Tonga society. But most of all I have to thank Elizabeth Colson who not only gave inspiring advice but allowed me to look into and to use her fieldnotes for quotation which is a most generous gesture.

Notes

1 Fieldwork was undertaken between 1988 and 1990 and again in 1993 in the two southernmost chieftaincies of the Valley, Sinazongwe and Mweemba.
2 According to Colson the word *basangu* may be derived from *kusanguna* which means to initiate. It is important to note that the same term *basangu* applies to the spirits as well as to the medium. The *ba*-suffix refers to the word as plural.
3 Similar observations of scepticism were already made by Elizabeth Colson in 1977. I quote her unpublished fieldnotes according to the date of her recording.
4 Although this differentiation was given up some time ago by most scholars because of a feeling that there are no clear cut differentiations, I find the term for my case study still useful. I differentiate spirit mediumship from spirit possession in regard of the subject of communication between the spirits and the medium/healer. Collective problems, like lack of rain, the invasion of locusts or epidemic diseases are treated by spirit mediums through direct public interrogations by the spirits whereas individual problems like illness or infertility, are personally discussed with healers and remedied through public dances. Spirit possession is therefore oriented to the healing of the individual while spirit mediumship deals with public collective problems.
5 I am aware that Gupta and Ferguson contest vigorously the isomorphism of space, place and culture (1992: 7) which in a way is still the precondition of this chapter. But this difference relates rather to local variations than to theoretical disagreements.
6 Colson stresses that the Tonga only fairly recently considered themselves as one ethnic group but there is no other adequate term to describe them as a group of actors.
7 For nuanced disagreement on the question of centralization of power see Matthews (1976) and O'Brien (1983).
8 For a similar form of continuity see Feierman (1990).
9 I take this term from Schoffeleers (1979).
10 The neat distinction I have drawn here is not acknowledged everywhere. In the more complex situations of life relations between *basikatongo* and *basangu* often overlap and, depending on local conditions and individual personalities, can result in deep felt animosity.
11 In contrast to the *mhondoro* mediums in Zimbabwe with whom they otherwise have many things in common it appears, although more research is needed, that the *basangu* cannot cleanse the land from the violent deaths of war or other 'unjust deaths' caused by *ngozi*, an evil spirit (see Schmidt 1997).

12 There is a considerable debate about the 'scientific' in local knowledge. In my view it is important to contextualize this debate since African rain prophets are very much able to judge the
conditions for rain in scientific terms as well. But these are not the only parameters for them, but
have to be set in relation to the overall conditions in the neighbourhood.
13 'Control over healing is important also in shaping ideology. The power to name an illness, to
identify its causes, is also the power to say which elements in the experience of life lead to suffering' (Feierman 1985: 75).
14 In Mweemba area, however, several people insisted that the selection of *basangu* mediums was
transmitted through lineage membership. This would suggest a greater amount of institution-
alization and linkage with the chieftaincy.
15 I take this term from Appadurai (1993).
16 Cipito means a place of peace where it is forbidden to hunt.
17 I use this rather unusual term because among the Tonga social and political relations are not yet
sufficiently hierarchized in order to speak from a history from below.
18 List of spirits

	NAME	IDENTIFICATION
Animals	cisimbwe	mongoose ?
	sokwe	baboon
	ceta	monkey
	inzovu	elephant
	suntwe	hyena
	mwaba	jackal
	silue	leopard
	bashumbwa	lion
	ingulube	pig
	basikompoli	crane
	induba	lourie
	madada	duck
Tribal	makolekole	korekore
	manyai	banyai
	mangoni	ndebele
	mazulu	ndebele
	mazezulu	zezuru
	masala	sala
	mazungu	europeans
Statuses	mapolis	the police
	matingatinga	the carrier
	matobela injanji	railroad followers
	maregimenti	soldiers
	madyabantu	cannibal
Vehicles	citima	train
	incinga	bicycle
	indeki	aeroplane
	kanamenda	motor boat
	siacilipwe	bush clearer
	kandimu	boat engine
Symbolic Actions	impande	shell ornament
	ketani	chain- ox chain
	pumpi	pump
	guitar	guitar
	madance	European dancing
	cilimba	accordion
Spirits	bamooba	bush spirit
	madilidili	?
	mangelo	angel
	mauba	?

(Shortened version of Colson 1969: 83ff; in her fieldnotes she cites more spirits whose interpretation has to await another publication.)

19 It was spread presumably by the neighbouring Shona from where the name *mashave* may have originated.

20 According to Colson (1969: 85) informants denied that 'they learn new dances in the cities of Rhodesia' which seems to be a contradiction to my argument. However, I am not suggesting here that labour migrants brought these dances with them, but that they recounted their experiences to their wives and other kin. In this way did they become mediators of the strange world outside the Valley which was forbidden for female migrants during colonial times.

21 Prominent among them were spirits of emotion, of pain and suffering, but also more complex spirits like a (new) *mangelo* and *mizimu* (see description below). These examples could be multiplied, but for reasons of economy of space I concentrate here only on those spirits which played a direct role in the construction of locality.

22 These last three spirits are not newly created but existed already during the first half of this century in other regions of Zambia. What is 'new' about them is that they are integrated into the *masabe* spirit pantheon.

23 All songs which are quoted were recorded by Ute Luig between 1988 and 1990; their transcription and translation was done together with participants of the dances.

References

Appadurai, Arjun (1993) 'The production of locality'. ASA Fourth Decennial Conference. Oxford: unpub. manuscript.

—— (1995) 'The production of locality', *Counterworks: Managing the Diversity of Knowledge*, Richard Fardon (ed.), 204–25. London & New York: Routledge.

Arendt, Hannah (1986) 'Communicative power', *Power*, Stephen Lukes (ed.) Oxford: the Clarendon Press.

Arens, W. & Ivan Karp (1989) *Creativity of Power: Cosmology and Action in African Societies*, Washington & London: Smithsonian Institution Press.

Bachelard, Gaston (1957) *La poetique de l'éspace*, Paris: Presses Universitaires de France.

Beattie, J. & J. Middleton (eds) (1969) *Spirit Mediumship and Society in Africa*. London: Routledge & Kegan Paul.

van Beek, Walter E. A. & Pieteke M. Banga (1992) 'The Dogon and their trees', *Bush Base: Forest Farm: Culture, Environment and Development*, 57–75, Elisabeth Croll & David Parkin (eds), London & New York: Routledge.

Beidelman, Thomas O. (1986) *Moral Imagination in Kaguru Modes of Thought*, Bloomington, IN: Indiana University Press.

Colson, Elizabeth (1955, 1956 and 1982) Unpublished Fieldnotes.

—— (1960) *The Social Organization of the Gwembe Tonga*, Manchester: Manchester University Press

—— (1962) *The Plateau Tonga of Northern Rhodesia: Social and Religious Studies*. Manchester: Manchester University Press.

—— (1969) 'Spirit possession among the Tonga of Zambia', *Spirit Mediumship and Society in Africa*, J. Beattie & J. Middleton (eds), 69–103. London: Routledge & Kegan Paul.

—— (1971) *The Social Consequences of Resettlement*, Manchester: Manchester University Press.

—— (1977) 'A continuing dialogue: prophets and local shrines among the Tonga of Zambia', *Regional Cults*, Richard Werbner (ed.), 119–40, London & New York: Academic Press.

—— (1997) 'Places of power and shrines of the land', *The Making of African Landscapes*, Ute Luig & Achim von Oppen (eds.), 47–58, special issue of *Paideuma*, Mitteilungen zur Kulturkunde 43, Stuttgart: Franz Steiner Verlag.

Feierman, Steven (1985) 'Struggles for control: the social roots of health and healing in modern Africa', *African Studies Review* 28, 2/3: 73–147.

—— (1990) *Peasant Intellectuals: Anthropology and History in Tanzania*, Madison: University of Wisconsin Press.

Gupta, Akbar & James Ferguson (1992) 'Beyond "Culture": space, identity, and the politics of difference', *Cultural Anthropology* 7, 1: 6–23.

Jacottet, E. (1899) *Études sur les langues du Haut-Zambèze. Textes originaux*, 2 vol. Paris: Textes Soubiya.

Janzen, John M. (1992) *Ngoma: Discourses of Healing in Central and Southern Africa*, Berkeley, CA: University of California Press.

Jaspan, M.A. (1953) *The Ila-Tonga of North Western Rhodesia*, London: Oxford University Press for the International African Institute.

Kramer, Fritz W. (1984) 'Notizen zur Ethnologie der passiones', *Ethnologie als Sozialwissenschaft*, by *Ernst W. Müller, René König et al.* (eds), 297–312, Opladen: Westdeutscher Verlag, Sonderheft der Kölner Zeitschrift für Soziologie und Sozialpsychologie vol. 26.

—— (1987) *Der rote Fes. Über Besessenheit und Kunst in Afrika*, Frankfurt: Athenäum.

Lancaster, Chet S. (1981) *The Goba of the Zambezi: Sex Roles, Economics and Change*, Norman: University of Oklahoma Press.

Lienhardt, Godfrey (1961) *Divinity and Experience: The Religion of the Dinka*. Oxford: Oxford University Press.

Luig, Ulrich (1997) *Conversion as a Social Process. A History of Missionary Christianity among the Valley Tonga, Zambia*. Münster: Lit-Verlag.

Luig, Ute (1993a) 'Gesellschaftliche Entwicklung und ihre individuelle Verarbeitung in den affliktiven Besessenheitskulten der Tonga', *Tribus* 42: 109–20.

——(1993b) 'Besessenheitsrituale als historische Charta: Die Verarbeitung europäischer Einflüsse in sambianischen Besessenheitskulten', *Paideuma, Mitteilungen zur Kulturkunde* 39: 343–56.

——(1995a) 'Naturaneignung als symbolischer Prozeß in afrikanischen Gesellschaften', *Naturaneignung in Afrika als sozialer und symbolischer Prozeß*, 29–50, Ute Luig and Achim von Oppen (eds), Berlin: Das Arabische Buch.

——(1995b) 'Gender Relations and Commercialization in African Possession Cults', *Gender and Identities in Africa*, 33–50, G. Ludwar-Ene and M. Reh (eds), Münster: Lit-Verlag.

——(1996) 'Wanderarbeiter als Helden: Zwischen kolonialer Entfremdung und lokaler Selbstvergewisserung', *Historische Anthropologie 3, Jg. 4, S.359–82*, Ute Luig & Heide Wunder (eds). Köln: Böhlau Verlag.

Luig, Ute & Achim von Oppen (eds) (1995) 'Einleitung: Zur Vergesellschaftung von Natur in Afrika', *Naturaneignung in Afrika als sozialer und symbolischer Prozeß*, 29–50, Berlin: Das Arabische Buch.

Maddox, Gregory, James Giblin & Isaria N. Kimambo (eds) (1996) *Custodians of the Land. Ecology and Culture in the History of Tanzania*, London: James Currey.

Matthews, Timothy Ian (1976) 'The historical tradition of the peoples of the Gwembe Valley, Middle Zambezi', unpublished PhD Thesis, School of Oriental and African Studies, University of London.

O'Brien, D. (1983) 'Chiefs of rain – chiefs of ruling: a reinterpretation of pre-colonial Tonga (Zambia) Social and Political Structure', *Africa* 53: 23–41.

Okoye, Ikemefuna Stanley (1997) 'History, æsthetics and the political in Igbo spatial heterotopias', *The Making of African Landscapes*, Ute Luig & Achim von Oppen (eds), 75–91, special issue of *Paideuma, Mitteilungen zur Kulturkunde 43*, Stuttgart: Franz Steiner Verlag.

Prins, Gwyn (1980) *The Hidden Hippopotamus. Reappraisal in African History: The Early Colonial Experience in Western Zambia*, Cambridge: Cambridge University Press.

Schieffelin, Edward L. (1985) 'Performance and the cultural construction of reality', *American Ethnologist* 12, 4: 707–24.

Schmidt, Heike (1997) 'Healing the wounds of war: memories of violence and the making of history in Zimbabwe's most recent past', *Journal of Southern African Studies* 23, 2: 301–10.

Schoffeleers, J.M. (1979) *Guardians of the Land*, Gwelo: Mambo Press.

Scudder, Thayer (1962) *The Ecology of the Gwembe Tonga*, Manchester: Manchester University Press.

Smith, E.W. and A. M. Dale (1920) *The Ila-speaking Peoples of Northern Rhodesia*, London: Macmillan.

Turner, Victor (1968) *The Drums of Affliction: A Study of Religious Process among the Ndembu of Zambia*, Oxford: The Clarendon Press.

10

Spirit Possession & the Symbolic Construction of Swahili Society

Linda L. Giles

Although scholarly literature on spirit possession has tended to adopt a functional approach that explains individual involvement in sociological and psychological terms, an increasing number of studies have begun to focus on possession as a culturally-constructed symbolic medium that must be related to the wider society and its systems of meaning (e.g., Lambek 1981; Boddy 1989; Sharp 1993; Kapferer 1983; Giles 1987, 1989b). This relationship holds true even in societies where possession affects only a small number out of the total population or is predominantly associated with certain distinctive categories within it. Many studies have noted that possession is frequently associated with women, lower class members of stratified societies, and other low status, subordinate, or deviant groups and individuals. In such cases, possession has often been explained as an expression of, as well as a compensatory mechanism for, marginality, providing a therapeutic outlet for psychological frustration, a means to command attention, redress grievances and gain material benefits, and an alternative way to achieve some measure of status and power (e.g., Kennedy 1967; Ferchiou 1972; Crapanzano 1973; and various works by I. M. Lewis 1966, 1971, 1986).[1] Although possession may indeed serve these functions for various individuals and subgroups in certain circumstances, it cannot be explained adequately in these terms, as Michael Lambek pointed out in his 1981 case study. One must also address the symbolic medium which is employed and hence the question of meaning rather than merely that of function (Lambek 1981: 69).

The analysis of spirit possession as a symbolic system conveying meaning has proved to be very fruitful, opening up new interpretations of possession and its role in society as well as of the social and cultural system of which it is a part. Edwin Ardener (1972), for instance, finds that female possession among the Bakweri of Cameroon reveals alternative cognitive models which run counter to dominant male models of society. A number of other scholars have stressed possessive events as communicative texts and applied various techniques of textual and semiotic analysis. Many also add the critical point that the idiom of these texts – possession, is culturally constructed (e.g., Crapanzano 1977; Zempleni 1977). Several scholars, including myself, have pursued this point further by adopting Clifford Geertz's

142

seminal concept of the 'cultural text' (1972). Cultural texts are 'written' and 'read' by the society concerned; they are stories that the society tells itself about itself. Since the 'language' employed is highly symbolic, it can associate many different levels of meaning and accommodate many different personal interpretations. Moreover, it can reflect non-avowed aspects of society which could not be stated through other means and actively restructure them into a metaphorical dramatic form. This form facilitates the affirmation of models of society that run counter to formal ideological statements without requiring public recognition.

Spirit possession provides an ideal medium for the creation of cultural texts. It creates powerful metaphorical dramas that are enacted in human form but attributed to the spirit world. The human actors are not actors in the conventional sense but a stage – the human body becomes a vehicle for the spirits to communicate with and interact with the human world. Some scholars have noted that the human vehicles often occupy a structural position that makes them culturally appropriate to play this role (Nicholas 1972; Lambek 1981; Kapferer 1983; Giles 1987). Hence participation in spirit possession can be seen as a positive social role rather than an indication of their social deprivation and possession itself as an 'integral part of the whole culture' rather than an isolated 'subculture' (Lambek 1981: 63).

Textual analyses of possession often interpret the meaning of the texts in terms of the personal lives of those possessed, including specific interpersonal relations or the relation of the individual psyche to the expectations of society. Those that pursue Geertz's notion of the cultural text as a self-reflective commentary on the sociocultural structure still tend to focus more on social relations than on wider systems of cultural meaning. In addition, many analyses try to isolate a specific message or set of messages as the core meaning encoded in the possession texts of a specific society. In line with Geertz's own analysis of cultural texts, this message is often identified as the dialectic expression of basic societal, cultural, or cosmic contradictions (Lambek 1981; Kapferer 1983; Boddy 1989). Although Boddy's (1989) analysis of female possession in a Sudanese village and Kapferer's (1983) analysis of Sinhalese possession in Sri Lanka still follow these general patterns, they begin to go beyond them by also relating possession texts to more diverse and comprehensive aspects of the cultural system. Thus whereas Boddy sees possession as expressing the conflict between village women's experiences and their self-image as defined by the gender ideals of their society, she relates this to the wider symbolic dialectic of enclosure and openness which permeates both internal village culture and their historical consciousness of relations with powerful outsiders. The issue of historical consciousness is also addressed by Kapferer in a more inclusive manner. Although he identifies the core symbolic meaning of Sinhalese possession as a cosmic dialectic between the forces of destruction and those of divine order, he notes that the symbolic organization 'reflect(s) Sinhalese historical consciousness and the diverse influences that have acted upon the forming of this consciousness,' bringing participants 'into vital contact with a specific cultural conception of their history' (1983: 12).

My own study of spirit possession in the Swahili coastal area of East Africa suggests that the symbolic expression of cultural identity and historical consciousness lies at the very heart of possession. I propose that Swahili possession texts do not merely express a limited number of basic cultural themes and contradictions but a

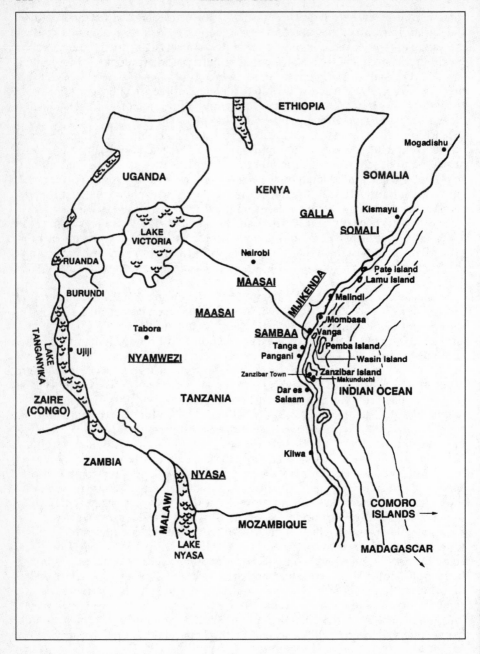

Figure 10.1 East Africa and the Swahili coast: places and peoples noted in text (ethnic groups underlined).

whole range of diverse and often contradictory elements which have entered into the cultural and historical construction of Swahili coastal society. This chapter will demonstrate how Swahili coastal history and identity are represented in the spirit world and the symbolic realms of specific spirit types.

An overview of the Swahili coast

The Swahili coast is an area of considerable cultural and historical complexity. In geographic terms, it refers to the narrow coastal strip of East Africa where a distinctive language and culture developed that represented a dynamic synthesis of 'foreign' and indigenous African elements. This synthesis resulted from a long history of maritime trade and urban settlement in prolonged contact with the wider world of the Indian Ocean, especially the Persian Gulf and later the southern Arabian peninsula. Whereas some scholars prefer to restrict the term 'Swahili' to the geographical area and the language, it is also applied to the distinctive coastal Islamic culture which came to characterize the indigenous Swahili-speaking peoples. Although there has been considerable debate about the use of the term 'Swahili' to refer to the coastal people themselves, 'a Swahili' can best be defined in the manner of Prins (1967), Eastman (1971) and others who combine the geographical, linguistic and cultural aspects of the term to refer to a person from the East African coastal area who speaks Swahili as a first language and who participates in the distinctive Muslim syncretic culture of the area. (See Figure 10.1.)

Much of the problem of defining the Swahili as a people results from the fact that they are by definition a composite group of diverse origins. Whereas Marc Swartz (1979: 32) has aptly pointed out that this is true to some degree of all ethnic groups, in the case of the Swahili it is the *key* element in their definition. Hence Nurse and Spear have pointed out that the Swahili are not so much a people as 'a historical phenomenon' (1985: 96).[2]

The early history of the Swahili coast is a topic of considerable interest and debate among historians, linguists and archaeologists. The Swahili language is clearly an African Bantu language with considerable Arabic (and some other foreign) vocabulary. Linguists view Swahili as one of the five languages in the Sabaki subgroup of Northeast Coastal Bantu. The Sabaki languages are spoken in the coastal and riverain areas of southern Somalia, the Kenyan coast, eastern Tanzania, and the Comoro Islands, and include Mijikenda (spoken by nine Mijikenda groups who currently occupy the Swahili hinterland), Pokomo and Elwana (spoken in the Tana river valley of northern Kenya) and Comorian in addition to Swahili. Nurse and Spear suggest that the early Sabaki speakers were mixed Bantu-speaking agriculturalists and fishermen and Cushitic-speaking pastoralists, who had contact with sailors and traders from the Persian Gulf. The ancestors of the Swahili and Comorians became increasingly involved in maritime fishing and trading and established settlements and towns throughout the Swahili coastal area (Nurse & Spear 1985). Pouwels (1987) distinguishes a second period in early Swahili history from 1100 to 1300, marked by increased trade with Middle Eastern and Indian merchants, growing wealth as evidenced by imported trade goods, 'stone' buildings, expanding urbanization, and most importantly, Islamization. During this time, powerful city

states under Arab ruling clans from Yemen and Oman developed in Mogadishu,
Kilwa and Pate, and by the fourteenth and fifteenth centuries the Swahili coast
entered its 'Golden Age' with a number of 'Shirazi' city states throughout the coast
enjoying a peak period of affluence and refinement, with multi-storeyed coral
houses and large quantities of imported trade goods. By the sixteenth century, the
towns showed considerable economic and political stratification. The dominant
ideological feature of Swahili society at this time was the concept of *uungwana*, the
cultured life style of the freeborn Muslim town dweller. Scholars (Allen 1974: 134,
1981a: 222–3; Pouwels 1987: 72) have recently pointed out that *uungwana* was not
equivalent to Arab culture but to the distinctive local coastal culture which had
evolved among long-established elite lineages in Swahili towns. This included distinctive forms of architecture, material wealth, dress, linguistic arts (using local
dialects of Swahili) and regalia. Both Pouwels (1987) and Nurse and Spear (1985)
also point to a very significant non-Islamic African contribution in the realm of religious belief and ritual, including propitiation of ancestors and spirits which control
harvests and the general well-being of the people as well as rainmaking, and systems of medicine, healing, divination, and so on.

In the sixteenth century, Swahili coastal development entered a period of major
disruption due to the arrival of the Portuguese (who attacked, sacked and sometimes ruled various Swahili cities), the invasion of the pastoral Galla under Somali
pressure from the north, and the depredations of the mysterious Zimba 'cannibals'
from the south. The Portuguese were finally expelled by the Yarubi Omani dynasty
in the eighteenth century, which initiated a period of Omani influence. At first
many of the older ruling families of the coast successfully resisted control by the
Omani newcomers, and even the Omani governors of Mombasa declared themselves independent when the Yarubi dynasty in Oman was displaced by the
Busaidi. The Busaidi, however, controlled Zanzibar and Kilwa and began to steadily
increase their control over the coast in the nineteenth century. The Busaidi Sultan
Sayyid Said further consolidated his rule by moving his court from Muscat to Zanzibar in 1840, initiating a new period of Zanzibari ascendancy that still colours present-day conceptions of Swahili culture and society. Arab cultural influence gained
unprecedented dominance and the coastal economy flourished. By the end of the
nineteenth century the commonly-used Swahili word for the cultured way of life
changed from 'uungwana' to 'ustaarabu,' literally meaning 'Arabness' (Allen 1981a:
222; Pouwels 1987: 128). Moreover, the increased prosperity of the coast drew a new
wave of non-Omani Arab immigrants, including many Islamic scholars and *sharif*
(descendants of the prophet) who brought renewed links with the Middle Eastern
literate Islamic tradition. At the same time, however, contact with the African interior increased as Arab and Swahili traders established direct caravan routes through
Maasai territory into Central Africa, where they obtained valuable supplies of ivory
and slaves. Although many slaves were exported, others remained in the coastal
area where they were assimilated into Swahili society. The demand for slave labour
increased further with the development of agricultural plantations in some coastal
areas, including Arab clove plantations in Zanzibar and Pemba. Hence, non-Islamic
African elements continued to be assimilated into Swahili culture. (See Cooper 1977,
1980; Strobel 1979; and Mirza and Strobel 1989 on slaves and slavery in Swahili
coastal society.)

By the end of the nineteenth century Zanzibari and Arab/Swahili power had already begun to decline, largely due to European interference. The British interfered with the slave trade and Britain and Germany began to compete for influence in the area, eventually resulting in the British colony of Kenya, the German colony of Tanganyika, and a British protectorate over Zanzibar (including Pemba). The Germans and the British fought a bush war in East Africa during World War One and Tanganyika came under British rule after the German defeat. Whereas the imposition of German rule had been brutal and traumatic, Arab and Swahili influence was undercut more under British rule, which not only favoured Westernized Christians over coastal Muslims but also exacerbated ethnic cleavages among the population. The British colonial period officially ended during the 1960s when Kenya, Tanganyika and Zanzibar became independent. Zanzibar gained independence under the Busaidi Sultan as constitutional monarch but one month later his government was overthrown. The new Zanzibari government soon entered into a merger with Tanganyika to form Tanzania but kept considerable autonomy.

In these complex historical circumstances, the definition of Swahili ethnicity and cultural identity is contested not only by scholars but by the Swahili themselves. The Swahili have always tended to differentiate themselves from their non-Muslim neighbours, contrasting the cosmopolitan 'civilized' culture of the trading ports with the 'uncivilized' lifestyle of the African farmers and pastoralists. During the period of extensive Omani Arab influence, this distinction became even more pronounced as Swahili society emphasized Arab cultural and ethnic identity. The non-Islamic, African, rural and slave components of Swahili coastal culture have thus often remained unarticulated or at least devalued in Swahili ideology. They are recognized, however, in symbolic form in Swahili possession cults, wherein one finds elaborate expression of Swahili identity in all of its historical and cultural complexity.[3]

Field sites and data collection

I conducted fieldwork on possession cults in the Swahili coastal area for three years from 1982 to 1984. The length of the research period allowed me to combine intensive field study with a regional overview which sampled the diversity of spirit beliefs and practices found in this area. Research was conducted at a number of different field sites in the coastal area of Kenya and Tanzania. My major field site was the urban port city of Mombasa in Kenya, which was originally one of the many 'Shirazi' city states that developed during the 'Golden Age' of the Swahili coast. Other primary and secondary sites included small towns and rural villages that were formerly Shirazi settlements in the Kenyan-Tanzanian border region (Vanga and Wasin), the area south of Pangani in northern Tanzania, the Makunduchi area in the southeastern corner of Zanzibar Island, and the island of Pemba (especially in the Wete and Chake Chake areas), as well as the more recent port cities of Tanga (established as a German colonial centre in northern Tanzania) and Zanzibar (which developed under the Busaidi Omani Sultans). Field data were gathered through participant observation in a number of possession cult ceremonies as well as formal and informal interviews with cult members and leaders, other spirit mediums and practitioners (including Muslim healers and diviners who use more religiously sanctioned methods), local community historians, and other members of the general populace.

The Swahili spirit world

The spirit world, in accord with the historical worldview of Swahili coastal society, is divided along two key dimensions. The first of these contrasts Muslim (or *kiislamu*) spirits with pagan (*kafiri*) spirits, which are also frequently described as 'kishenzi,' i.e., 'uncivilized', thus shifting the discourse slightly to focus on standards of uncivilized and civilized behaviour rather than on religions *per se*. ('*Ki-*' is the Swahili class marker that denotes manner, hence spirits are often typed using this prefix.) The second dimension contrasts the spirits of the East African interior (*bara*) with those of the coast (*pwani*). Contrary to the spirit categorizations of neighbouring non-Swahili peoples, these two dimensions only partially coincide. All inland spirits are described as *kafiri* and *kishenzi*, but coastal spirits are diverse in character: whereas some are civilized Muslims, others are uncivilized pagans; some are Muslim but nonetheless *behave* like uncivilized pagans ('*kiislamu lakini kishenzi*') and many are explicitly categorized as hybrid spirits with a dualistic nature – part *pwani* and part *bara*.

Within these broad oppositions, spirits are further differentiated into more specific categories that are the focus of particular cults. I believe that these categories can be understood as ethnic groups within the spirit world. Many spirit categories, in fact, are specifically identified with human ethnic groups, including Arabs, Comorian-Malagasy, Pemba,[4] Segeju, Mijikenda, Sambaa, Maasai, Nyamwezi and more generalized categories such as Congolese, Nyasa and Europeans.[5] I view many of these spirit groups as representing Swahili conceptualizations of various peoples who have impinged upon Swahili experience throughout their history. In this way Swahili society constructs the image of the other, but in a dialectical process also constructs the image of the self through opposition.[6] Hence many characteristics emphasized in spirit portrayals are those that differentiate the group in question most dramatically from Swahili conceptions of themselves. However, these spirit categories should not be viewed only as outside groups, for most spirit types also represent the diverse socio-cultural components that have entered into the formation of Swahili society itself, not only the diverse ethnic origins of the Swahili population (both as specific individuals and as a group) but also the various and often conflicting components of the syncretic Swahili culture. What emerges is a symbolic construction of the Swahili socio-cultural universe. This universe includes both external and internal aspects, and moreover, displays that the boundary between the external and the internal is not just imprecise but by definition extremely permeable. Swahili coastal society as portrayed in the texts of the spirit world is inclusive rather than exclusive.

The best quantitative data that I collected on distribution of spirit types is from Mombasa. By far the most prevalent types of spirits found are *kiarabu* (Arab) and *kipemba* (spirits from the off-shore island of Pemba). Out of 41 individuals surveyed in four different cult associations (*kilinge*), I found 35 with *kiarabu* spirits (a category which tends to include Somali as well as Arab spirits), with the total number of *kiarabu/kisomali* spirits being at least 42. The figures for *kipemba* spirits are similar, with 32 to 36 cult members having a total of at least 46 spirits.[7] If someone has only one possessive spirit, it is most likely to be a *kiarabu* spirit, but it is far more common to have both, since one type is generally followed by the other. There is also a marked tendency for people in the upper ranks of the cult hierarchy to have more *kipemba* spirits than *kiarabu*.[8]

Whereas the *kiarabu/kipemba* diad forms the basic spirit core throughout the Swahili area, other spirits may be added. In Mombasa, Mijikenda (*kinyika*) and Maasai (*kimasai*) spirits appear as a substantial minority. Other spirit types appear in Mombasa as scattered cases, often among elderly cult members, and seem to represent traces of spirit traditions that were more prevalent in the past.[9] In other field sites, different spirit types may become significant, including Malagasy/Comorian (*kibuki*) and Ethiopian (*Habeshia*) spirits in Zanzibar town,[10] Nyamwezi (*kinyamwezi*) and Sambaa (*kisambaa*) spirits in Pemba, and a unique hybrid type of Maasai spirit (*Jini Bara kiswahili*) in Tanga that will be discussed below.

Swahili spirit ceremonies are divided into two contrasting sections – the *dhikri* and the *ngoma*, which forcefully express the dualistic oppositions within the Swahili world view. The *dhikri* focuses on Middle Eastern, Islamic, and urban socio-cultural elements whereas the *ngoma* focuses on an opposing symbolic set of non-Islamic African socio-cultural elements. The *dhikri* consists of popular Islamic ritual forms (either the Sufi-inspired *dhikri*[11] itself or the *maulidi*[12]) in contrast to the *ngoma* which utilizes more indigenous African forms of dancing and instrumentation that are inappropriate to Islamic ceremonies. The *dhikri* utilizes vocal chants praising Allah and the Prophet or, if the *maulidi* form is used, religious songs accompanied by the tambourine (*tari*), one of the few instruments permitted in popular Islamic ritual.[13] The *ngoma* uses songs with non-Islamic themes, puts much more emphasis on instrumental music, and utilizes instruments that are not permitted in popular Islamic ritual – especially the drums and rattles typical of indigenous African music. Whereas the predominant language utilized in the *dhikri* is Arabic (which suits both its Islamic and Middle Eastern character), Arabic is never used in the *ngoma*. (See Table 1.) The spirits that require *dhikri* ceremonies are Muslim spirits from the Middle East and North Africa, who are lumped together as 'kiarabu' spirits, even if they are not specifically Arab in ethnicity. The spirits that require non-Islamic *ngoma*, however, are varied. Here one finds the pagan *bara* spirits of the interior,[14] as expected, but also a number of coastal spirits – not only the Mijikenda and other

TABLE 1 *Ceremonial oppositions*

	Dhikri	Ngoma
ceremonial style	Islamic: *dhikri*, *maulidi, tari*	most African styles of music & dance
instrumentation	Islamic: none or tambourine	non-Islamic: drums, rattles, gong, *zumari*
main language	Arabic	Swahili & other
spirit types	Muslim 'kiarabu'	*bara*, Mijikenda, non-Muslim coastal, *kipemba*

non-Swahili coastal spirits but also the *kipemba*. Moreover, the *kipemba* spirits do not just appear in the *ngoma*, they dominate it, especially in Mombasa, where approximately 70 per cent of the *ngoma* is devoted to *kipemba* spirits. This is very interesting because the *kipemba* are the only spirits that cult participants define as Swahili in nature ('*kiswahili*'). Hence whereas the Swahili people are Muslim and have historically emphasized their Middle Eastern ancestry, Swahili spirits require non-Islamic African-style ceremonies which are symbolically opposed to those held for Muslim Middle Eastern spirits. (See Table 1 above.)

The ideological superiority of the Islamic/Middle Eastern/upper-class element in Swahili culture is given some symbolic recognition in the fact that the *dhikri* must always precede the *ngoma*. Nonetheless, the *ngoma* clearly does not assume secondary importance in cult practice. In fact, much more time is usually devoted to the *ngoma* than the *dhikri*, and the non-Islamic *ngoma*, especially the *kipemba* section, shows a very high degree of ritual elaboration which equals, and in many ways surpasses, that of the Islamic *dhikri*.

The symbolic realm of key spirit types

Let us now look in more detail at the symbolic realm represented by some of the key spirit types.

Kiarabu *spirits*

The symbolic realm associated with the *kiarabu* spirits represents the wider world of the Indian Ocean that has long been associated with the Swahili coastal towns. All *kiarabu* spirits are hence categorized as *pwani* (coastal) and are often more specifically associated with the sea. They are strongly associated with the Arabic language; and hence, in addition to utilizing ceremonies conducted in Arabic, they usually speak Arabic themselves whenever they possess their mounts. Although most Swahili can recite Arabic religious texts and phrases, few possess any conversational ability in the language. Arabic speech is thus diagnostic of possession by *kiarabu* spirits, and observers (including one professional linguist)[15] note that possessed individuals demonstrate a competence with the language that they do not possess under normal circumstances.

Kiarabu spirits are generally ascribed a very dominant position in the spirit hierarchy, which seems directly to express the ideological hegemony and political power of Muslims of Middle Eastern descent in Swahili society, particularly during the historical period of Omani ascendancy, as well as the religious dominance of Islam.[16] *Kiarabu* spirits can be quite powerful and thus can be valuable allies, but they can also be quite dangerous – hence their power has a negative as well as a positive aspect.[17] Even the most esteemed Islamic types are hard task masters who punish their human associates severely when they displease them.

The danger of *kiarabu* spirits is even more pronounced in the case of true *jini*, opportunistic types of spirits that are cultivated by individuals in their own homes outside of possession cult contexts. Whereas these spirits can bring their human partners riches and personal gain, they will feed off the blood of family members if they are not given appropriate sacrifices. These *jini* may express the ultimate degree

TABLE 2 Kiarabu, kinyika & bara *spirit traits*

	kiarabu	*kinyika*	*bara*
character	civilized	uncivilized	uncivilized
domain	sea (and coast/town)	hinterland *nyika* ('bush')	interior *nyika*
religious nature	Muslim	pagan	pagan
ritual purity	pure	polluting	polluting
power	much	little	little but some fierce & strong fighters

of danger and betrayal that can result from bringing powerful Middle Eastern outsiders into Swahili coastal society and striking bargains with them.

Most *kiarabu* spirits exhibit the sophistication and refinement associated with the
cosmopolitan world of the urban elite, emphasizing imported, manufactured and
store-bought items and a great concern with physical and ritual purity. (See Table 2.)
Their colour association is white. During the *dhikri*, cult members possessed by
kiarabu spirits wear white clothes, prayerbeads and Quranic amulets and show a
great fondness for rosewater and perfume. Although there is some variation in
incense, *kiarabu* spirits are most often associated with *udi* (rosewood).

Kiarabu food and drink preferences are also quite revealing. They frequently ask
for *kombe*, a medicinal drink made from the ink of Quranic texts. Their most characteristic offering plate is the *upatu*, a small silver tray containing substances associated with the consumption of betel nut. They may also be given a larger metal tray
(*sinia*) containing imported nuts and fruits together with popped millet, cube sugar,
and sweet delicacies such as *halua*, followed by coffee served in the Arab style.[18] (See
Table 4, page 153.)

The term '*kiarabu*' is extended to include all spirits that require Islamic ceremonies
of *dhikri*, *tari*, or *maulidi* or that show Middle Eastern characteristics, thus underscoring the two basic associations which underlie this category. By extension of the
Middle Eastern criteria, cult informants will classify a number of spirits from north-
east Africa as '*kiarabu*.' These spirits represent the various peoples from this region
who have influenced or otherwise made a lasting impression on the Swahili – the
Somali, the Galla, the 'Nubian' slaves and soldiers brought to East Africa by the
Egyptians and the Omani Busaidi and the Ethiopian slaves and concubines valued
throughout the Islamic world and brought into the harems of the Zanzibar court.
There are even vague references to Bedouin nomads (*bedui*). These spirit types,
however, occupy a rather ambiguous position in the classification system which
varies according to location and historical period. At present, only the Somali spirits are portrayed as typical *kiarabu* spirits with an Islamic character, especially in
Mombasa spirit cults where they are commonly found. Hence, whereas Somali spirits are often referred to by the more generic designation of '*kiarabu*' spirits, the other
spirit types in this group are always designated more specifically as, for example,

TABLE 3 Kiarabu, kipemba & bara *spirit traits, Chart 1*

	kiarabu	*kipemba*	*bara*
ethnicity	Arab	Swahili, native	non-Swahili African
main language	Arabic	Swahili	various African languages
character	civilized	unique, includes 'uncivilized' elements, syncretic	uncivilized
domain	sea (& coast/ town)	coast (natural features)	interior *nyika*
religious nature	Muslim	mostly pagan	pagan
ritual purity	pure	ambiguous, with many non-Islamic elements; *rubamba* subtype: polluting	polluting
power	much	much	little but some fierce & strong fighters
ceremonial style	Islamic	non-Islamic *ngoma*	non-Islamic *ngoma*
themes	Islamic supernatural: Quran	non-Islamic supernatural: *panga*, medicine bag (*mkoba*), witchcraft	natural world, physical strength & aggression
	Arab cultural traits	distinctive Swahili cultural traits	distinctive non-Swahili cultural traits
	urban environment	natural coastal environment, fields/fish, communal welfare fertility	interior bush, wilderness

TABLE 4 Kiarabu, kipemba & bara *spirit traits, Chart 2*

	kiarabu	*kipemba*	*bara*
colour	white	tri-colour: red, white & black	black or red
instruments	none or tambourine	'Swahili': *zumari* (oboe), *upatu* (gong), & drums; may have other percussion	drums may have gong & rattle
dance style	orchestrated, *dhikri*	orchestrated, African-style	unorchestrated
costume	white cloth	tri-colour cloths	black cloth,
	white turban	tri-colour braid turban, tri-colour shirt & trousers	red cloth for *kimasai* types bells
regalia	Quranic amulets, prayerbeads	fly whisks, 'Shirazi' items: e.g., seats, drums, canopies	fly whisks (*mibwisho*)
medicines	rosewater, *kombe*	infusions of local plants & roots: *vuo*	
scent	sweet-smelling (rosewater, perfume)	sweet-smelling (flowers), *rubamba* subtype foul-smelling	foul-smelling
primary incenses/ fumigation	imported incense, mostly *udi*	combination of imported incense: *udi*, *ubani* (*kinyika*), with focus on *uvumba*	bush plants (*mafusho*)
offering plates	refined, often sweet; more foreign cosmopolitan; metal tray; coffee	coastal: sweet, semi-refined some foreign cosmopolitan items; coastal fruits & flowers raw eggs; wooden tray	staples: agricultural & pastoral beer, repugnant & impure foods

kigala or *kinubi*. Moreover, they have distinctive cult requirements that focus on the non-Arab and non-Islamic aspects of their identity, often associating them more with *bara* rather than *kiarabu* spirits, or, in the case of the *Habeshia*, placing them in their own unique realm (see below). Even the Somali spirits in Mombasa cults are sometimes given their own section of the Islamic ceremony after the *dhikri* proper, when they reveal their own special characteristics: a preference for the *tari* ritual form utilizing tambourines, melodic songs that are said to be in the Somali language, orchestrated dance movements and an excitable nature demonstrated by frequent verbal exclamations and a concluding volley of rapid chattering speech.

Bara *spirits*

The *kiarabu* symbolic universe is totally opposed by that of the *bara* spirits, representing the non-Swahili world of the African interior. The *bara* world is the epitome of 'the other' – wild, uncivilized, pagan; not only dangerous but also physically and ritually polluting. *Bara* spirits are almost always categorized as extremely dirty spirits. Cult members possessed by such spirits do not wash themselves during their initiation ceremonies. The spirits enjoy ill-smelling items and often engage in religiously polluting behaviour – eating impure food and drinking intoxicating beverages. Among them are powerful groups in the interior, most notably the formidable Maasai and Nyamwezi, who played a significant role in the caravan trade, either as direct participants or as raiders and demanders of tribute, and peoples of the Congolese and Nyasaland areas who were raided for slaves, as well as several animal spirits such as the lion, cow, donkey and snake. The inclusion of these animal spirits is consistent with the emphasis on uncultured behaviour as well as the nature of the *bara* itself, filled with game animals of the bush and the herds of pastoralists. They are mentioned in several accounts of Swahili coastal possession in previous times[19] but seem to be rarely encountered today. (See Table 2, page 151.)

Bara spirits are usually portrayed as very aggressive. Their pagan and uncivilized nature is usually quite evident in cult practice. They never wear white like Muslim *kiarabu* spirits but are strongly associated with black and red. Their dances are vigorous, seldom orchestrated, and accompanied by drums. They hold flywhisks (*mibwisho*) made from animal tails, a distinctive African symbol of rank. Medicines and fumigations are usually made from native wild plants, in contrast to the storebought items used by *kiarabu* spirits. The offering plates emphasize simple staple foods typical of agricultural or pastoral peoples (e.g., corn, millet, milk, ghee) instead of the more complicated culinary items preferred by Arabs and Swahili, and almost always include native beer. One also finds symbolic references to various cultural traditions such as initiation rituals and dances that entered Swahili society through the agency of peoples from the interior. (See Table 4, page 153.)

Jini Bara kiswahili *spirits: a syncretic type*

The symbolic nature of the *bara* portrayals is further accentuated by the creation of a spirit category in the Tanga area that has no relation to reality at all but represents the merging of the *kiarabu* and the *bara* spirit worlds. These spirits are perceived as Maasai spirits that have moved to the coast and adopted Islamic coastal attributes in a syncretic manner. Whereas regular Maasai spirits are called '*Jini Bara kimasai*,' these spirits are, quite significantly, called '*Jini Bara kiswahili*.'

Kinyika *spirits: coastal spirits with* Bara *traits*

Jini Bara kiswahili spirits are a unique subtype that appears to be limited to one specific Swahili locality; however, there is an entire category of coastal spirits with *bara* traits that is found throughout the Swahili area. In contrast to the *Jini Bara kiswahili* spirits, this category is conceptualized as native spirits of the coast or its immediate hinterland who are decidedly non-Islamic and totally African in character. Like the *bara* spirits of the interior, they represent 'the other' in the Swahili world view, but in this case within the coastal context itself. This category of spirits includes those that represent the Mijikenda peoples of the Kenyan coast and hinterland, who are closely related to the Swahili in terms of historical origin, political and economic relations, cultural exchange, and intermarriage (Spear 1978; Abdulaziz 1979; Willis 1993).[20] Like many of the other spirit representations, that of the Mijikenda represents their historic rather than their current positions vis-a-vis the Swahili. Thus, in spite of the fact that many of the Mijikenda peoples, especially the Digo, have converted to Islam and adopted many elements of Swahili culture, the Swahili categorize Mijikenda spirits as pagan and uncivilized and stress the indigenous non-Islamic and non-Swahili aspects of Mijikenda culture which historically differentiated them from their Swahili neighbours. Accordingly, Mijikenda spirits are still called by the pejorative term the Swahili have traditionally used for the Mijikenda peoples – '*Nyika*', meaning bush area. *Nyika* spirits dance to fast exuberant rhythms accompanied with drums and rattles. They wear distinctive Mijikenda cloths (*kitambi* and *msimbiji*) and beads, although many cult members make do with a simple black cloth (*kaniki*) that symbolizes the spirit's pagan and rural nature. *Kinyika* spirits use *ubani* (frankincense) incense together with other fumigants and medicines made from native plants, particularly those growing in ponds and bogs. Their most distinctive food request is palm wine, and informants warned that if one gives in to this non-Islamic behaviour, they may go on to ask for rats, which is even more disgusting to Swahili sensibilities. (See Table 2, page 151.)

Although Mijikenda spirits are portrayed negatively, many cult members are possessed by them, and the part of the *ngoma* devoted to them is considered essential. This prominent role in Swahili cult practice seems to give symbolic recognition to the important contribution of the Mijikenda, not only to the general history of the coastal area but also to Swahili society and culture, especially in the Mombasa area. Moreover, the close relationship between the Swahili and Mijikenda peoples is expressed in spirit behaviour during the actual performance of the cult ceremonies, since *kinyika* spirits often dance to the rhythms of *kipemba* spirits and vice versa.[22]

Kipemba *spirits*

This brings us to the most important spirit category of all – the *kipemba*. As noted above, *kipemba* spirits not only dominate current Swahili spirit practice together with the *kiarabu* spirits, but they are the only spirits that are conceptualized as '*kiswahili*' in nature. Hence they provide the most powerful statement of Swahili self-identity within the cult context. Although they are said to originate from the island of Pemba, many *kipemba* spirits are thought to have migrated to other Swahili areas long ago and thus seem to be viewed as native spirits throughout the Swahili area. In Pemba itself, they are often simply referred to as '*wenyeji*', i.e., 'native residents' or 'owners of the land'.

The symbolic realm of the *kipemba* spirits provides a representation of Swahili society that differs markedly from the one generally found within the dominant ideology of the urban elite. It portrays a coastal identity that is strikingly non-Islamic in character. Furthermore, although it acknowledges a syncretic blend of Middle Eastern and African elements as one of the defining characteristics of Swahili culture, it puts considerable stress on the indigenous nature of this formulation and gives full recognition to the African influences involved.

The colour symbolism of *kipemba* spirits indicates their special syncretic character in that it is usually tri-colour – red, white and black, thus combining the colour association of the Islamic *kiarabu* spirits with those of the pagan *bara* spirits. In the Tanga area, cult members wear especially elaborate tri-colour costumes including a distinctive turban of braided red, white and black cloth. (See Table 4, page 153.)

The incense utilized in the *kipemba* cult displays a similar combination of symbolic elements. Spirits are generally given a combination of three incenses, the *udi* (rosewood) preferred by *kiarabu* spirits as well as the *ubani* favoured by *kinyika* spirits but focusing on *uvumba*, an aromatic gum. These incenses are used in addition to *vuo*, the special mixture of herbs and water that replaces rosewater in the *bara* spirit category. (See Table 4.)

The language and music, though non-Islamic, are distinctively coastal Swahili. The songs, which are often sung in Pemba or archaic Swahili dialects, emphasize the natural environment of the coast – i.e., the sea shore, fruits, flowers, birds or crops, instead of its urban or Islamic features. The instrumentation, which is unique to the *kipemba* category, adds the piercing *zumari* oboe[22] and the raucous *upatu* gong to the drums that typify non-*kiarabu* spirits. (See Tables 3 and 4, pages 152 and 153.)

The offering plates show a similar coastal character, consisting of sweet tasting and smelling items but utilizing more native fruits and flowers than *kiarabu* offerings. Thus the usual offering plates focus on bananas, honey, sugarcane, betel nuts, Swahili-style sweets and breads, raw eggs, several types of flowers and screwpine (*mkadi*), combined with lesser amounts of distinctly *kiarabu* items. In addition, the offering plates themselves are frequently made out of wood instead of metal, once again underscoring the more natural and local nature of *kipemba* spirit imagery compared to *kiarabu*. (See Table 4.)

The central themes of *kipemba* cult practice concern the non-Islamic world of the supernatural. *Kipemba* spirits are strongly associated with the *panga*, natural features such as caves and trees, often found on the sea shore, which act as spirit residences. Spirits of the *panga* often act as guardian spirits and traditionally were objects of communal rituals that ensured village welfare and controlled the fertility of both land and sea, a practice that can still be found at some Tanzanian sites.[23] The *kipemba* cult also shows an ambiguous relationship with witchcraft and evil spirits, which it both controls and uses, and utilizes herbal medicines and inherently powerful ritual objects which would be considered pagan fetishes or idols in orthodox Muslim thought. Instead of the emphasis on Quranic texts (including direct consumption in the form of *kombe*), the curative power of the *kipemba* cult focuses on the *mkoba* or medicine bag, which contains many of the same items used by traditional healer/diviners (*waganga*) among the non-Muslim African neighbours of the Swahili – i.e., medicines composed of native plants and certain animal parts, contained in special ritual gourds and animal horns, anointed in sacrificial blood. (See Table 3.)

The *kipemba* symbols of rank also show a striking African character. In addition to the flywhisks used by the *bara* spirits, these include a number of items used as seats – mats, roughly carved pieces of wood and coral and drums. Moreover, most of the ritual regalia are also items which were part of the distinctive set of regalia utilized by the Shirazi city states that ruled the coast before the Omani Arabs – not only special chairs and drums but also fine cloths, turbans, canopies, wooden sandals and *zumari*, for example. (Mtoro 1981: 148–52; Velten 1903: 225–9; Hollis 1900: 279–82; Prins 1967: 93–7; and especially Nurse and Spear 1985: 92–3 and Pouwels 1987: 28).[24] The *kipemba* cult also devotes specific sections of the *ngoma* to other distinctive Swahili practices of the past, such as the girls' and boys' initiation ceremonies (*unyago* and *unjuguu*) with their African and slave origins,[25] the Pemban bull-baiting ceremonies,[26] and the *kirumbizi*[27] stick dance. (See Tables 3 and 4.)

The *kipemba* spirit world hence gives symbolic expression to a Swahili history and identity that reaches far into the past and out into the fields and villages. It transcends the ideology of the urban elite and the historical period of Arab cultural ascendancy to reclaim an older, more syncretic, more indigenous tradition. It is, in fact, a counter-hegemonic statement of what is truly Swahili.

Other types of spirits

Finally, one should note several spirit types that represent cultural contacts with peoples who are not defined in terms of the usual *kiislamu/kafiri* (Islamic/pagan), *pwani/bara* (coastal/up-country) classification system – *kizungu* (European) spirits, *Habeshia* (Abyssinian) spirits, and *kibuki* (Malagasy) spirits. These peoples are neither Islamic nor part of Swahili coastal or Arab culture, yet they are not regarded as uncivilized in the same way as pagan peoples of the interior and hinterland.[28] Whereas these spirit types are not presently widespread, they have assumed importance during certain historical periods or in certain localities.

Kizungu spirits seem to have been significant in most coastal areas during the period of European penetration and colonial domination,[29] although they are rarely found today. In accord with colonial experience, most are portrayed as either British or German, the latter limited to the former German area of mainland Tanzania (Tanganyika) and focusing on locations where the German presence was most pervasive (such as Tanga, a major German administrative centre). *Kizungu* spirit cults, like those for other spirit types, stress distinctive dietary items and consumptive practices (toast, biscuits, cake, alcoholic beverages, cigars, pipes, cigarettes, and currently, store-bought white bread and soft drinks) as well as selected items of dress (pith helmets and black coats with tails, for example). The general cult practice of providing culturally-specific regalia often takes on special significance and focuses on items of European technology, utilizing wooden models of guns, airplanes, merchant ships, and more recently, flashlights. The military nature of many items probably reflects the experience of European military technology during the World Wars as well as during the period of colonial exploration and imposition of political rule.

The character of European spirits is portrayed as powerful, fierce, and authoritarian, reflecting the position of Europeans as conquerors and rulers. These character traits are most pronounced in the case of German spirits, in accord with the forceful and often brutal nature of German colonialism in the area. Moreover, I found that German spirits were always dominant over other spirit types, whereas this was not always true in the case of British spirits.[30] The greater impact of German spirits on cultural memory can also be seen in the fact that *kizungu* spirits still express themselves as German in former German areas, even though a longer period of British colonial rule followed.

The *Habeshia* and *kibuki* cults come from a different historical process. Contrary to most Swahili spirit cults, they are actually adaptations of non-Swahili possession cults, the Ethiopian *zar* and the Malagasy/Comorian *tromba*, brought to the Swahili coast by immigrants from those areas. As noted above, the Ethiopian *zar* was brought by Abyssinian concubines of the Arab/Swahili elite, especially the Omani rulers of Zanzibar. Malagasy influence, on the other hand, was brought by immigrants from the Comoro Islands, who also settled in the town of Zanzibar. These immigrants were absorbed into Swahili society but continued to be possessed by spirits inherited from their ancestors. *Habeshia* and *kibuki* spirits hence act as historical markers of the incorporation of these groups into the Zanzibari population, and in the former case, into the ruling family itself. The symbolic realms of both cults are derived substantially from the ancestral cults outside of the Swahili area (see Sharp 1993 and Lambek 1981), but they take distinctive form in the Swahili milieu.

Instead of the many different types of spirits that are found in the *zar* cults of Ethiopia and other areas of northeastern Africa, the Zanzibari *Habeshia* cult concentrates on two opposing types: refined Abyssinian royalty and unrefined slaves. This division reflects the nature of Omani Zanzibari society itself, with its ruling Omani dynasty and its very large slave population. The royal spirits dominate *Habeshia* ritual, which is described as very lavish and elegant, whereas the slave spirits are given token parts to highlight the contrast between them and their masters. After the 1995 revolution which overthrew the Omani rulers, the *Habeshia* cult went into decline but was still functioning at the time of my research.

The *kibuki* cult seems to have kept more of its original (Comorian and Malagasy) cosmological and ritual structure than the *Habeshia*, probably due to its more recent derivation, continuing influx of immigrants and constant utilization. The cult members identify the spirits as Malagasy kings, but have lost the more specific connection with the royalty of the Sakalava kingdoms in Madagascar. In addition, they no longer know the meaning of many of the words contained in the cult songs.[31]

The character of the *kibuki* spirits is strikingly non-Islamic and non-African, including a fondness for imported alcohol, attraction to Europeans and their material items, and accordion dance music, the same traits which Sharp (1993) describes as the most common spirit types in current-day *tromba* possession among the Bemazava Sakalava in northwestern Madagascar.[32] These traits probably account for the conceptualization of *kibuki* spirits in Zanzibar as Christians, and more specifically as French Catholic priests. In contrast to refined *kiarabu* spirits or the royal spirits of the *Habeshia* cult, *kibuki* spirits, like many of their Comorian and Malagasy counterparts, are arrogant, boisterous, and prone to undisciplined and immodest behaviour. The younger males show a striking resemblance to the 'playboy' spirits that Sharp (1995) notes in her Malagasy study, splashing whisky about and chasing women in the audience. *Kibuki* spirits in Zanzibar thus seem to a be a further elaboration of the process already present in the Malagasy spirit tradition, blending indigenous Malagasy spirit practices with the symbolic representation of European hegemony and material culture. Moreover, contrary to the *kiarabu* or *Habeshia* cults, the *kibuki* cult has no connection to the former royal family nor with the status symbols of the Omani Sultanate. It undermines the cultural refinement and restraint that typified the behaviour of the former Zanzibari aristocracy and offers a totally different expression of status that is strikingly non-Islamic and non-Arab in origin, based on unrestrained power, self-indulgence, and a non-Zanzibari royal tradition. The *kibuki* cult seems particularly well-suited to the cultural and socio-political conditions of post-revolutionary urban Zanzibar, where, contrary to other possession cults, it enjoys widespread popularity.

Conclusion

Swahili possession cults generate a number of different symbolic texts through the agency of different spirit categories. Through these multiple texts, the possession cult gives dialectical expression to the often contradictory elements which have formed the socio-cultural universe of Swahili society throughout its history, defining both self and other, present and past. Such texts can challenge as well as reflect dominant cultural models and formulations of history and identity. Whereas they emphasize the differences between Swahili coastal society and other African societies in the neighbouring hinterland or the interior, they also call attention to the integration of individuals and cultural influences from these societies into Swahili society. Whereas they portray the worldview of the Swahili urban elite, they also reveal those of the lower classes, villagers, and people of slave descent. Whereas they express the ideological emphasis on Middle Eastern, Islamic and urban culture – '*ustaarabu*', through the symbolic realm of the *kiarabu* spirits, they counter it with the older, more syncretic 'Shirazi' ideology of '*uungwana*', which permeates the symbolic realm of the *kipemba* spirits. They portray the Ethiopian heritage which entered the bloodlines of the Omani rulers of Zanzibar, but also express an alternative royal tradition and status system through the *kibuki* cult.

The type of symbolic discourse expressed in Swahili possession cults changes according to time, period and locality. The dominant discourse currently centres around the opposing representations of Swahili society expressed in the *kiarabu* and *kipemba* spirit realms, but other discourses pertaining to different aspects of Swahili experience have emerged in the past and continue to be formulated in the present. New texts and new discourses are constructed within the context of each cult performance, providing an ever-ready source of interpretation of Swahili history and identity.

Acknowledgements

This chapter is a revised version of a paper presented for the panel 'Belonging to an Ethnic Group: The Swahili Case' at the American Anthropological Association meeting in Chicago, Illinois, on 22 November 1991. It is based on material found in my doctoral dissertation (1989) on Swahili spirit possession cults and focuses in particular on a summary of the symbolic analysis of cult cosmology and ritual which constitutes Part II. Some of this information has been mentioned previously in my earlier publications. The research project was funded by doctoral dissertation grants from Fulbright-Hays, the Social Science Research Council, and the National Science Foundation and conducted in affiliation with the Department of Sociology at the

University of Nairobi, the Department of Sociology at the University of Dar es Salaam, the Eastern African Centre for Research on Oral Traditions and African National Languages (EACROTANAL) in Zanzibar as well as the Ministry of Tradition, National Culture, and Sports (*Wizara ya Mila, Utamaduni wa Taifa, na Michezo*) and the Institute of Swahili and Foreign Languages (*Taasisi ya KiSwahili na Lugha za Kigeni*) in Zanzibar and Pemba. I also wish to thank my local research assistants (among them John Baya Mitsanze [Mombasa], Hatibu Pashua [Vanga and Tanga], Al-Amin S. Abadi [Wasin], Patrick Ditfurth [Tanga], and Mwalimu and Momadi Shehe Yahaya [Tungamaa-Pangani]) as well as Ahmed Sheikh Nabhany, Mohammed Abdulaziz, Hamo Sassoon, Jim Berg, James de Vere Allen, David Fawcett and my many host families, and especially the *waganga, watege,* and other informants who made this project possible.

Notes

1 Lewis has developed one of the most influential elaborations of such arguments in his theory of peripheral possession, whereby persons in 'peripheral situations' are afflicted by 'peripheral' spirits, i.e., spirits which are not central to the maintenance of the society's system of morality and are, in fact, often of extraneous origin.

2 This following historical outline is based on various sources on Swahili coastal history, e.g., Nicholls 1971 and Salim 1973, but focuses on several recent reassessments by Allen (1974 and 1981a), Nurse and Spear (1985), and Pouwels (1987) as noted.

3 See Giles (1987) for an earlier statement of this interpretation.

4 Denoting the indigenous Swahili population of the island of Pemba.

5 The '*ki-*' prefix is almost always used to indicate such spirit groups, hence Arab spirits are designated as '*kiarabu,*' spirits from Pemba as '*kipemba,*' Maasai spirits as '*kimasai,*' etc.

6 See Giles (1989a) for an analysis of this process between the Giriama and the Mombasa Swahili, with each group representing the other within their spirit cosmologies.

7 Cf. Topan's earlier study of Mombasa spirit cults groups conducted from 1966 to 1970, in which he also finds a similar preponderance of *kiarabu* and *kipemba* spirits but notes that *kipemba* spirits rank first in popularity – 83 cult members and associates with *kipemba* spirits compared to 52 with *kiarabu* spirits (1970: Appendix).

8 Cf. Topan, who notes that *kipemba* spirits are the most powerful spirits and that *waganga* (the highest rank who often act as cult leaders) with *kipemba* spirits are thus the most powerful *waganga* (1970: 60–2).

9 Topan also observes that cult groups other than *kiarabu* and *kipemba* seem to be in decline. In contrast to my findings, however, he notes only one person with a Mijikenda spirit in his cult membership analysis and does not mention Maasai spirits at all (1970: 59, 459–61).

10 See Giles 1995 as well as 'Spirits, Class, and Status in Swahili Society,' paper presented for the panel 'Status Markers in Swahili Towns' at the American Anthropological Association meeting, Washington, DC, 18 November 1989 (and subsequently rewritten in expanded form) for a discussion of these two Zanzibari spirit cult types.

11 The *dhikri* (cf. *zikr*) consists of repetitive rhythmic chanting of certain words or formulas in praise of God and involves rhythmic breathing and bodily movements, often leading to trance in Sufi and spirit cult practice.

12 The *maulidi* is a ritual honouring the Prophet Mohammed, generally performed during religious ceremonies which mark his birthday (see Franken 1986). In addition to chants, prayers and songs, *maulidi* are usually characterized by the recital of panegyric poems praising Mohammed and his birth.

13 Cf. Franken 1986.

14 Including northeast African spirits that exhibit a non-Muslim character and hence resemble *bara* spirits (see below).

15 Personal communication from Mohammed Abdulaziz, Department of Linguistics, University of Nairobi.

16 Cf. Pouwels' suggestion that the Swahili town-dwellers pre-empted the threat of Arab cultural supremacy to their more syncretic life style during the ascendancy of the Zanzibari Sultanate through possession by Arab spirits (1987: 121). Although I would agree with this assessment I would argue that the symbolic representations of other spirit types must also be considered in order to apprehend the larger system of symbolic meaning.

17 Although Islamic identity is one of the most characteristic traits of *kiarabu* spirits, they nonetheless can show a wide range of religious behaviour. Many *kiarabu* spirits exhibit a very strict Islamic character, especially the most powerful, most esteemed, and probably the most common subcategory of *kiarabu* spirit, the *ruhani*. Other *kiarabu* spirits, however, may not be particularly religious, and some, including entire subcategories of *kiarabu* spirits, are definitely considered *kafiri*. These latter types are often typified as quite evil, a characterization which generally seems to originate directly from Middle East spirit traditions. In many cases no useful relationship can be established with such spirits, and thus whereas they may play a significant role in the spirit cosmology of Quranic *waganga* (ritual experts) specializing in exorcism, they are not very important in the cult context except as a generalized form of *sheitani* or *jini* which the cult spirits help to combat and expel.

18 There are, however, variations in this general pattern which point to differences in the conceptualization of the various subtypes of *kiarabu* spirits, depending on how closely they fit the core characteristics of Middle Eastern origins, Islamic behaviour, and 'civilized', cultured traits.

19 For example, Koritschoner (1936) and Skene (1917).

20 Abdulaziz (1979: 23) points out that the Mijikenda thus often refer to the Swahili as '*adzomba*,' meaning 'uncle' or 'nephew,' a usage that my Giriama research assistant John Mitsanze also called to my attention. Intermarriage has tended to be unidirectional, with Swahili men marrying Mijikenda women, but its extent can be judged from Abdulaziz' observation that 'there would hardly be an indigenous Swahili family in Mombasa which could not trace some Mijikenda blood in them' (1979: 23).

21 See Giles (1989a) for a more detailed discussion of the portrayal of Mijikenda spirits in Mombasa Swahili spirit cult practice.

22 Allen not only points out the antiquity of the *zumari* on the Swahili coast but also observes that the *zumari* is 'an unclean instrument' in the Islamic view and hence unsuitable for mosque functions. (1981b: 239–40)

23 See Trimingham 1964: 17, 20; Skene 1917: 420 (in reference to the '*kinyago*'); Pakenham 1959: 112; and Gray 1955 and 1980 in regard to communal spirit ceremonies held in the recent past. Some sources also mention spirit propitiation by individual hunters, fishermen, and cultivators (Pakenham 1947: 8–9; Gray 1955: 8; and Trimingham 1964: 117). I found a strong historical tradition of *kipemba* spirits as village guardians in Pemba and the Tanzanian coast south of Pangani, where informants often reported that communal spirit *ngoma* to promote the general welfare of the community were still held for these spirits several times a year. In the Makunduchi area of Zanzibar and in Pemba (especially on the island of Kojani), I found spirit propitiation and possession still associated with communal ceremonies in celebration of the traditional Swahili New Year (*Siku ya Mwaka*, often referred to as *Nairuz* in the literature), performed to cleanse the community of harmful and polluting influences and to ensure its protection during the coming year (cf. Gray's description [1955] of earlier ceremonies at Makunduchi). (The communal ceremonies for *Siku ya Mwaka* in Mombasa no longer involve the spirits or the spirit cult groups, but the latter still hold their own ceremonies of renewal and purification at this time.) I also found that *kipemba* spirit ceremonies still had some connection with planting and harvesting in Pemba and with fishing in the Pangani area. The latter was especially striking in one village where informants told of a *kipemba* guardian spirit of the village who had formerly brought a communal harvest of stunned fish to the area after the villagers performed the spirit's annual *ngoma*.

24 Whereas the English translation of Mtoro bin Mwinyi Bakari's *Desturi za Waswahili* notes that the local rulers (*jumbe*) are accompanied by 'a pipe and horn' (1981: 150), the Swahili text published by Velten identifies these specifically as the *zumari* and *siwa* (1903: 15). Allen in his appendix to the English edition notes the imprecise translation. He also points out that the 'oboes and trumpets' mentioned as regalia of the Mogadishu ruler by Ibn Battuta in the fourteenth century were 'doubtless' the *zumari* and 'probably' the *siwa* (1981b: 240).

25 See Caplan 1976; Strobel 1979 (Chapter 8), and Mirza and Strobel 1989: 70–73. See also Cory

1947/48; Hinawiy 1964: 30–34; Lambert 1965; Strobel 1975 (Appendix B); Lienhardt 1968: 68–70; Prins 1967: 108–9; Mtoro 1981: 45–59; and Mirza and Strobel 1989: 74–88 for descriptions of these rites at various sites and time periods.

26 See Gray 1980.

27 See Mtoro 1981: 87–8 and Franken 1986: 108–9 for descriptions of the *kirumbizi*.

28 Like *kiarabu* spirits, they enter Swahili society from overseas. They are associated with powerful, politically centralized societies with complex social structures. Both European and Abyssinian societies possess complex technologies and traditions of urban life. Moreover, they are Christian, 'People of the Book', who are not categorized as pagans. The situation for the *kibuki* cult with its indigenous Malagasy origins is less well defined, but it is clear that the cult entered Swahili society via the Comoro Islands (themselves an extension of the wider Swahili world) and carries strong associations of French colonialism (see below).

29 The written literature on *kizungu* spirits, however, seems to be scarce. I found only two sources which mentioned them for the Swahili area – Mtoro 1981(1903) and Charles Sacleux' *Dictionnaire Swahili-Français* (Paris: Institut d'Ethnologie, 1939), although my informants in many areas reported that *kizungu* spirits used to be common.

30 In the Makunduchi region of Zanzibar, British spirits were sometimes portrayed as secondary to Arab spirits. This ranking is not surprising for 'Shirazi' areas of Zanzibar, where the imposition of Arab rule under the Omani Sultanate was more traumatic and far-reaching than the later imposition of British rule.

31 After listening to my recordings of *kibuki* ritual performances, Didier Rapanoel, a Malagasy scholar working with the East African Centre for Oral Traditions and African National Languages in Zanzibar, reported that the words still retain a strong resemblance to the Sakalava language.

32 Sharp reports that *tromba* spirits are classified into three generations that represent different epochs of Sakalava history. Most *tromba* spirits today are children and grandchildren, who portray the colonial and post-colonial epochs.

References

Abdulaziz, Mohammed H. (1979) *Muyaka: Nineteenth Century Swahili Popular Poetry*, Nairobi: Kenya Literature Bureau.

Allen, James de Vere (1974) 'Swahili culture re-considered', *Azania* 9: 105–38.

—— (1981a) 'The Swahili World of Mtoro bin Mwinyi Bakari, Appendix I', in *The Customs of the Swahili People*; Mtoro bin Mwinyi Bakari *et al.*, J.W.T. Allen *et al.*, (eds), 211–46. Berkeley: University of California Press.

—— (1981b) 'Ngoma: music and dance, Appendix III', in *The Customs of the Swahili People*: Mtoro bin Mwinyi Bakari *et al.*, J.W.T. Allen *et al.*, (eds), 233–46. Berkeley: University of California Press.

Ardener, Edwin (1972) 'Belief and the problem of women', in *The Interpretation of Ritual*, J.S. LaFontaine, (ed.) 135–8, London: Tavistock.

Boddy, Janice (1989) *Wombs and Alien Spirits: Women and Men in the Zar Cult in Northern Sudan*, Madison: University of Wisconsin Press.

Caplan, Ann Patricia (1976) 'Boys' circumcision and girls' puberty rites among the Swahili of Mafia Island, Tanzania', *Africa* 46: 21–33.

Cooper, Frederick (1977) *Plantation Slavery on the East Coast of Africa*, New Haven: Yale University Press.

—— (1980) *From Slaves to Squatters: Plantation Labor and Agriculture in Zanzibar and Coastal Kenya, 1890-1925*, New Haven: Yale University Press.

Cory, Hans (1947/48) Jando *JRAI* 77: 159–68 & 78: 81–95.

Crapanzano, Vincent (1973) *The Hamadsha: A Study of Moroccan Ethnopsychiatry*, Berkeley: University of California Press.

—— (1977) 'Introduction', in *Case Studies in Spirit Possession*, Vincent Crapanzano and Vivian Garrison (eds), 1–40. New York: Wiley & Sons.

Eastman, Carol M. (1971) 'Who are the WaSwahili?' *Africa* 41 (3): 228–36.

Ferchiou, Sophie (1972) 'Survivances mystiques et culte de possession dans le maraboutisme Tunisian', *L'Homme* 12: 47–69.

Franken, Marjorie Ann (1986) 'Anyone can dance: a survey and analysis of Swahili Ngoma, past and present', PhD dissertation. Department of Anthropology, University of California, Riverside.

Geertz, Clifford (1972) 'Deep play: notes on the balinese cockfight', *Daedalus* (Winter): 1–37.

Giles, Linda (1987) 'Possession cults on the Swahili coast: a re-examination of theories of marginality', *Africa* 57 (2): 234–58.

—— (1989a) 'The dialectic of spirit production: a cross-cultural dialogue', *Mankind Quarterly* 33 (3): 243–65.

—— (1989b) 'Spirit possession on the Swahili coast: peripheral cults or primary texts?' Doctoral dissertation, University of Texas at Austin.

—— (1995) 'Sociocultural change and spirit possession on the Swahili coast of East Africa', *Anthropological Quarterly* 68 (2, April): 89–106.

Gray, John M. (1955) 'Nairuzi or Siku ya Mwaka', *Tanganyika Notes and Records* 38: 1-22 and 41: 89–92.

—— (1980) 'Bull-baiting in Pemba', *Azania* 15: 121–9.

Hinawiy, Mbarak Ali (1964) 'Notes on customs in Mombasa', *Swahili* 34 (1): 17–34.

Hollis, A. J. (1900) 'Notes on the history of the Vumba, East Africa', *JRAI* 30: 275–97.

Kapferer, Bruce (1983) *A Celebration of Demons: Exorcism and the Aesthetics of Healing in Sri Lanka*, Bloomington: Indiana University Press.

Kennedy, J. G. (1967) 'Nubian Zar ceremonies as psychotherapy', *Human Organization* 26: 185–94.

Koritschoner, Hans (1936) 'Ngoma ya Sheitani', *JRAI* 66: 209–19.

Lambek, M. (1981) 'Human spirits: a cultural account of trance in Mayotte', Cambridge: Cambridge University Press.

Lambert, H.E. (1965) 'Initiation songs on the southern Kenya coast', *Swahili* 35 (1): 50–67.

Lienhardt, Peter, ed., trans., and introduction (1968) *The Medicineman*, Oxford: The Clarendon Press.

Lewis, I.M. (1966) 'Spirit possession and deprivation cults', *Man* 1(3): 307–29.

—— (1971) *Ecstatic Religion: An Anthropological Study of Spirit Possession and Shamanism*, Harmondsworth: Penguin Books.

—— (1986) *Religion in Context: Cults and Charisma*, Cambridge: Cambridge University Press.

Mirza, Sarah, and Margaret Strobel (eds). (1989) *Three Swahili Women*, Bloomington: Indiana University Press.

Mtoro bin Mwinyi Bakari (1981) *The Customs of the Swahili People: The Desturi za Waswahili of Mtoro bin Mwinyi Bakari and Other Swahili Persons*. J.W.T. Allen (ed. and trans.), Berkeley: University of California Press. (Published in Swahili as Desturi za WaSuaheli na khabari za desturi za sheria za WaSuaheli by Carl Velten. Goettingen: Vandenhoeck & Ruprecht, 1903.)

Nicholas, Jacqueline (1972) *Ambivalence et culte de possession*, Paris: Anthropos.

Nichols, Christine S. (1971) *The Swahili Coast: Policy, Diplomacy and Trade on the East African Littoral 1798–1856*, London: George Allen & Unwin.

Nurse, Derek, & Thomas Spear (1985) *The Swahili: Reconstructing the History and Language of an African Society, 800-1500*, Philadelphia: University of Pennsylvania Press.

Pakenham, R. H. W. (1947) *Land Tenure among the Wahadimu at Chwaka, Zanzibar Protectorate*, Zanzibar.

—— (1959) 'Two Zanzibar ngomas', *TNR* 52 (March): 111–16.

Pouwels, Randall (1987) *Horn and Crescent: Cultural Change and Traditional Islam on the East African Coast, 800–1900*, Cambridge: Cambridge University Press.

Prins, A. H. J. (1967) 'The Swahili-speaking peoples of Zanzibar and the East African coast'. *Ethnographic Survey of Africa*. East Central Africa, Part XII. Daryll Forde (gen. ed.) London: International African Institute.

Salim, A. I. (1973) *The Swahili-speaking Peoples of Kenya's Coast: 1895–1965*, Nairobi: East African Publishing House.

Sharp, Lesley A. (1993) *The Possessed and Dispossessed: Spirits, Identity, and Power in a Madagascar Migrant Town*, Berkeley: University of California Press.

—— (1995) 'Playboy princely spirits', *Anthropological Quarterly* 68 (2 April): 75–88.

Skene, R. (1917) 'Arab and Swahili dances and ceremonies', *JRAI* 47: 413–34.

Spear, Thomas T. (1978) *The Kaya Complex: A History of the Mijikenda Peoples of the Kenya Coast to 1900*, Nairobi: Kenya Literature Bureau.

Strobel, Margaret (1975) 'Muslim Women in Mombasa, Kenya, 1890–1973', PhD dissertation, Department of History, University of California, Los Angeles.

—— (1979) *Muslim Women in Mombasa, 1890–1975*, New Haven: Yale University Press.

Swartz, Marc (1979) 'Religious courts, community, and ethnicity among the Swahili of Mombasa: a historical study of social boundaries', *Africa* 49 (1): 29–41.

Topan, Farouk Mohamedhussein T. (1971) 'Oral Literature in a ritual setting: the role of spirit songs in a spirit-mediumship cult in Mombasa, Kenya', PhD dissertation, University of London.

Trimingham, John Spencer (1964) *Islam in East Africa*, Oxford: The Clarendon Press.

Velten, Carl (see Mtoro bin Mwinyi Bakari) (1903) *Desturi za WaSuaheli na khabari za desturi za sheria za WaSuaheli*, Goettingen: Vandenhoeck & Ruprecht.

Willis, Justin (1993) *Mombasa, the Swahili, and the Masking of the Mijikenda*, Oxford & New York: The Clarendon Press.

Zempleni, Andras (1977) 'From symptom to sacrifice: the story of Khady Fall', in *Case Studies in Spirit Possession*, Vincent Crapanzano & Vivian Garrison (eds), 87–140. New York: Wiley & Sons.

Index